Rethinking Responsibility

Rethinking Responsibility

K. E. Boxer

OXFORD
UNIVERSITY PRESS

OXFORD
UNIVERSITY PRESS

Great Clarendon Street, Oxford, OX2 6DP,
United Kingdom

Oxford University Press is a department of the University of Oxford.
It furthers the University's objective of excellence in research, scholarship,
and education by publishing worldwide. Oxford is a registered trade mark of
Oxford University Press in the UK and in certain other countries

British Library Cataloguing in Publication Data
Data available

Library of Congress Cataloging in Publication Data
Data available

ISBN 978-0-19-969532-4

Printed in Great Britain by
MPG Books Group, Bodmin and King's Lynn

For Savan and Eishan

Preface

When I first started thinking about moral responsibility, it struck me as obvious that moral responsibility was incompatible with determinism. To be truly morally responsible for her actions, an agent would have to be ultimately responsible for her actions. She would have to be responsible for their ultimate causes. Yet, if the thesis of determinism is true, then no agent is ultimately responsible for her actions. All of an agent's actions ultimately trace back to events long antedating her birth. Hence, if the thesis of determinism is true, no agent is morally responsible for her actions. Or so I 'argued'. When I returned to the question several years later, I came to realize that, as wielded by me, this knockdown argument was less an argument than it was a matter of stipulation—that, in fact, I had no real sense of what it was for an agent to be *morally* (as opposed to *ultimately*) responsible for her actions. Actually, that's not quite accurate. I had, or thought I had, some sense of what it was for an agent to be morally responsible for her actions. An agent's being morally responsible for her actions was a matter of her being the type of agent who could be truly deserving of moral praise or blame, or of reward or punishment, for her actions. So far so good. However, when I went on to claim that, if the thesis of determinism is true, then no agent is ever truly deserving of blame (or truly to blame) for her actions, I think that what I actually meant was that no agent is ever to blame for her actions 'all the way back' i. e., for her actions' ultimate causes. In short, I came to realize that I had been writing an ultimate responsibility requirement into my conception of moral responsibility—defining 'true' moral responsibility as responsibility that extended all the way back to the ultimate causes of an action. In doing so, I had been begging the question against my compatibilist opponents. What compatibilists claim is not that we are ultimately responsible for our actions; it is that ultimate responsibility is not required for moral responsibility for actions. If I wanted to show that ultimate responsibility is required for moral responsibility, I would first have to come to a clearer understanding of what it is for an agent to be morally responsible for an action—an understanding that did not write responsibility for an action's ultimate causes into the definition of moral responsibility.

So began a philosophical journey that, after many fits and starts, cul-
minated in publication of this book in its current form. During the first
years of this journey, I remained committed to incompatibilism. I was
confident that in order to be morally responsible for an action, an agent
would have to be ultimately responsible for the action. I had only to come
up with a non-question-begging specification of moral responsibility
that would enable me to show that this was the case. That my goal was
to come up with such a specification and thereby vindicate my incompatibilist convictions helps to explain why the book's argument takes the
shape that it does. The further I progressed, however, the less certain
I became that my incompatibilist convictions were well grounded. On
virtually every non-question-begging specification of moral responsibility
that I could think of, it seemed that moral responsibility did not require
ultimate responsibility. There were two possible exceptions. The first
involved thinking of moral blame as attaching not to the empirical self,
but rather to a metaphysically distinct noumenal self capable of choosing its
initial characteristics. Even if it were possible to make sense of the idea of
such a self, there would remain the problem of explaining how it could be
blamed for what it chose. Hence, I dismissed the first possibility. (Though
some might attribute the conception I dismissed to Kant, it is, I believe,
not a view with which Kant should be saddled.) The second possible
exception involved accepting what might be thought of as a traditional
moral retributivist understanding of the moral desert of punishment.
On the understanding I have in mind, wrongdoers deserve to be made
to suffer *simpliciter*. Punishment is an instrument for bringing it about
that wrongdoers are made to suffer as they deserve. For moral as well as
non-moral reasons, this was not an understanding of the moral desert of
punishment that I could accept. It was not an understanding of which
I could make moral sense. If it did not make sense, then it could not be
used to justify an ultimate responsibility requirement for moral responsibility. And so eventually I gave up my incompatibilism. The project
that I had hoped might bear the title 'Justifying Incompatibilism' came
to bear the title *Rethinking Responsibility*. Others with incompatibilist
sympathies will undoubtedly look at the same arguments that convinced
me that moral responsibility does not require ultimate responsibility and
remain unconvinced. I hope that for them I have at least identified points
at which further arguments must be brought to bear.

Over the course of this journey, I have benefited greatly from informal discussions with, and comments from, others. These others include my teachers at Oxford—Jonathan Glover, Martha Klein, Derek Parfit, Joseph Raz, and Galen Strawson—who first introduced me to the problem of moral responsibility, and, more recently, friends, students, and colleagues including Sarah Buss, Kenneth Ehrenberg, Jennifer Frey, Barbara Herman, Kristen Inglis, Mike Otsuka, Hille Paakkunainen, Kieran Setiya, Michael Thompson, Jay Wallace, and Andrea Westlund. I wish separately to thank Ian Blecher for his superb editorial advice and assistance and Gila Issenberg and Vanessa Wills for their many hours of proofreading and formatting in the leading up to final submission of the manuscript. Finally, there are three people to whom I owe my greatest thanks and gratitude: my late friend and confidant, Jerry Cohen, who managed to pry text from my fingers when no one else could; my very much alive friend and former colleague, Jerry Massey, who sacrificed much of a summer helping me to prepare an earlier version of the manuscript for submission and who has since provided me with countless hours of counsel and support; and my dear friend and colleague, Stephen Engstrom, whose patience in discussing this material, and insights into Kant and other things philosophical elevated the level of discourse in the manuscript beyond measure.

Contents

'We cannot expect to reach a satisfactory conclusion concerning whether determinism is or is not compatible with moral responsibility unless we know what it is with which its compatibility is in question. We require a clear idea, in other words, of the nature of this "moral responsibility" whose relationship to determinism is in question'.

Harry Frankfurt, 'Reply to John Martin Fischer

Introduction

This book is about moral responsibility and whether such responsibility is compatible with causal determinism. It is written by a philosopher who began with deeply incompatibilist intuitions, but became dissatisfied with the arguments that she and other contemporary incompatibilists marshaled in support of incompatibilism. The book evolved out of her search for a more adequate argument. The question it ultimately seeks to answer is whether a more adequate argument can be advanced. Just as important, however, is the question that the book addresses along the way, viz., what is the disagreement between compatibilists and incompatibilists concerning moral responsibility a disagreement about? What are we talking about when we speak of moral responsibility?

In recent decades, disputes having to do with putative 'alternative possibilities' and 'ultimate responsibility' conditions of moral responsibility have had a tendency to take on lives of their own. Disputants argue over the best way to interpret their favored condition, and whether and under what circumstances the condition would or could be satisfied, in virtual isolation from any consideration of what the putative conditions are meant to be conditions *of*. Although we may have started with a well-defined debate, or series of debates, concerning the causal and capacity conditions an agent would have to satisfy to be morally responsible for her actions, we've ended up with no such thing. The core concept of moral responsibility—as distinct from the putative causal and capacity conditions of such responsibility—all too frequently drops out of the discussion or plays no substantive role in the arguments offered. Yet, without the core concept of moral responsibility anchoring the discussion, there is no way to determine the causal and capacity conditions an agent would have to satisfy to be morally responsible for her actions. It is not even clear what type of question, a metaphysical question or a moral one—much less what specific question we are trying to answer.

One of the main aims of this book is to remedy this defect. Chapter 1 examines the attempts of four contemporary incompatibilists—Galen Strawson, Robert Kane, Saul Smilansky, and Derk Pereboom—to justify incompatibilism concerning moral responsibility and determinism (henceforth simply 'incompatibilism') by appeal to the idea that for an agent to be morally responsible for her actions, she must be ultimately responsible for her actions. That is, she must herself be, or be responsible for, the ultimate (determining) cause(s) of her actions, having personally determined their (determining) causes 'all the way back'. The decision to focus on these attempts reflects my conviction that there is not an independent alternative possibilities condition for moral responsibility.[1] Beyond this, I am convinced by the arguments provided by Martha Klein and Kane, among others, that once the ultimate responsibility and alternative possibilities conditions are disentangled from one another, the former is shown to be more basic to incompatibilist thinking than the latter.[2] Worries about ultimate responsibility seem to explain incompatibilist demands for alternative possibilities and, also, the rejection by incompatibilists of compatibilist analyses of 'could'. Hence, if there is reason to be an incompatibilist concerning moral responsibility and determinism, it is because moral responsibility requires ultimate responsibility and not because of an independent requirement for 'strong' alternative possibilities, i.e., alternative possibilities of a sort incompatible with determinism.[3]

Note that, throughout the book, I shall use the term 'incompatibilist' to refer to anyone who believes that the freedom required for moral responsibility is incompatible with determinism, irrespective whether she believes it would be attainable under indeterminism. The term should thus be taken to cover not only libertarians and those traditional hard determinists who believe that the freedom necessary for moral responsibility is possible under indeterminism, but also 'no-free-will-either-way' theorists, who

---

[1] My conviction that there is not an independent alternative possibilities condition for moral responsibility is based in large part on Frankfurt-style counterexamples to the Principle of Alternative Possibilities. Though I agree with Widerker (1995b) that there are structural problems with Frankfurt's original counterexample, I believe that is possible to construct counterexamples that do not suffer from the same problems. See, e.g., Pereboom (2003).

[2] See Klein (1990) and Kane (1996).

[3] Throughout the book, I shall use 'moral responsibility requires ultimate responsibility' as shorthand for 'in order for an agent to be morally responsible for an action, she must be ultimately responsible for the action'. Unless otherwise specified, I will always have as my focus moral responsibility, and ultimate responsibility, for *actions*.

believe that the freedom in question is impossible under indeterminism as well as determinism.[4] Importantly, I do not regard compatibilism and incompatibilism as exhausting the positions one might take with respect to moral responsibility and free will. There is a third possibility: that of maintaining that our ideas of moral responsibility and desert are hopelessly confused even apart from concerns about freedom. If the dispute between compatibilists and incompatibilists is to be meaningful, this third position must be defeated.

Though I remain sympathetic to the intuitions underlying the claim that to be morally responsible for her actions, an agent must be ultimately responsible for them, I am skeptical of the arguments that have been produced up to this point in defense of the claim. If incompatibilists wish to show that moral responsibility presupposes ultimate responsibility, then they will have to adopt a new approach. It will not help simply to adduce additional problem cases or to delve deeper into the metaphysics of freedom or causation or the self. Incompatibilists need to shift their focus away from such concerns and back to what H. L. A. Hart identifies as the primary sense of the concept of responsibility: the 'liability' sense. To say that an agent is responsible for an action in the liability sense is to say that she satisfies the necessary causal and capacity conditions of liability to, or, in the case of moral liability-responsibility, desert of, certain forms of response, whatever the conditions turn out to be.[5] Put slightly differently,

---

[4] I borrow the label 'no-free-will-either-way' from Double. See his (1996). I distinguish the position of the 'no-free-will-either-way' theorist—here represented by Galen Strawson—from that of someone who believes our ideas of moral responsibility and desert are hopelessly confused even apart from issues of freedom. The former is engaged in a debate with compatibilists concerning the type of freedom required for moral responsibility while the latter is not. As for the two other incompatibilist positions I mentioned, whereas libertarians affirm that we are morally responsible for our actions and so deny the truth of determinism, hard determinists affirm the truth of determinism and so deny moral responsibility.

[5] See Hart (1967), 265. As Hart notes and I further discuss in Chapter 1, the liability sense of responsibility is no longer the most commonly used sense. Rather than being used to refer to an agent's meeting the necessary capacity and causal conditions (whatever they might be) of liability, to or desert, of some form of response, responsibility terms are now more commonly used to refer directly to the capacities or form of causal connection normally required for liability or desert, or to causal connection more generally. That is, they are now more commonly used in what Hart refers to as the 'capacity' and 'causal' senses of responsibility. In describing the liability sense as the primary sense of responsibility, Hart seems largely to be making an etymological point. The point I mean to be making is additionally a conceptual and methodological one: that there is no way to determine the causal and capacity conditions an agent would have to satisfy to be morally responsible for her actions other than by reference to the liability sense.

it is to say that she possesses the capacities that she would have to possess, and stands in the relation to the action in which she would have to stand, for the action to open her to desert of certain types of response in the event that the action is commendable or condemnable. Focusing on the liability sense highlights and clarifies the respect in which the concept of moral responsibility is a *moral* concept, and the question which causal and capacity conditions an agent must satisfy to be morally responsible for her actions a *moral* question: one concerning the conditions an agent must satisfy to be (capable of being) deserving of certain responses for her action.[6] If incompatibilists wish to establish that an ultimate responsibility condition is among these conditions, they must first clarify how they understand the concept of desert and the precise forms of response they take to be at issue in discussions of moral responsibility. They must supply an analysis of moral liability-responsibility.

Some will deny the need to engage in such analysis, insisting that we already have an adequate understanding of what I am calling 'moral liability-responsibility'. To say that an agent is morally responsible for an action in the liability sense, they will tell us, is to say that she satisfies the necessary causal and capacity conditions for desert of moral praise and blame and reward and punishment, with moral desert being a matter of justice and, indeed, pre-institutional justice or 'fittingness', as opposed to utility. The problem with remaining content with this answer is not just that it leaves many of the central questions concerning desert unanswered.

---

[6]   I am by no means the first author to emphasize that the concept of moral responsibility is, in the first instance, a moral concept, and the question of the necessary conditions of moral responsibility, in the first instance, a moral (or at least a normative) question. Others include Glover (1970), Korsgaard (1992), and Wallace (1994). My own realization that the question is, in the first instance, a moral question and not a metaphysical one owes much to Wallace's discussion. Nevertheless, the specific moral question that I take it to be—viz., that of the causal and capacity conditions an agent must satisfy to be capable of being deserving of certain responses—and the way in which I understand the concept of desert differs from Wallace's understanding. (For Wallace, the central question concerns the conditions under which it is fair to hold someone morally responsible, where fairness is taken to encompass more than desert.) These and other differences between my view and Wallace's will be discussed in Chapters 3 and 4. I hope that what I've been arguing makes it apparent that when I say that the question of the necessary conditions of moral responsibility is, in the first instance, a moral question, I do not mean to suggest that it is somehow up to us to decide what the pertinent conditions are or should be—as, for example, Glover seems to suggest in his (1970). Nor do I mean to suggest that there are no facts about moral responsibility. There are. They are simply moral facts: facts about desert.

(Perhaps it is enough to say that desert is a matter of what is pre-institutionally just or intrinsically fitting when we are discussing moral praise (or moral 'credit') and blame, understood as forms of non-overt moral appraisal.[7] But what about when we are considering overt moral praise and blame? Or when we are considering reward and punishment? What is the force of desert claims, as compared to other justice-related claims, where overt treatment is concerned? Do desert claims automatically outweigh other justice-related claims or are the reasons they provide merely *pro tanto*? In claiming that a person is deserving of some mode of overt treatment, are we merely claiming that she lacks ground for complaint of injustice if she is subjected to such treatment, or are we further pointing to a positive ground for affording her such treatment?) Beyond this, there is more than one conception of moral praise (credit) and blame, and of the relation between desert of moral praise and blame and desert of reward and punishment, as well as disagreement as to whether reward and punishment are among the responses whose desert should be seen to be at issue in discussions of moral responsibility. Hence, there is more than one conception of moral liability-responsibility itself. And which conception one has in mind might well affect the causal and capacity conditions that an agent would have to satisfy to be morally responsible for her actions in the liability sense. Prior to investigation, at least, we should not rule out the possibility that the conditions that an agent would have to satisfy to be capable of being deserving of one form of response might differ from those she would have to satisfy to be capable of being deserving of another.

There may be those who, despite the considerations just advanced, remain skeptical of the need to engage in an analysis of the concept of moral liability-responsibility. To determine whether moral responsibility requires ultimate responsibility, they may insist, we need only analyze our actual attributions of moral responsibility and pinpoint what is missing in those cases in which we excuse or exempt an agent from moral responsibility. There are several difficulties with this suggestion. Agents we excuse or exempt in the course of our actual practices typically lack not just ultimate responsibility, but a number of other capacities that might be deemed necessary for moral responsibility and that, unlike ultimate responsibility, are perfectly compatible with determinism. Compatibilists will insist that it

---

[7] Insofar as praise is often thought of as spoken or expressed, 'credit' seems a more perspicuous term to use when discussing unspoken and non-overt positive appraisal.

is the lack of one of these other capacities and not the lack of ultimate responsibility that grounds our ordinary excuses and exemptions. In the end, our intuitions concerning such cases are not sufficiently fine-grained to determine which explanation is correct. True, we can introduce cases in which an agent possesses all of the capacities that compatibilists claim to be necessary for moral responsibility but in which it is made explicit from the outset that the agent is not ultimately responsible for her behavior. Those who believe that moral responsibility requires some form of ultimate responsibility will insist that when presented with such cases, their intuition that the agent is not morally responsible for her actions remains unchanged. Their insistence, however, will hardly persuade compatibilists. To the contrary, compatibilists will maintain that insofar as the agent under consideration possesses the capacities that they (i.e., compatibilists) view as necessary and sufficient for moral responsibility, the intuition that the agent is not morally responsible should disappear. If it persists, they will argue that this is a sign of some sort of conceptual confusion. (Recall the once common charge that incompatibilists confound causation and compulsion.) And, as we shall see in Chapter 1, there is some reason to suspect that the intuition that moral responsibility presupposes ultimate responsibility in part reflects the ease of sliding from talk of agents being 'truly' morally responsible for their actions (or 'truly' deserving of blame) to talk of their being 'ultimately' responsible (or ultimately to blame) for their actions. Once one clearly distinguishes moral responsibility from the ultimate responsibility that is meant to be among its necessary conditions—and one of the main benefits of focusing on the liability sense of moral responsibility is that it forces one to distinguish them—it begins to look less obvious that ultimate responsibility is required for 'true' moral responsibility. Indeed, it becomes somewhat unclear what proponents of an ultimate responsibility condition have in mind when they speak of 'true' moral responsibility and 'genuine' desert. This brings us back to the need for incompatibilists to provide an analysis of moral liability-responsibility.

Compatibilists have long had things to say about the nature of moral liability-responsibility. Unlike the accounts and analyses provided by compatibilists like Moritz Schlick in the first half of the twentieth century—accounts and analyses that, today, even compatibilists acknowledge to have been far too crude—the accounts provided by more recent compatibilists are often quite rich.[8] Indeed, the principal problem facing anyone wishing to defend an ultimate-responsibility (or a 'strong' alternative possibilities) condition for moral responsibility is that many of the things that contemporary compatibilists identify as at issue in discussions of moral responsibility—e.g., desert of 'deep' moral appraisal, punishment without grounds for complaint of being treated unjustly, perhaps even desert of the reactive attitudes—seem not to require ultimate responsibility (or strong alternative possibilities). Moreover, I take it that with respect to at least some of the things that compatibilists point to, many of those who believe that moral responsibility requires ultimate responsibility could be brought to agree with this claim. That is, I take it that many proponents of an ultimate responsibility requirement for moral responsibility could be brought to agree that, as understood by compatibilists, moral liability-responsibility does not require ultimate responsibility. They would simply insist that the compatibilist understanding fails to capture true moral liability-responsibility. If proponents of the ultimate responsibility condition wish to defend this further claim, then they must provide an alternative account of the nature of moral liability-responsibility—one that makes clear (a) how they understand desert, (b) the precise forms of response that they have in mind when they speak of 'true' moral responsibility, and (c) why desert of these forms of response presupposes ultimate responsibility.

The remaining chapters of the book are devoted to discovering whether an account of the requisite type can be provided. Chapters 2, 3, 4, and 5 each discuss a different conception of the desert at issue, or partly at issue, in discussions of moral responsibility. In all four chapters, I focus on ill-desert or desert for wrongdoing. Incompatibilists tend to be more worried about ill-desert than they are about good-desert. Focusing on ill-desert will enable us to better pinpoint their worries. Chapters 2 and 3 discuss two different understandings of the nature of moral blame. Chapters 4 and 5 discuss competing understandings of the moral desert of punishment. I do not take a stand on which understanding of moral blame best corresponds to the ordinary understanding—I'm not sure that there is an

---

[8] According to Schlick, 'the question of who is responsible is the question concerning the *correct point of application of the motive*. It is a matter only of knowing who is to be punished or rewarded, in order that punishment and reward function as such—be able to achieve their goal' of discouraging certain types of acts and encouraging the performance of others. See Schlick (1939), 153.

answer to this question. Nor, until the closing pages of the book, do I take a stand on which understanding of the moral desert of punishment better reflects the ordinary understanding (though I do earlier take a stand on the force of desert claims). The crucial question for our purposes is whether on any of the understandings discussed, moral liability-responsibility would require ultimate responsibility. Given my belief that if there is reason to be an incompatibilist concerning moral responsibility and determinism, it is based on moral responsibility's requiring ultimate responsibility and not an independent requirement for strong alternative possibilities, I take this question to be equivalent to the question whether there is reason to be an incompatibilist at all.

Chapter 2 explores desert of moral blame on a pure belief-based account of moral blame. On the account in question, to morally blame an agent for an action is to judge that her action reflects badly on her as a moral agent. More specifically, it is to judge that her action reflects a defect in her as a moral agent: a moral defect or defect of character. I argue that what distinguishes defects of character from other types of defect and appraisals involving the attribution of such defects from other forms of negative appraisal, qualifying both the defects and the appraisals as distinctively moral, is that the defects in question are ones that their possessor is unconditionally obligated to eliminate. This creates an opening for incompatibilists to argue that unless agents are ultimately responsible for their characters, there could be no moral blame or moral defects, properly speaking. For, they might argue, unless agents are ultimately responsible for their characters, there can be no unconditional obligations to have a certain character. (This is how I interpret Kant's claim that '[m]an *himself* must make or have made himself into whatever, in a moral sense, he is or is to become. Either condition must be an effect of his own free choice; for otherwise he could not be held responsible for it and could therefore be *morally* neither good nor evil'.[9]) After arguing against the claim that unless agents are ultimately responsible for their characters, there can be no unconditional obligations to have a certain character, I consider a second argument that incompatibilists might put forward: viz., for there to be unconditional obligations with respect to character, it must be the case that all normal adult human beings under normal circumstances possess the

---

[9] Kant (1960), 40.

'specific ability' to eliminate their moral defects, where this would require alternative possibilities of a sort incompatible with determinism. I argue that there is a sense of 'can' that corresponds to the incompatibilist's interpretation of 'can',—viz., the theoretical sense—but that it is not the sense implied by moral oughts. The sense of 'can' implied by moral oughts is the practical sense: the sense internal to the practical standpoint, the standpoint of the agent facing moral oughts. 'Can' in this sense is compatible with determinism.

Chapter 3 explores desert of moral blame on a different understanding of the nature of blame, one on which to morally blame an agent for an action is to hold a negative moral reactive attitude towards her on account of what she has done. The reactive attitudes are among the attitudes that bear what Philippa Foot calls an 'internal relation' to their object. That is, there are certain conditions that the subject of such an attitude must believe its object to meet for the attitude to be the attitude in question. These conditions give rise to internal standards of appropriateness for the reactive attitudes, that fully determine when a particular attitude is deserved. It is because of the nature of desert—the fact that desert is a matter of what is *intrinsically* just or fitting—that the standards that determine desert of the reactive attitudes are those internal to the attitudes themselves. And by the moral reactive attitudes' internal standards, desert of the moral reactive attitudes does not require ultimate responsibility. Or, at least, desert of the moral reactive attitudes appears not to require ultimate responsibility. There is a further aspect of the reactive attitudes that must be taken into account, viz., the link between the negative moral reactive attitudes and certain retributive sentiments. Insofar as it is of the nature of the negative moral reactive attitudes, where strong, to involve some desire to see their target punished or some thought that punishment is deserved, it will only be possible for the negative moral reactive attitudes to be morally deserved if it is possible for punishment to be morally deserved.[10] To determine whether desert of the negative moral reactive attitudes presupposes ultimate responsibility, we therefore need to determine whether moral desert of punishment presupposes ultimate responsibility.

[10] P. F. Strawson (1962), 90.

Chapter 4 takes up the question of the moral desert of punishment. After providing a provisional working definition of punishment, I turn to the question of the meaning and force of the claim that S morally deserves to be punished. I argue that the claim is roughly equivalent to the claim that it is *pro tanto* (and pre-institutionally) morally fitting that the agent be punished, where this constitutes a positive ground for punishment and not merely a ground for the agent's being unable to complain of being treated unjustly if she is punished. Towards the end of the chapter, I distinguish two different ways of thinking about the moral desert of punishment. On the first, which I label the 'communicative' understanding, desert of punishment derives from desert of the negative moral reactive attitudes, with punishment serving as a vehicle for communicating to the wrongdoer the negative moral reactive attitudes she deserves. On this understanding, the fact that the negative moral reactive attitudes involve a readiness to punish is explained by punishment's communicative role. On the second understanding, the 'non-communicative' understanding, it is *pro tanto* just, in and of itself, that those who culpably engage in moral wrongdoing be deliberately made worse off than they would have been had they not engaged in wrongdoing. The difficulty with the non-communicative understanding, I suggest, is that there is little to distinguish it from the traditional moral retributivist understanding of desert of punishment according to which what morally culpable wrongdoers deserve is, simply, to be made to suffer. As I note in Chapter 1, there are incompatibilists who understand the moral desert of punishment in such terms and who take moral responsibility to require ultimate responsibility for this very reason. Yet, as I also note, many philosophers—including, I believe, the majority of incompatibilists—would be loathe to ally themselves with this understanding of the moral desert of punishment, finding it morally problematic.

Chapter 5 explores whether the communicative understanding of desert of punishment is capable of serving as a viable, less morally problematic, alternative to the non-communicative understanding. I argue that it is. More specifically, I argue (1) that desert of the negative moral reactive attitudes entails desert of an overt response that serves to communicate to the wrongdoer the negative moral reactive attitudes she deserves, (2) that in cases of serious public wrongdoing, punishment is necessary to communicate adequately to wrongdoers the negative moral reactive attitudes they deserve, and (3) that the reason that condition (2) holds is not that the negative moral reactive attitudes involve the belief that those who culpably engage in moral wrongdoing non-communicatively deserve to be made to suffer. However, as I also argue, there is no reason to believe when understood in communicative terms, desert of punishment requires ultimate responsibility.

The concluding chapter of the book explores what, in light of the discussion of the previous five chapters, incompatibilists are to do. Incompatibilists, I suggest, have four options: (1) align themselves with the traditional moral retributivist understanding of moral responsibility and desert of punishment despite finding it morally problematic (that is, if they do find it morally problematic), arguing that it alone adequately captures the ordinary understanding; (2) show that the traditional moral retributivist of the moral desert of punishment is not morally problematic (and presupposes ultimate responsibility); (3) show that it is wrong to assimilate the non-communicative (or, perhaps, the 'non-derivative') understanding of the moral desert of punishment to the traditional moral retributivist understanding and that, when not so assimilated, desert of punishment requires ultimate responsibility; or (4) abandon incompatibilism.

There may be incompatibilists who think that they can dismiss the book's conclusion on the ground that they base their incompatibilism on an independent requirement for strong alternative possibilities rather than on the need for ultimate responsibility. In case there are, it is worth emphasizing that proponents of a strong alternative possibilities requirement face the same argumentative burden as proponents of an ultimate responsibility requirement: they, too, must adduce a conception of moral liability-responsibility that makes clear why such responsibility requires freedoms beyond those compatible with determinism. If the arguments advanced in the book are correct, proponents of a strong alternative possibilities requirement will be left with much the same options as those who base their incompatibilism on a requirement for ultimate responsibility.

1

Moral Responsibility and Ultimate Responsibility

In this chapter, I examine the attempts of four contemporary incompatibilists—Galen Strawson, Robert Kane, Saul Smilansky, and Derk Pereboom—to justify incompatibilism concerning moral responsibility and determinism by appeal to the idea that moral responsibility presupposes some form of 'ultimate responsibility'. Before I turn to the attempts themselves, it will be useful to situate them in the history of the larger debate concerning the compatibility of moral responsibility and determinism.

Prior to 1969, it was nearly universally assumed that moral responsibility presupposes 'the ability to act (or to choose) otherwise' or, as many now say, 'alternative possibilities'. Debate between compatibilists and incompatibilists centered on whether universal causal determinism would preclude this ability. Incompatibilists argued that it would. Compatibilists argued that it would not. Harry Frankfurt's 1969 paper 'Alternate Possibilities and Moral Responsibility' changed all this. There, Frankfurt provides an apparent counterexample to what he refers to as the 'Principle of Alternate Possibilities': the principle that 'a person is morally responsible for what he has done only if he could have done otherwise'[1]. The example involves an agent, Jones, who performs an act entirely on his own. Unbeknownst to Jones, there exists a second agent, Black, who would have prevented Jones from performing (or even choosing to perform) any act other than the one he in fact chose to perform had he been about to choose otherwise. Given the set-up of the example, it seems that Jones could have neither acted otherwise nor chosen to act otherwise. At the same time, his inability plays no role in explaining his action. Black never

---

[1] Frankfurt (1969), 1.

intervenes in the causal chain leading up to Jones's action. Unaware of Black's presence, Jones performs the same action, in the same manner, and for the same reasons, as he would have done if Black had never existed. Insofar as Jones's inability to do otherwise plays no role in explaining his action, it would, Frankfurt argues, be 'quite gratuitous to assign it any weight in the assessment of his moral responsibility'.[2] Rather, we should conclude that Jones is morally responsible for his action despite his inability to act otherwise. Contrary to what had always been assumed, moral responsibility does not presuppose the ability to act otherwise. To the extent that the traditional rationale for incompatibilism concerning moral responsibility and determinism had been tied to the assumption that moral responsibility presupposes the ability to act otherwise, Frankfurt's example calls the traditional rationale seriously into question.

Incompatibilists have offered several responses to Frankfurt's example and to 'Frankfurt-style examples' more generally.[3] Some question whether the examples are genuine counterexamples to the principle of alternative possibilities, arguing that although they exclude alternative possibilities of the traditional type, they do not exclude all alternative possibilities. In a related move, some incompatibilists accept that the examples are genuine counterexamples to the principle of alternative possibilities as originally formulated, but argue that there are close cousins of the principle that are not susceptible to counterexample.[4] Still other incompatibilists question whether it is possible to ensure that the agent could not have chosen to act otherwise without presupposing that his choice is causally determined,

---

[2] Frankfurt (1969), 8.

[3] The term 'Frankfurt-style counterexamples' was originally coined by van Inwagen to refer to 'counterexamples that are directed at principles similar to but distinct from PAP [Frankfurt's Principle of Alternate Possibilities], and which are as strategically similar to Frankfurt counterexamples as is possible' (van Inwagen (1978), 203). An example of the type of principle van Inwagen has in mind is his own PPA (Principle of Possible Action), which reads: 'A person is morally responsible for failing to perform a given act only if he could have performed that act' ((1978), 204). Van Inwagen attempts to show that even if PAP is vulnerable to counterexamples, other similar principles (such as PPA) are not. Frankfurt replies to van Inwagen in Frankfurt (1983). For a detailed discussion of Frankfurt-style counterexamples and the debate concerning them, see Fischer (1994) and (1999). A recent volume of articles devoted to Frankfurt-style counterexamples is Widerker and McKenna (2003). The volume includes a brief reply by Frankfurt.

[4] For one of the earliest challenges to Frankfurt's argument along these lines, see van Inwagen (1978), discussed in n. 3 above. More recent challenges along these lines include Wyma (1997) and Otsuka (1998).

thereby begging the question against the incompatibilist if one nevertheless assumes that the agent is morally responsible.[5] However, there are incompatibilists who accept the counterexamples or, at least, the primary lesson Frankfurt draws from them: that what matters in deciding whether a person is morally responsible for an action is not the presence or absence of alternative possibilities per se, but how the action is brought about.[6] Rather than abandoning their incompatibilism, members of this final group maintain that concerns about the origins of our actions provide independent grounds for espousing incompatibilism concerning moral responsibility and determinism. For, they maintain, these concerns point to a separate condition of moral responsibility: an 'ultimate responsibility' condition.[7] To be morally responsible for her actions, they argue, an agent must be 'ultimately responsible' for them: roughly, she must herself be, or be responsible for, the ultimate (determining) cause(s) of her actions, having personally determined the (determining) causes of her actions 'all the way back'.[8] Yet, if the thesis of determinism is true, then no agent is ever the ultimate (determining) cause of her actions, for all actions are causally determined by the laws of nature and events long antedating the agent's birth.[9] Hence,

---

[5] For challenges of this sort, see Widerker (1995a), (1995b), (2000); Ginet (1996); and Wyma (1997). For Frankfurt's response to Widerker, see Frankfurt (2003). While I agree with Widerker that Frankfurt's original counterexample suffers from this difficulty, I believe that it is possible to construct versions of the counterexample that do not suffer from it. (See, e.g., Pereboom (2003).) Beyond this, I, like the incompatibilists I am about to discuss, accept the primary lesson that Frankfurt draws from the original counterexample: that what matters in connection with moral responsibility is not the presence or absence of alternative possibilities per se, but what happens in the causal sequence leading up to the agent's action. (See Frankfurt (2003) and Fischer (2002).) It might turn out that one of the actual-sequence conditions that an agent must fulfill to be morally responsible for her actions requires the existence of indeterminism. (An ultimate responsibility condition would be one such condition.) In this case, the presence of 'strong' alternative possibilities would be a necessary consequence of an agent's being morally responsible. Still, such possibilities would not independently be required for moral responsibility. For an argument along these lines, see Klein (1990).

[6] See Frankfurt (2003).

[7] See, for instance, G. Strawson (1986), (1994), (1998), (2000), (2001); Klein (1990); Kane (1994), (1996), (2000), (2004); Smilansky (2000); Pereboom (1995), (2001), (2005); and Bernstein (2005).

[8] The roughness of my formulation reflects the fact that proponents of an ultimate responsibility condition for moral responsibility formulate the condition in different ways. Some of the different formulations will be discussed shortly.

[9] More carefully, if determinism holds, then no agent is ever ultimately responsible for her actions in the backtracking sense described above. There may be ways of defining the term

if the thesis of universal determinism is true, no agent is ever morally responsible for her actions, irrespective of whether moral responsibility requires alternative possibilities. The idea that moral responsibility requires some form of ultimate responsibility has long been part of incompatibilist thinking. Bramhall insists that man must have a power to move himself originally and without 'extrinsical necessitation'; that if the will were extrinsically necessitated to evil, then the necessitating force would be 'the true cause of evil, and ought rather to be blamed than the will itself'.[10] Reid argues that 'if, in every voluntary action, the determination of [a man's] will be the necessary consequence of something involuntary in the state of his mind, or in his external circumstance, he is not free; he has not what I call the Liberty of a Moral Agent'; as such, he is incapable of 'justly merit[ing] disapprobation and blame' or 'esteem and moral approbation'.[11] Kant insists that 'man *himself* must make or have made himself into whatever, in a moral sense, whether good or evil, he is or is to become . . . for otherwise he could not be held responsible for it and could therefore be *morally* neither good nor evil'.[12] In the twentieth century, the idea that moral

'ultimate responsibility' that do not build this backtracking component into the definition of ultimate responsibility and on which it would not follow from the truth of determinism that no agent is ever ultimately responsible for her actions. Haji (2009) suggests that we think of Frankfurt's account of when an agent's desires are 'truly her own' and, similarly, Fischer and Ravizza's account of when the mechanism that issues in an agent's action is the agent's 'own' as attempts to spell out a compatibilist conception of 'ultimate responsibility' or ultimate origination. See Frankfurt (1971) and Fischer and Ravizza (1998). It is certainly true that such compatibilist accounts attempt to spell out the sense in which an agent's actions must have their source in the agent for her be morally responsible for them. As I define 'ultimate responsibility', they are attempts to show that an agent need not be ultimately responsible for her actions in order to be their source in the relevant sense. Throughout the book, I shall use the term 'ultimate responsibility' in the backtracking sense defined above. This corresponds to the way the term is generally used in the literature.

[10] Bramhall (1999), 56.
[11] Reid (2011), 267, 269.
[12] Kant (1960), 40. Although Kant is often characterized as an incompatibilist, his position is more complex, and less clear-cut, than this suggests. Wood (1984) describes Kant as being committed to the 'compatibility of compatibilism and incompatibilism' ((1984), 74). How one understands this compatibility will depend on whether one views Kant's distinction between the noumenal and the phenomenal as a distinction between two worlds or between two standpoints on a single world. For discussion of the two ways of understanding the distinction in connection with Kant's views of freedom, see Wood (1984), Korsgaard (1989), (1992), and Keller (2010). If the two standpoints view is correct, then the compatibilist position that I develop in Chapter 2 in (seeming) opposition to Kant may resemble Kant's true view.

responsibility requires some form of ultimate responsibility finds expression in the works of C. A. Campbell, Roderick Chisholm, and Richard Taylor, among others.[13] It underwrites Peter van Inwagen's 'Direct Argument' for the incompatibility of moral responsibility and determinism, and its crucial 'Principle of the Transfer of Non-Responsibility'.[14] Likewise, it is the driving force behind what Susan Wolf, a compatibilist, refers to as the 'Dilemma of Autonomy' and also behind Nagel's despair of the 'problem of responsibility' ever being solved.[15] More generally, echoes of the idea can be heard in incompatibilists' talk of 'origination', 'self-creation', 'uncaused causes', and 'prime movers unmoved'. Prior to Frankfurt's article and the attention that it drew to the difference between what happens in the causal chain leading up to an action, on the one hand, and the availability of alternative causal sequences, on the other, the alternative possibilities requirement and the requirement for ultimate responsibility were never clearly distinguished from one another. Once they were, many incompatibilists came to regard the ultimate responsibility requirement as the more fundamental.[16]

Whether there are any circumstances under which the ultimate responsibility requirement might be satisfied—and if so, what they are—is a subject of dispute among proponents of the requirement. The answer depends in large part on how the requirement is formulated. Strawson formulates the requirement in terms of an agent's having to be responsible for the crucial (determining and non-determining) mental causes of her actions all the way back. As such, she must be responsible for the initial mental nature with which she was born. Formulated in these terms, the requirement is impossible to satisfy. Kane, by contrast, formulates the requirement in terms of an agent's having to be responsible for anything that is a sufficient reason, cause, or motive for her action.[17] If the requirement is formulated in these terms, then an absence of sufficient

---

[13] See Campbell (1938), Chisholm (1964), Taylor (1966).

[14] Van Inwagen first presents the 'Direct Argument' in his (1980). He there refers to its crucial principle as 'Principle B'. Ravizza coined the name 'Principle of the Transfer of Non-Responsibility' in his (1994).

[15] See Wolf (1990); Nagel (1986).

[16] To the best of my knowledge, Klein (1990) was the first to explicitly distinguish the ultimate responsibility requirement from the alternative possibilities requirement. For the idea that the ultimate responsibility requirement is the more fundamental of the two, see additionally Kane (1996), (2000), (2004) and Pereboom (2001).

[17] See Kane (2000) and (2005).

reasons, causes, and motives at the right point in the causal chain leading up to an action—the point of choice—would suffice for the requirement's being satisfied. The same is true if the requirement is formulated in terms of an agent's actions having to not be determined by any factor that the agent did not herself determine. Here, too, an absence of determinism at the right point in the causal chain would suffice for satisfaction of the ultimate responsibility requirement. However, it is for precisely this reason that Pereboom rejects such formulations. As he argues, the mere absence of determinism (or of sufficient reasons and motives) does not add up to additional agential control.[18] Pereboom himself formulates the ultimate responsibility requirement in terms of our actions and choices having to be neither:

alien-deterministic events—events such that there are causal factors beyond our control by virtue of which they are causally determined, [n]or truly random events—those that are not produced by anything at all, [n]or partially random events—those for which factors beyond the agent's control contribute to their production but do not determine them, while there is nothing that supplements the contribution of these factors to produce events.[19]

Pereboom maintains that when formulated in these terms, the requirement is satisfiable, but only by a form of agent-causation that, for empirical reasons, he believes unlikely to exist. Much of what is written about the requirement focuses on the question whether and under what circumstances it might be satisfied. The question I want to focus on is whether there is an ultimate responsibility requirement for moral responsibility in any of these forms.

The claim that an agent must be ultimately responsible for her actions to be morally responsible for them is one that I, like many others, intuitively find plausible. It seems to capture the idea that if we are to be accountable for our actions, then our actions must originate in ourselves in some absolute, buck-stopping way. Our actions and characters must be ultimately 'up to us' and not trace back to causes outside of us. True responsibility and blame lie with the ultimate cause.[20] If asked how agents can be morally responsible for their actions if their actions are caused by factors for

18 Pereboom (2001), 39–54.
19 Pereboom (2001), 127.
20 See Kane (1996), 33–5. In explaining his position, Kane writes: 'The basic idea is that the ultimate responsibility lies where the ultimate cause is' (35).

which they are not responsible, or how agents can be morally blamed for actions caused by factors for which they are not to blame, many instinctively answer that the agents in question cannot be morally responsible, cannot be morally blamed. One of the principal arguments in favor of the ultimate responsibility requirement is that ordinary intuitions strongly support it. Strawson writes that the demand for ultimate responsibility 'lie[s] deep in ordinary moral thought and feeling'; Kane maintains that the idea that moral responsibility requires ultimate responsibility reflects 'the way most people think about genuine desert before they are corrupted by philosophical doubts about the possibility of ultimate responsibility and underived origination'.[21] They may be right. At the same time, I've come to suspect that part of the intuitive plausibility of the requirement stems from the ease of conflating the concepts of moral responsibility and ultimate responsibility, inadvertently sliding from talk of the one form of responsibility to talk of the other.[22] It is all too easy to move from talk of an agent's being 'truly or ultimately' morally responsible or deserving of moral blame for an action—in the sense of being genuinely and full-fledgedly morally responsible or genuinely and full-fledgedly deserving of moral blame for an action—to talk of her being 'ultimately responsible' or 'ultimately to blame' for an action—where one now has in mind the agent's being, or being responsible for, the action's ultimate cause(s). I take the ease of conflating the two types of responsibility largely to account for the 'lure of pure indeterminism'. Apart from this it is difficult to see why one might think that the insertion of a degree of indeterminism at a certain point in the causal sequence leading up to an action would be enough to render an agent morally responsible for the action when she would not have been morally responsible for the action without it. Again, as Pereboom emphasizes, the addition of indeterminism affords an agent no additional control. However, as I said above, the question I want to focus on is not whether or under what circumstances it would be

---

[21] G. Strawson (2001), 453; Kane (1996), 82–3.

[22] I say that I've come to suspect that *part* of the intuitive plausibility of the ultimate requirement reflects the ease of conflating the concepts of moral and ultimate responsibility. There are other factors, including I suspect, a less than clear (and, arguably, quasi-mechanistic) understanding of determinism and of causation more generally, as well as a mistaken picture of the relation between agents, actions, and the causes of agents' actions that obscures agents' ineliminable role as actors. On the latter mistake, see Hornsby (2004a), (2004b).

possible to fulfill an ultimate responsibility requirement, but whether there is an ultimate responsibility requirement for moral responsibility.

With this in mind, let us turn to the first two steps of Galen Strawson's 'Basic Argument' for the impossibility of moral responsibility. I quote Strawson directly:

(1) When you act, you do what you do, in the situation in which you find yourself, because of the way you are.

It seems to follow that:

(2) To be truly or ultimately morally responsible for what you *do*, you must be truly or ultimately responsible for the way you *are*, at least in certain crucial mental respects.[23]

From these first two steps, Strawson goes on to argue that you can never be truly or ultimately responsible for the way you are in any respect at all, and so can never be truly or ultimately morally responsible for what you do. For, to be truly or ultimately responsible for the way you are, you would have to be *causa sui* and this is impossible. What is most significant for our purposes is not the further steps of the argument, but the transition from step (1) to step (2).

Strawson appears to take (2) to follow straightforwardly from (1).[24] In a later paper he remarks that, to him, the transition seems 'obvious'—so obvious that he 'do[es] not really think that it needs defense'.[25] (Strawson goes on to say that his characterization of ultimate responsibility as 'heaven-and-hell' responsibility 'can be taken as a defense if one is felt to be needed'. This characterization is discussed below.) Yet, in the eyes of compatibilists, the transition will be far from obvious.[26] In fact, (2) only follows from (1) if either (a) it has already been assumed that genuine moral responsibility for a given act presupposes responsibility for the ultimate

---

[23] G. Strawson (1998), 746. The Basic Argument first appeared in G. Strawson (1986). It has since appeared, with minor changes in wording, in G. Strawson (1994), (1998), (2000), and (2001).

[24] In other versions of the Basic Argument, Strawson uses 'Hence' or 'So' to describe the transition between the first two steps, rather than the relatively more cautious 'It seems to follow' quoted above. See, e.g., G. Strawson (1994).

[25] G. Strawson (2001), 443, 451.

[26] Compatibilists might agree that for agents to be morally responsible for their actions, they must in some sense be responsible for their characters. What they will deny is that agents must be regressively responsible for the causes of their characters in the manner claimed by proponents of an ultimate responsibility requirement. Responsibility for character will be discussed in Chapter 2 and, again, in the conclusion.

causes of that act or (b) what is meant by 'truly or ultimately morally responsible for one's actions' is 'responsible (morally or otherwise) for the ultimate causes of one's actions'. Whereas (a) assumes precisely what is meant to be in question (and what compatibilists deny), (b) either conflates 'true' moral responsibility with some form of ultimate responsibility or simply changes the topic.

Put somewhat differently, what the considerations Strawson highlights in the remaining steps of his Basic Argument show, at least in the first instance, is that an agent cannot be responsible for the ultimate causes of her actions; she cannot be causally responsible for her actions 'all the way back'. This point might be restated in terms of its being impossible for the agent to be ultimately responsible for her actions. The form of responsibility in question, however, is, in the first instance, simply causal.[27] We can happily grant to Strawson that if an agent is not ultimately causally responsible for her actions, in the sense of not being causally responsible for their ultimate causes, then she is not ultimately morally responsible for her actions (in the sense of not being morally responsible for their ultimate causes). But saying an agent is not ultimately morally responsible in this sense for her actions is not the same as saying she is not truly morally responsible for her actions in the sense of being genuinely and fully capable of deserving reward or punishment, or praise or blame, for the actions themselves. It is this latter form of responsibility that we were meant to be discussing. What compatibilists claim is not that determinism is compatible with an agent's being responsible for the ultimate causes of her actions, but that an agent needn't be responsible for the ultimate causes of her actions in order to be genuinely and fully morally responsible or capable of deserving reward or punishment, or praise or blame, for her actions.

To be clear, I am not presently suggesting that full-fledged moral responsibility for one's actions does not presuppose ultimate responsibility for one's actions; nothing I have said thus far tells against there being such a requirement. The point is simply that, *pace* Strawson, the claim that moral responsibility requires ultimate responsibility is one that demands serious

---

[27] In some of the statements of the Basic Argument, Strawson emphasizes not just the need to have brought about one's original mental nature, but the need to have brought it about in a *conscious, reasoned* fashion. In this case, the responsibility being declared impossible would be more than simply causal. We might call it 'intentional causal' responsibility. However, it would not yet amount to moral responsibility.

defense, for it is a claim compatibilists reject. Yet apart from appeals to the 'intense naturalness' of the supposition that moral responsibility requires ultimate responsibility and his later reference to 'heaven-and-hell' responsibility, no real defense is provided by Strawson.[28]

Before moving on, it is worth emphasizing that while the use of modifiers like 'truly' and 'ultimately' undoubtedly facilitates slides between talk of 'true' moral responsibility and ultimate responsibility, it is not the only facilitating factor. Another is the language of responsibility itself. It is an unfortunate feature of this language that statements of the form 'S is responsible for x'—where S stands for an agent and x for the agent's action(s) or some consequence of her action(s)—have a number of different senses. When used in its primary sense—viz., the liability sense—the statement that 'S is responsible for x' indicates that the agent satisfies the necessary causal and capacity conditions for liability to, or desert of, some form of response to x. However, as is often pointed out, such statements can also be used in a purely causal sense—i.e., simply to indicate that S caused x to occur—in which case S needn't stand for a rational agent at all.[29] Less often noted is that statements of this form can be used in a third sense, which Hart terms the 'capacity' sense. When used in this third sense, the statement that 'S is responsible for x' might be used to indicate that the agent stands in some morally or legally significant causal relation to x, or possesses a particular capacity or set of capacities normally required (or alleged to be required) for liability or desert. Thus it might be used to

[28] In his (1994), G. Strawson dismisses compatibilist challenges to the second step of the Basic Argument with the following:

Clearly this sort of compatibilist responsibility [i.e., the sort that merely requires the absence of certain constraints] does not require that one should be truly responsible for how one is in anyway at all, and so step (2) of the Basic Argument comes out as false. One can have compatibilist responsibility even if the way one is is totally determined by factors entirely outside one's control...It is for this reason, however, that compatibilist responsibility famously fails to amount to any sort of true *moral* responsibility...One does what one does entirely because of the way one is, and one is in no way ultimately responsible for the way one is. So how can one justly be punished for anything one does? Compatibilists have given increasingly refined accounts of the circumstances in which punishment may be said to be appropriate or intrinsically fitting. But they can do nothing against this basic objection. ((1994), 16–17)

In the next paragraph, Strawson states that '[m]any compatibilists have never supposed otherwise. They are happy to admit the point' ((1994), 17). That he takes this to be the case may explain his not offering a stronger defense. Whether he is correct in taking it to be the case is discussed below.

[29] See, e.g., Glover (1970) and Wolf (1990).

indicate that S is the proximate cause of some harm, or the ultimate cause of her actions, or that she possesses the capacity to distinguish right from wrong, or the capacity to recognize and act in accordance with 'the True and the Good', or even the ability to act otherwise.[30] These multiple uses are hardly a coincidence. As Hart emphasizes, it is perfectly natural that responsibility terms should have been extended from their primary use—viz., that of referring to an agent's liability to, or desert of, some form of response or, more accurately, to an agent's meeting the necessary causal and capacity conditions of such liability or desert—to instead refer directly to the causal connection or capacities normally required for liability or desert, and then, by a further extension, to causal connection more generally.[31] As Hart further notes, the later uses may have even supplanted the original use as the most common—hence the tendency to speak of responsibility as a *condition* of liability or moral desert. Still, as natural as this tendency might be, it is not without risk— particularly in contexts such as ours where the conditions required for liability or desert have yet to be determined. The more accustomed one becomes to thinking of responsibility as a causal relation or capacity or form of control, the easier it becomes to slip into thinking that questions concerning the possibility of moral responsibility and its compatibility with determinism, are purely *metaphysical* questions—i.e., questions that can be answered simply by establishing that a specific type of causal connection or control is, or is not, possible or compatible with determinism, and so without recourse to *moral* argument.

I do not mean to deny that metaphysical considerations have a crucial role to play in determining whether anyone is, or could be, morally responsible for his or her actions and, if yes, then under what circumstances. The answers to these questions will depend on metaphysical matters—on whether the causal and capacity conditions of moral responsibility are compatible with determinism or possible to fulfill under any set of circumstances. My point is that the question 'What are the necessary

[30] For the idea that to be morally responsible, an agent must possess the capacity to recognize and act in accordance with 'the True and the Good', see Wolf (1990). Hart's discussion of the different senses of 'responsibility' is to be found in Hart (1967). Hart there also discusses a fourth sense of responsibility: the role-responsibility sense. Used in this fourth sense, to say S is responsible for *x* is to say that S has a duty of care or oversight with respect to *x*. We will return to this sense in Chapter 2.

[31] Hart (1967), 265.

causal and capacity conditions of moral responsibility?' is not a metaphysical question. It is a moral question: a question about the capacities an agent must possess and the causal relation she must bear to her actions in order for her to be capable of being morally deserving of certain types of response. For this reason, the disagreement between compatibilists and incompatibilists concerning the compatibility of moral responsibility and determinism cannot be settled by metaphysics alone. To know which metaphysical questions to ask, we must first answer the moral question. And, to return to what I said in the Introduction, to answer—or even to know how to go about answering—the moral question, we must first clarify what it is to be morally deserving of a certain response, and the types of response at issue when we speak of moral responsibility. Only then will we be in a position to tell whether full-fledged moral responsibility presupposes ultimate responsibility.

In fact, Strawson does say several things about the forms of response he takes to be in question in discussions of moral responsibility. As noted earlier, at one point he suggests that his characterization of 'true' or 'ultimate' moral responsibility as 'heaven-and-hell' responsibility—i.e., 'responsibility of such a kind that, if we have it, it *makes sense* to propose that it could be just to punish some of us with (eternal) torment in hell and reward others with (eternal) bliss in heaven'—can be taken as a defense of the ultimate responsibility requirement 'if one is felt to be needed'.[32] If such heaven-and-hell responsibility is what Strawson has in mind when he speaks of 'true' moral responsibility, then his accompanying claim that many compatibilists are happy to admit that their accounts of liberty do not afford 'true' moral responsibility is relatively uncontroversial. At the

---

[32] For the suggestion that his characterization of true or ultimate responsibility can be taken as a defense of the ultimate responsibility requirement if one is felt to be needed, see G. Strawson (2001), 451. The characterization quoted is from his (1994). Strawson there emphasizes the importance of the words 'makes sense': 'for one certainly does not have to believe in any version of the story of heaven and hell in order . . . to believe in the existence of true moral responsibility' (9–10). Just how much of a concession this is meant to be is somewhat unclear. Immediately after this statement, Strawson writes that '[o]n the contrary, many atheists have believed in the existence of true moral responsibility' (10). This seems to indicate that what he means to step away from is the idea that there exists a God who might literally sentence one to eternal torment in hell, not the idea that it might be just to impose such a sentence. Indeed, Strawson goes on to say that the 'story of heaven and hell is useful simply because it illustrates, in a peculiarly vivid way, the kind of absolute or ultimate accountability or responsibility that many have supposed themselves to have, and that many do still suppose themselves to have. It very clearly expresses its scope and force' (10).

same time, these compatibilists will insist that the fact that their accounts do not afford such 'heaven-and-hell responsibility' is not a shortcoming of their accounts; as they see it, the claim that it could be just deliberately to subject someone to eternal torment in hell is morally indefensible. It does not follow that the compatibilists in question would be similarly happy to admit that in the absence of ultimate responsibility 'no punishment or reward is ever truly just or fair'—much less that it is 'exactly as just to punish and reward people for their actions as it is to punish or reward them for the (natural) color of their hair or the (natural) shape of their faces'.[33] The 'less colorful' characterization Strawson offers of 'true or ultimate moral responsibility and desert'—viz., as 'responsibility and desert of such a kind that it can exist if and only if punishment and reward can be fair or just without having any pragmatic justification, or indeed any justification that appeals to the notion of distributive justice'—is not equivalent to his initial characterization.[34]

There are proponents of ultimate responsibility conditions who are fully cognizant of the need to defend the condition against compatibilist challenges. Kane and Pereboom are among them. Smilansky may be, too; though whether he fully appreciates the need is a bit unclear. However, in the end, the arguments that all three provide rely on claims no less controversial than those they set out to defend—claims that compatibilists will reject—or else smuggle in their original claims. I turn first to Kane.

Kane believes, as I do, that in order adequately to defend the claim that moral responsibility requires ultimate responsibility, incompatibilists must adopt a new approach. It is not enough for incompatibilists simply to cite ordinary intuitions or to declare that compatibilist accounts of moral responsibility and desert cannot provide for 'true' moral responsibility and desert, i.e., responsibility and desert of the most 'exalted' kind or the kind most worth-wanting. As Kane emphasizes, compatibilists will reply that neither moral responsibility, nor moral desert, requires ultimate responsibility or, as Kane calls it, 'underived origination', and that repeated incompatibilist references to 'true' responsibility and 'genuine' desert and to 'true' or 'genuine' versions of such goods as autonomy, creativity, self-worth, and uniqueness as a person simply beg the question. For, compatibilists will continue, when one analyzes what incompatibilists mean by

---

[33]   G. Strawson (1998), 749; (1994), 15; (2001), 458.
[34]   G. Strawson (2001), 452.

'true' responsibility and autonomy, and 'genuine' desert and creativity, one finds that they simply have in mind versions of these goods that satisfy the requirements of ultimate responsibility and underived origination.[35] Kane refers to this stage of the back-and-forth between compatibilists and incompatibilists as the 'dialectic of origination'.[36] To move beyond it, Kane argues, we need to 'take seriously the metaphysical depths of the free will issue'.[37] Once we do, we come to recognize that the incompatibilist's desire for ultimate responsibility and underived origination traces back to two more elemental desires:

(i) the desire to be an independent source of activity in the world, which is connected . . . to the sense we have of our uniqueness and importance as individuals; and (ii) the desire that some of our deeds and accomplishments . . . have objective worth—worth not just from one's own subjective point of view but true (i.e., non-deceptive) worth from the point of view of the world.[38]

It is because we desire these other things that we want to be ultimately responsible for our actions and are dissatisfied with any form of moral responsibility or desert that does not involve ultimate responsibility.

There are several difficulties with this argument, at least if it is intended to supply a non-question-begging defense of the idea that true moral responsibility and genuine desert—and true versions of the other goods on Kane's list—presuppose ultimate responsibility. First, it is somewhat unclear how the claim that the desire for ultimate responsibility traces back to these two more elemental desires is meant to relate to the question whether moral responsibility requires ultimate responsibility. (Perhaps the thought is that objective desert of moral praise and blame presupposes that our deeds and accomplishments possess objective worth?) The most serious difficulty with Kane's argument, however, is that unless there is independent reason to believe that the objective worth of our deeds or the independence necessary to secure our uniqueness and importance as individuals depends on our being ultimately responsible for our actions, the fact that our desire for ultimate responsibility traces back to desires for these other goods will be irrelevant. Surely the fact that we desire ultimate responsibility because we wrongly suppose it to be required for some other good cannot vindicate the desire for ultimate responsibility. While

[35] Kane (1996), 91. [36] Kane (1996), 91.
[37] Kane (1996), 92. [38] Kane (1996), 98.

the claim that we must be ultimately responsible for our actions for them to have 'objective, non-illusory, significance in the world' is just as, if not more, controversial than the claim Kane sets out to defend, the claim that ultimate responsibility is a precondition of the sort of independence necessary to secure our genuine uniqueness and importance as individuals appears simply to be a restatement of part of the original claim.[39]

Perhaps Kane is right that from early childhood onwards '[o]ur full sense of *being a distinct self is tied up with the conception of our being a distinct source of motion or activity in the world*, such that what goes on behind the screen of the mind can have effects out there in the world'.[40] And perhaps he is right that our growing understanding of the world and of the ways in which we are influenced by it threatens this sense, leading to the worry that '[p]erhaps we are not really independent sources of motion in the world at all, but are entirely products of the world, or of the not-self. Perhaps we only *seem* to "move ourselves" in a primordial way, when our motions are in fact caused by forces in the world of which we are unaware'.[41] And perhaps he is right that it is in response to this and other perceived threats to our status as distinct selves that we come to desire ultimate responsibility and thereafter resist attempts to undermine the belief that we are ultim- ately responsible for our actions, fearing that this would entail that our activities have 'merely illusory and not real significance or worth *for* the world'.[42] Still compatibilists will insist that such worries and fears are ill- grounded—that the perceived threats are *merely* perceived—and so the appeal to ultimate responsibility is unnecessary.

---

[39] Interpreted as a claim concerning the preconditions of our actions' making an objective difference in the world or having value 'over and above the felt-satisfaction the acts have or bring' to us ((1996), 97)—as many of Kane's comments suggest we ought to interpret it—the claim that ultimate responsibility is required for our deeds to have 'objective, non-illusory, significance' is one that other proponents of an ultimate responsibility requirement for moral responsibility reject. There is no reason to think that in the absence of ultimate responsibility, all value would be subjective. (On this point, see Fischer (2002)). There is perhaps another way of interpreting Kane's references to our deeds having objective worth 'over and above the felt satisfaction the acts have or bring' to us, namely, as a reference to our deeds being such as to render *us* objectively worthy of praise or blame or moral praise or blame. On this interpretation, the claim that ultimate responsibility is a precondition of our deeds having objective worth—like the claim that it is a precondition of our having the sort of independ- ence necessary to secure our genuine uniqueness and importance as individuals—is merely a reworded version of part of the original claim that Kane sets out to defend.

[40] Kane (1996), 93.   [41] Kane (1996), 94.   [42] Kane (1996), 100.

We could, of course, define an agent's being an 'independent source of activity' in terms of some of her deeds originating ultimately in herself rather than being ultimately determined by sources external to her and beyond her ultimate control. And at times this appears to be what Kane has in mind when he speaks of 'being an independent source of activity'. However, thus defined, it is an open question whether being an independent source of activity is a necessary condition of genuine uniqueness and importance as an individual—unless, that is, we similarly define 'genuine uniqueness and importance' in terms of (at least some of) the agent's deeds or traits having their ultimate source in herself rather than being determined by sources beyond her ultimate control. Within the present context, however, to interpret 'genuine uniqueness and importance' in this way would beg the question.

Similarly, we might insist with Kane that 'the possession of independent selfhood . . . is a precondition for moral agency in the fullest sense' and then define 'moral agency in the fullest sense' in terms of an agent's 'being selfish or having moral concern for others in a way that emanates ultimately from [her]'[43] or in terms of an agent's vices and virtues ultimately tracing back to her and her alone. However, thus defined, it is an open question whether moral agency in the fullest sense is a precondition for true moral responsibility or moral responsibility in an ultimate sense—unless of course what we mean by 'true moral responsibility' or 'moral responsibility in an ultimate sense' is moral responsibility that extends to the ultimate sources of an agent's vicious and virtuous traits and actions. But, once again, to interpret 'true' moral responsibility or 'moral responsibility in an ultimate sense' in this fashion is either to conflate true (i.e., genuine, full-fledged) moral responsibility with some form of ultimate responsibility or else simply to change the topic.

I turn next to the work of Smilansky.[44] Unlike Strawson and Kane (and Pereboom, as we shall see), Smilansky considers himself a dualist concerning moral responsibility rather than a straight incompatibilist. As he sees it, questions concerning the control required for moral responsibility can legitimately be asked and answered on two different levels and, thus, from two different perspectives: the 'local compatibilist' perspective and the 'ultimate hard-determinist' incompatibilist perspective. Both perspectives, he thinks, are partially valid. On the one hand, we need to take seriously distinctions in local compatibilist control and organize our communities and practices of responsibility around them. On the other hand, we must recognize that in organizing our communities and practices around distinctions in local compatibilist control, we shall inevitably treat people in ways that are unjust. No matter how just or deserved a particular instance of punishment or blame might be on the local compatibilist level, on the hard determinist level no one ultimately deserves to be blamed or punished for his or her actions and so all blame and punishment are ultimately unjust.[45]

Whether Smilansky fully appreciates the need to defend the incompatibilist half of his dualism is unclear. At times he appears to believe that once he grants the partial validity of the compatibilist perspective on responsibility and justice—i.e., its validity on the non-ultimate level—compatibilists will have no reason to deny the incompatibilist claim that in the absence of ultimate responsibility all adverse treatment must be considered ultimately undeserved and so ultimately unjust.[46] Yet unless 'ultimate desert' and 'ultimate justice' are defined in such a way as to render the claims in which they appear trivially true, it is far from clear why compatibilists should be willing to grant the claim in question. It may be true that '[b]lameworthiness requires desert, desert requires responsibility, and responsibility requires control'.[47] It may also be true that 'holding people responsible for what was not in any sense under their control constitutes almost a paradigm of injustice'.[48] However, it does not follow from these claims that ultimate blameworthiness and ultimate desert require ultimate responsibility and ultimate control, or that absent ultimate

---

[45] See Smilansky (2000), 97–100, (2003a), 262–6.

[46] E.g., in his (2000), Smilansky writes:

once we grant the compatibilist that his distinctions have some foundation and are partially morally required, there is no further reason to go the whole way with him, to claim that the absence of libertarian free will is of no great moral significance, and to deny the fact that without libertarian free will even a vicious and compatibilistically free individual is in some important sense a victim of his circumstances ... There is a sense in which 'compatibilist justice' is very often, at best, 'justified injustice', and in which the proper compatibilist order can be seen as, in one way, morally outrageous. (99)

Whether compatibilists would be willing to grant these claims is, Smilansky concedes, a different matter.

[47] Smilansky (2000), 17.

[48] Smilansky (2000), 16.

responsibility and control, all blame and punishment are ultimately unjust. Or, at least it does not follow if what we mean by 'ultimate blameworthiness and desert' and 'ultimate injustice' is genuine blameworthiness and desert and genuine injustice. The claims concerning ultimate blameworthiness and desert *would* follow if what we meant by 'ultimate blameworthiness and desert' was blameworthiness and desert for the ultimate causes of one's actions. However, it remains an open question whether genuine blameworthiness and desert are in any way undermined by an agent's not being blameworthy for the ultimate causes of her actions. Similarly, we can stipulate, with Smilansky, that what we mean by 'ultimate injustice' is the injustice that, from a hard-determinist perspective, is involved in all acts of blame and punishment in the absence of ultimate responsibility and control.[49] But such a stipulation does not entail that 'ultimate injustice' is a genuine form of injustice that must be acknowledged when assessing the overall justice of blaming or punishing agents for actions under their immediate control.

At other times, Smilansky appears to recognize the need to provide some sort of argument in support of his claims concerning the necessity of ultimate responsibility. The arguments he supplies, however, turn out not to be arguments for the necessity of ultimate responsibility, but rather arguments for its impossibility that are then conjoined with reassertions of his initial claims concerning the necessity of ultimate responsibility or with claims that presuppose the truth of his initial claim. The two following passages are representative:

The question of justification based upon desert, which is founded on being 'under someone's control' or 'up to someone', can be asked up to the highest level. When moral and intellectual capacities are developed, and illusion does not dominate, these questions will be asked and pursued. And if they are not asked up to that level, then the moral sense, not being consistent, will not be what it should be ... Without libertarian free will, however sophisticated the compatibilist formulation of control in the broad sense, and whether it focuses on character, reflection, ability to follow reasons, or anything else available at the compatibilist level, in the end *no one can have ultimate control over that for which one is being judged* ... The fact remains that if there is no libertarian free will, a person being punished *may suffer justly* in compatibilist terms for what is ultimately her luck, for what follows from being what she is—ultimately without her control, a state which she had no

[49] See, e.g., Smilansky (2000), 106. For further discussion of ultimate injustice, see Smilansky (2003a) and (2003b). The latter piece is a response to criticisms raised by Lenman in his (2002).

real opportunity to alter, hence not her responsibility and fault. We must recognize the fundamental unfairness and injustice that appear from common practices, the particular ways in which compatibilistically free people so often become *victims* of the forces which have made them what they are, if they are harmed and the moral significance of the absence of libertarian free will is not taken into account.[50]

Even if our criminal [the 'fortunate' or non-deprived criminal who receives a harsh prison sentence for cheating many people out of their life savings] significantly shaped his own identity he could not, in a non-libertarian account, have created the original 'he' that formed his later self (an original 'he' that could not have created his later self differently). If he suffers on account of whatever he is, he is a victim of injustice, simply by being. Again, this does not eliminate the difference between his being a victim and the way in which he victimized his victims. It does not eliminate the moral propriety of punishing him, if he possessed compatibilist free will. Indeed, we might be required to maintain the moral order and punish him . . . [But] . . . [e]ven compatibilistically justified institutions of re-tributive justice create grave ultimate injustice on the hard determinist level. Even if people can be morally responsible in compatibilist terms they lack ultimate responsibility: this lack is often morally significant, and in cases such as the one we have considered, having people pay dearly for their compatibilistically responsible actions brings forth injustice. To risk an aphorism: not to take the absence of libertarian free will seriously is not to take justice seriously. Positions that fail to do so and remain on the compatibilist level will inevitably be morally superficial.[51]

It is undeniable that 'we can ask the question about control also on the ultimate level', querying the sources of an agent's character and motiv-ation, rather than limiting our enquiry to the local compatibilist level.[52] It may also be true that 'when the moral and intellectual capacities are developed, and illusion does not dominate, these questions will be asked and pursued' at the ultimate level, and that when they are, we are forced to admit that 'ultimately there can be no control'.[53] However, *pace* Smi-lansky, it does not follow from these claims that compatibilists who care about issues of control ought, on pain of inconsistency, to acknowledge that even compatibilistically justified institutions are in one way unjust— that, insofar as they do not, their position 'is morally, even humanly, shallow, for it depends on our remaining on the level of people as more or less "givens"; i.e., on blindness as to what we learn when we push our enquiries further, into the causes of this "given"'.[54] These claims assume that there is a regress condition on moral responsibility—that facts about

---

[50] Smilansky (2000), 47–8.   [51] Smilansky (2000), 52.
[52] Smilansky (2003a), 262.   [53] Smilansky (2000), 47; (2003a), 262, 263.
[54] Smilansky (2000), 54.

the ultimate sources of our character and actions and our lack of ultimate control are morally significant and do affect the justice of practices such as punishment. But this is precisely what has yet to be shown.[55] I turn finally to Pereboom. Pereboom's defense of the idea that moral responsibility requires some form of ultimate responsibility relies on what he calls 'the four case strategy'.[56] The strategy—which he describes as a combined counterexample and generalization strategy—involves presenting an initial case expected to elicit the intuition that the agent described is not morally responsible for his actions even though he purportedly satisfies the four most prominent compatibilist conditions for moral responsibility. Via consideration of two intermediary cases, Pereboom argues that there is no morally significant difference between the initial case and one in which everything is 'ordinary from the compatibilist point of view' and determinism holds. He concludes that, to be consistent, compatibilists must concede that no agent is ever morally responsible for her actions if determinism holds. He further contends that the best explanation of this fact is that moral responsibility requires ultimate responsibility.

In all four of the cases that Pereboom describes, Professor Plum murders Ms. White for the sake of personal advantage. In all four cases, Plum is caused to do so by desires that (a) 'flow from his "durable and constant character"', (b) are not irresistible, (c) conform to his second-order desires, and (d) are modifiable by, or even the product of, a deliberative process that is moderately reasons-responsive. Beyond this, Plum is said to possess the capacity to 'grasp, apply, and regulate his behavior by moral reasons': 'when the egoistic reasons that count against acting morally are relatively weak, he will typically regulate his behavior by moral reasons instead'.[57] The only differences between the four cases have to do with the ultimate source of the egoistic desire upon which Plum is acting when he kills White.

---

[55] That one can ask the same question about the ultimate causes of one's actions as one can about the proximate causes of one's actions does not entail that if answers to the latter are morally significant, then answers to the former are morally significant. Smilansky might be right that facts about the ultimate sources of our character and actions and our lack of ultimate control are morally significant and affect the justice of our practices of punishment. Whether he is right will be discussed in later chapters. My present point is that Smilansky hasn't argued for these claims. Rather, he has assumed them.

[56] Pereboom (2001), 112. Pereboom appeals to an earlier version of the four-case argument in his (1995). He further defends the argument in his (2005) and (2008).

[57] Pereboom (2001), 111.

In Case 1, Plum was created by neuroscientists who '"locally" manipulate him to undertake the process of reasoning by which his desires are brought about and modified—directly producing his every state from moment to moment'.[58] In Case 2, Plum was also created by neuroscientists; this time, rather than locally manipulating his every state, they have simply programmed him to weigh reasons in a certain way, causing him often (though not always) to behave egoistically. In Case 3, Plum is 'an ordinary human being except that he was determined by the rigorous training practices of his home and community so that he is often but not exclusively rationally egoistic'; the training in question occurred too early in his life for him to have prevented or altered it.[59] In the final case, '[p]hysicalist determinism is true, and Plum is an ordinary human being, generated and raised under normal circumstances' who often, but not always, acts egoistically.[60] The question we are asked to consider is whether, in any of the four cases, Plum is morally responsible for murdering White.

As Pereboom sees things, intuitively Plum is not morally responsible for murdering White in either Case 1 or Case 2. He assumes that many compatibilists will share his intuition, at least in Case 1, and perhaps also in Case 2. To his mind, the only real difference between the two cases is in the length of time between the neuroscientists' programming and the resultant action. And, he maintains, 'it would seem unprincipled to claim' that the length of time between the neuroscientists' programming and the resultant action could affect Plum's moral responsibility.[61] Pereboom further maintains that the most plausible explanation of the intuition that Plum is not morally responsible in the two cases is that, in both cases, Plum's action is causally determined by factors beyond his control. But, of course, in Cases 3 and 4, Plum's action is also causally determined by factors beyond his control. Thus, unless compatibilists can point to some other feature to explain why Plum is morally responsible in the latter two cases but not the former—which Pereboom contends they cannot—they have no choice but to concede that Plum is not morally responsible in any of the four cases. Moreover, just as the most plausible explanation of Plum's lack of moral responsibility in Cases 1 and 2 is that his action is causally determined by factors beyond his control, so the most plausible explanation of his lack of responsibility in Cases 3 and 4 will be that his action is causally determined by factors beyond his control. As such, we may conclude that in order for an agent to be morally responsible for his actions, his actions must not be determined by factors beyond his control. Moral responsibility requires ultimate responsibility.[62]

By combining the counterexample strategy with the generalization strategy, Pereboom hopes to avoid the sorts of objections that the two strategies face when deployed separately from one another.[63] In the end, however, his four-case strategy inherits both sets of objections. The most serious objection is that even if a majority of compatibilists were willing to concede that Plum is not morally responsible for his action in Case 1—and based on early responses to Pereboom's argument, it's far from clear that the majority of compatibilists would be willing to concede this—they can credibly deny that the most plausible explanation of Plum's lack of moral responsibility in Case 1 is that his action is causally determined by factors beyond his ultimate control.[64] An equally credible explanation is that, insofar as neuroscientists directly produce his every state from moment to moment, Plum cannot properly be regarded as reasoning at all. It is not Plum who is processing the relevant information and recognizing rational relations and drawing inferences on the basis of that recognition. Not if his programmers are directly producing each discrete state. It is the programmers who are doing all the reasoning. Nor is this the only credible explanation compatibilists might offer of Plum's lack of responsibility in Case 1. I focus on this explanation in particular partly because it strikes me as the most obvious explanation, but also because, if what it alleges is true, then Plum does not meet (all of) the compatibilist conditions that Pereboom claims he meets. (Not if, e.g., the moderately reasons-responsive deliberative process modifying and/or producing the agent's desires is meant to be the agent's own.) Moreover, unlike most of the other explanations that compatibilists cite or might cite, this explanation of Plum's lack

---

[62] Pereboom (2001), 120.

[63] See the objections I raised in the Introduction on pp. 5–6.

[64] See, e.g., Haji (1998) and McKenna (2005), (2008). McKenna advocates a 'hard-line' reply to Pereboom's four-case argument. Rather than arguing, on the basis of the similarities between Case 1 and Case 4, that insofar as Plum is not morally responsible in Case 1, he cannot be considered morally responsible in Case 4, McKenna proposes arguing that since Plum is morally responsible in Case 4, he must be considered morally responsible in Case 1 despite the presence in Case 1 of local manipulation. This 'hard-line' reply seems far weaker than the reply that I am about to provide on behalf of compatibilists.

of responsibility cannot be ruled out simply by altering Case 1 in such a way that Plum satisfies the condition in question. The only way of accommodating the condition would be to eliminate Case 1 from the strategy. Yet, without Case 1, Pereboom would be in an even weaker position with respect to the other three cases than he already is; even with Case 1, many compatibilists do not share the intuition that Plum is not morally responsible in Case 2.

Pereboom could perhaps respond that his intuitions concerning Case 2 remain fully intact even if we omit Case 1. Yet, just as Pereboom dismisses the objection that, according to ordinary intuitions, Plum is morally responsible in Case 4 by contending that this subset of ordinary intuitions rests on a mistake—viz., our not recognizing that, under ordinary circumstances, our actions still trace back to factors beyond our control—so compatibilists will contend that Pereboom's own intuitions are based on some sort of mistake or confusion.[65] And this brings us back to the problem with which we began this chapter: there is reason to suspect that intuitions concerning the need for ultimate responsibility may stem from the ease of conflating the concepts of moral responsibility and ultimate responsibility and inadvertently sliding from talk of the one form of responsibility to talk of the other. Once 'true' moral responsibility is distinguished from ultimate responsibility, however, it starts to look less obvious that moral responsibility for one's actions requires ultimate responsibility. Indeed, it's not entirely clear what proponents of the requirement even have in mind when they speak of 'true' moral responsibility.

Again, none of this shows that true moral responsibility does not require ultimate responsibility. For all that's been said thus far, moral responsibility may well require ultimate responsibility. The point is that if incompatibilists are to show that this is the case, then they are going to have to provide a different type of argument from those that they have provided thus far— one that starts by providing a clearer account of what they have in mind when they speak of true moral responsibility and genuine moral desert. Strawson's heaven-and-hell-responsibility perhaps represents one option. However, I suspect that this understanding of true moral responsibility is one that the majority of incompatibilists, no less than the majority of compatibilists, would not want to accept. As libertarian Randolph Clarke writes:

---

[65] See Pereboom (2001), 116–17.

One might think that no sort of freedom that is possible for finite, human agents could ground a responsibility of this sort. One might think that if we are created beings, then there is no variety of freedom that our creator could possibly have given us that would justify that being's (or anyone's) rewarding us with eternal bliss or punishing us with eternal suffering. One might, it seems, very reasonably accept all this and still hold that the responsibility—true moral responsibility—of human agents is not ruled out. If any such agent is truly responsible, one might say, that fact provides us with a specific type of justification for responding in various ways to that agent, with reactive attitude of certain sorts, with praise or blame, with finite rewards or punishments. To be a morally responsible human agent is to be truly deserving of these sorts of responses, and deserving in a way that no agent is who is not morally responsible.[66]

The question is whether there is a way of understanding the nature of the responses that Clarke mentions and the nature of their desert such that, understood in this way, true moral responsibility would require ultimate responsibility. It is to the task of answering this question that I turn in the next four chapters.

---

[66] Clarke (2005), 21.

2

Moral Appraisal and Defects of Character

This chapter and the next discuss desert of moral blame, though on two different understandings of the nature of moral blame. In this chapter, I examine an account on which moral blame is understood as a form of cognitive judgment or appraisal. In Chapter 3, I explore an account of moral blame in terms of the negative moral reactive attitudes. I briefly discuss overt blame in Chapter 5. I shall not try to show that one of these understandings is the correct understanding of moral blame or *the* understanding at issue in discussions of moral responsibility. I do not believe there is one understanding that has a unique claim to being the correct understanding or the understanding at issue in discussions of moral responsibility.[1] The crucial question for our purposes is whether, on any of the understandings, an agent would have to be ultimately responsible for her actions (or character) to be deserving of moral blame for wrongful behavior.

On the assumption that moral blame is to be understood as a form of cognitive judgment or appraisal, or as the content of such judgment or appraisal, just how are we to understand the judgment or appraisal in question? A common answer is that moral blame is a form of 'deep' moral appraisal: appraisal that 'does more than record a causal connection' between an agent and the consequences of her action and that also 'goes

---

[1] Which understanding of blame is the predominant understanding seems to have changed over time. Etymology and blame's conventional pairing with praise suggest that blame was once understood, in the first instance, as overt criticism or censure, or the outward expression of disapproval. While P. F. Strawson's (1962) has inspired many contemporary philosophers to identify blame with certain negative reactive attitudes, Strawson himself appears to be referring to overt condemnation when he speaks of blame.

beyond mere evaluative description of what the agent has done'.[2] The talk of 'depth' traces back to Wolf. It is intended to capture the difference between moral praise and blame and the type of 'superficial' praise and blame that can be assigned to inanimate objects no less than to persons, e.g., when we 'blame' the rain for the cancellation of the picnic or the finicky carburetor for the vehicle's not starting. In Wolf's words:

When we say that an individual is responsible for an event in the superficial sense, we identify the individual as playing a causal role . . . of special importance to the explanation of that event. And when we praise or blame an individual in the superficial sense, we acknowledge that the individual has good or bad qualities, or has performed good or bad acts. But when we hold an individual morally responsible for some event, we are doing more than identifying her particularly crucial role in the causal series that brings about the event in question . . . When, in this context, we consider an individual worthy of blame or of praise, we are not merely judging the moral quality of the event with which the individual is so intimately associated; we are judging the moral quality of the individual herself in some more focused, non-instrumental, and seemingly serious way . . .[3]

Nagel makes a similar point in discussing moral blame. In his words: 'when we blame someone for his actions, we are not merely saying it is bad that they happened, or bad that he exists: we are judging *him*, saying he is bad, which is different from his being a bad thing'.[4] 'This kind of judgment', Nagel continues, 'takes only a certain kind of object'.[5] It takes as its object a person, a moral agent. To morally blame a person for his action is to judge him, on the basis of that action, to be a morally bad person, a bad moral agent.

Taken literally, Nagel's analysis of moral blame would not stand. The judgment with which it identifies moral blame is too strong. One wrong is typically not enough to render an agent a morally bad person, though it is normally enough to render her deserving of some degree of

---

    [2] The quoted material is from Wallace (1994), 52, 75. For similar descriptions, see Glover (1970) and Wolf (1990). Wallace believes that the only way to capture the special 'depth' of moral blame and the way in which moral blame goes beyond 'mere evaluative description of what the agent has done' is by understanding blame in terms of the negative reactive attitudes. See his (1994), 74–83.
    [3] Wolf (1990), 40.
    [4] Nagel (1979), 175. Nagel reiterates the point several pages later: 'Moral judgment of a person is judgment not of what happens to him, but of him . . . We are not thinking just that it would be better if he were different, or did not exist, or had not done some of the things he has done. We are judging *him*, rather than his existence or characteristics' (184).
    [5] Nagel (1979), 175.

moral blame. Nevertheless, what I take to be Nagel's intended point holds: in one sense of moral blame, to morally blame an agent for her action is to judge her action to reflect badly on her as a person or as a moral agent. (This is one way, though certainly not the only way, of cashing out the idea that to morally blame an agent for an action is to hold the action morally against her.) Put slightly differently, to morally blame an agent for her action is to judge her action to reflect a defect in her as a moral agent: a moral defect or defect of character.[6]

If this is the content of a judgment of moral blame—that an agent's action reflects a moral defect or defect of character—then at first glance it might seem unclear how an argument for an ultimate responsibility requirement for desert of moral blame is even to get off the ground. *Qua* cognitive judgment or appraisal, the judgment that an agent's action reflects a moral defect will be deserved just in case what it alleges is true, i.e., just in case the appraisal is accurate.[7] (This follows from the nature of desert—from the fact that desert is a matter of what is *intrinsically* just or fitting. A judgment is intrinsically just or fitting if it is true, an appraisal if it is accurate.) Hence, the judgment that an agent's action reflects a moral defect or defect of character will be deserved just in case the agent's action does reflect a moral defect or defect of character. Provided that one is prepared to allow—as many contemporary incompatibilists are—that an

---

[6] In his (2006), Sher maintains that it is a 'truism' that 'blaming a person for something involves taking its moral defects to reflect badly on him'. At the same time, he denies that to blame a person for an action is to take the action's defects to reflect a defect in the person's character. Or rather he rejects the claim, seemingly entailed by this view of blame, that a person is blameworthy for a bad action if and only if the action reflects a defect of character. Sher's understanding of what constitutes a defect of character differs from the understanding I introduce later in the chapter. In evaluating the defect of character view of blame, it is important to bear in mind that one can take an agent's action to reflect a defect of character without knowing precisely what defect it reflects—e.g., does it reflect cowardice or lack of compassion?—and also even if the defect does not neatly correspond to one of our standard vice terms. The first point must hold if we are ever to be in a position to blame agents of whose characters we do not have intimate knowledge. Having established that the agent is a normal adult and that the circumstances are normal and that none of the standard compatibilist excusing conditions obtains, there may be no other reasonable conclusion to reach than that the agent's action reflects a defect of character.

[7] On the idea that justice (or, more accurately, desert) in judgments is a matter of truth, see Kneale (1967), Feinberg (1974), and Zimmerman (1988). Expression of that truth—in the case of blame, overt criticism or condemnation—requires separate discussion. In connection with expression, it is especially important to keep in mind that desert 'represents only a part, and not necessarily the most important part, of the domain of justice' (Feinberg (1963), 56). This and other issues concerning the force of desert claims where what is deserved is a mode of overt treatment will be discussed in Chapter 4.

absence of ultimate responsibility would not undermine the judgment that an agent acted morally wrongly, it is far from clear why it should be thought to undermine the judgment that an agent's action reflects a moral defect or defect of character.[8]

That an absence of ultimate responsibility would not undermine this type of judgment is—ironically—the primary point that Hobart is making in the passage that prompts Wolf to distinguish 'deep' praise and blame from merely superficial praise and blame and to speak of an 'unbridgeable gulf' between Hobart's position and her own.[9] The passage (in which Hobart identifies blaming an agent with saying the agent is a 'bad act-maker') is part of Hobart's response to what he describes as 'a certain very familiar objection': '"How can any one be praised or blamed if he was framed by nature as he is, if heredity and circumstances have given him his qualities? A man can surely be blamed only for what he does himself, and he did not make his original character, he simply found it on his hands."' Hobart responds is as follows:

> A man can surely be blamed only for what he does himself, for that alone tells what he is. He did not make his character, no, but he made his acts. Nobody blames him for making such a character, but only for making such acts. And to blame him for that is simply to say that he is a bad act-maker. If he thinks the blame misapplied he has to prove that he is not that sort of an act-maker. *Are we to be told that we may not recognize what he is, with appropriate feelings for its quality, because he did not create himself—a mere contortion and intussusception of ideas?*[10]

In identifying 'blaming' with 'calling [someone] a bad act-maker', Hobart is not suggesting that blaming an agent is simply a matter of acknowledging that the agent 'made' a bad act, much less a bad act of the sort that

[8] Of the four incompatibilists whose views are discussed in detail in Chapter 1, only Pereboom raises the possibility that an absence of ultimate responsibility might undermine judgments of moral rightness and wrongness. He does not come down firmly on one side or the other. At the same time, he maintains that even if an absence of ultimate responsibility were to undermine judgments of rightness and wrongness, it would not undermine judgments of moral goodness or badness. See his (2001).

[9] Wolf (1990), 38. There is a further irony in Wolf's criticism of Hobart: on her own account of moral responsibility, it does not matter whether the agent created her own character. What matters is that the agent possesses the ability to appreciate and govern herself in accordance with 'the True and the Good' and that nothing prevents her from exercising this ability. Indeed, she explicitly argues against the view that moral responsibility requires an agent to be ultimately responsible for her character. See chapters 3 and 4 of her (1990) as well as her (1997).

[10] Hobart (1934), 83. Italics added.

might equally be made by '[e]arthquakes, defective tires...dogs [or] children'.[11] On the contrary, Hobart appears to be emphasizing precisely what critics like Wolf take him to have missed: that blaming a moral agent is a matter of judging *him*—of judging the moral quality of the agent himself—and not just the moral quality of his actions. In Hobart's words: 'It is self we are reproaching, *i.e.*, self that we are viewing as bad in that it produced bad actions. Except in so far as *what-it-is* produced these bad actions, there is no ground for reproaching it (calling it bad) and no meaning in doing so'. 'How do we reproach ourselves? We say to ourselves, "How negligent of me!" "How thoughtless!" "How selfish!"... In other words we are attributing to ourselves at the time of the act, in some respect and measure, a bad character...'[12] Hobart makes the same point in connection with praise: in praising a self 'because of [its] action you have implied that the action came from its goodness (which means its good character) and was a sign thereof'.[13] Where that self came from 'is another question... *Its origin cannot take away its value, and it is its value we are recognizing when we praise*'.[14]

How might proponents of an ultimate responsibility requirement for desert of moral blame respond to an argument like Hobart's? They have two options. First, they might admit that an absence of ultimate responsibility would not undermine desert of the judgment that an agent's action reflects a moral defect or a defect of character, but argue that this sort of judgment falls short of genuine moral blame. This is the option likely to be favored by most contemporary proponents of an ultimate responsibility requirement for desert of moral blame. Many contemporary incompatibilists are already willing to concede that determinism does not threaten judgments of moral goodness or badness, including judgments concerning the moral goodness or badness of agents and their characters. And even many of their compatibilist opponents would agree that the judgment that an agent's action reflects a moral defect in her or a defect of character does

---

[11] The list of other potential 'bad act-makers' is Wolf's. See her (1990), 40. Importantly, although earthquakes, defective tires, dogs, and very young children can behave in unwelcome ways and produce unwelcome results, they cannot behave in ways that are *morally* bad.

[12] Hobart (1934), 67. Italics added.

[13] Hobart (1934), 69.

[14] Hobart (1934), 84. I do not mean to suggest that Hobart's account of blame is free of shortcomings, but only that it does not suffer from the particular shortcoming that Wolf attributes to it.

not yet amount to a judgment of moral blame. However, there is also a second option. Proponents of an ultimate responsibility requirement for desert of moral blame might argue that, contrary to initial appearances, an absence of ultimate responsibility would undermine judgments concerning the moral goodness or badness of agents and their characters. More specifically, they might argue that unless agents are ultimately responsible for their characters, neither they nor their characters could be morally good or bad. This seems to be Kant's view.[15] In his words: 'Man *himself* must make or have made himself into whatever, in a moral sense, he is or is to become. Either condition must be an effect of his own free choice; for otherwise he could not be held responsible for it and could therefore be *morally* neither good nor evil.'[16] Absent ultimate responsibility, the defects that we ordinarily think of as defects of character would not be *moral* defects and hence appraisals involving the attribution of such defects would not be *moral* appraisals. The appraisals in question would lack moral force.

Most of the remainder of this chapter will be devoted to exploring the second option just described: that of arguing that unless agents are ultimately responsible for their characters, defects of character would not be moral defects and hence appraisals involving the attribution of such defects would not be moral appraisals. We shall briefly return to the first option at the end of the chapter; the material we discuss in the interim will place us in a better position to respond to the argument underlying it. In order to assess the second option, we need an account of what distinguishes genuinely moral defects from other types of defect and genuinely moral appraisal from other forms of appraisal. That is, we need an account of moral force. Towards this end, I want to begin by examining the account

---

[15] Whether it is in fact Kant's view that absent ultimate responsibility of the type required by contemporary incompatibilists, agents cannot be morally good or evil is unclear. It is clear that, for Kant, an agent must be ultimately responsible in some sense for her character if she or her character is to be morally good or bad. What this sense is and whether it supports incompatibilism concerning moral responsibility and determinism as incompatibilism is ordinarily understood is complicated by Kant's distinction between the noumenal and the phenomenal, and by his belief that noumenal freedom is compatible with the causal necessitation of phenomena. (See my remarks in n. 12 of Chapter 1.) If the distinction between the noumenal and the phenomenal is between two different standpoints on a single world and not between two different worlds, then the compatibilist position that I develop later in this chapter in seeming opposition to 'Kant's view' may be close to Kant's actual position.

[16] Kant (1960), 40.

of the distinctive force of moral appraisal that Scanlon advances in some of his earlier works on moral blame.[17] Although ultimately inadequate as an account of the special force of moral appraisal, identifying its central shortcoming will lead us to a more adequate account. With the latter account in place, we will be in a position to examine the charge that unless agents are ultimately responsible for their characters, defects of character would not be moral defects and appraisals involving the attribution of such defects would not be moral appraisals. After further argument, we will be in a position to refute it.

Central to Scanlon's earlier discussions is the idea that the distinctive force of moral judgment (including moral blame) is to be located not 'in what the moral judge is *doing*' in making or expressing her judgment, but rather in the content of the judgment or 'what is claimed about the person judged'.[18] In Scanlon's terms, to morally blame an agent for an action is to claim that the agent's action is the product of morally faulty rational self-governance and reflects 'judgment-sensitive attitudes' that themselves are morally defective.[19] In deciding to act as she did, the agent either failed to consider or knowingly disregarded 'a reason that should, according to any principles that no one could reasonably reject, have counted against [her] action'.[20] In so doing, the agent 'ignored or flouted requirements flowing from another person's standing as someone to whom justification is owed'.[21]

According to Scanlon, that the above is the content of moral blame distinguishes moral blame from other forms of unwelcome evaluative

---

[17]   I have in mind Scanlon (1988) and (1998). Within these earlier discussions, Scanlon understands moral blame in purely cognitive terms. While Scanlon moves away from a purely cognitive understanding of moral blame in his (2008), his new account suffers from the same shortcoming as I attribute to the original. In the interim different aspects of Scanlon's original account have been adopted and developed by Hieronymi and Smith, among others. See, e.g., Hieronymi (2004) and Smith (2008).

[18]   Scanlon (1988), 365.

[19]   Scanlon defines 'judgment-sensitive attitudes' as 'those attitudes that, in a rational creature, should be "under the control of reasons"' (Scanlon (1998), 272). They constitute the set of attitudes for which rational agents are answerable, i.e., for which such agents can, in principle, be asked to provide normative reasons and to modify or withdraw them if appropriate reasons cannot be provided. See Scanlon (1998), 20–4, 272. Scanlon's talk of 'morally faulty judgment-sensitive attitudes' roughly corresponds to my talk of 'defects of character'.

[20]   Scanlon (1998), 271.

[21]   Scanlon (1998), 271.

assessment—the examples he cites are negative appraisal of a person's appearance or talents—in two ways. First, *qua* criticism of an agent's rational self-governance, moral blame calls upon the agent to reconsider her judgment-sensitive attitudes and explain why the charge of faulty rational self-governance is mistaken or acknowledge its validity and modify her judgment-sensitive attitudes accordingly.[22] As Scanlon admits, this first feature is not unique to moral blame. All forms of criticism involving charges of faulty rational self-governance—from criticisms of an agent's mathematical or philosophical reasoning to criticisms of her unwary moves in chess—call upon the agent to reconsider her judgment-sensitive attitudes and either defend or modify them. What distinguishes moral blame from other forms of rational criticism is the second feature of moral blame that Scanlon cites: the particular kind of significance that the failings that moral blame points to have for the agent's relations with other people. This feature is tied to the grounds underlying moral blame— to the particular kind of reason to which the agent being morally blamed is alleged not to have given sufficient weight. As Scanlon emphasizes:

> What is special about violations of the morality of right and wrong is that the reasons one has failed to respond to are grounded not just in some value that others recognize, but in *their own* value as rational creatures. These violations therefore have particular importance for one's relations to them . . . If I have injured someone by failing to take her interests into account in the way one should, then my relation with her is already altered by that fact, whatever she does.[23]

While the first of the two features of moral blame that Scanlon cites is meant to differentiate moral blame (and rational criticism more generally) from what J. C. C. Smart describes as 'dispraise' or mere negative 'grading' (the primary function of which is 'just to tell people what people are like'[24]), the second is meant to differentiate moral criticism from other forms of rational criticism and to account for its peculiar 'sting'.

Measured solely against the two aims just mentioned, Scanlon's account is largely successful. That moral blame implicitly calls upon the agent to reassess her rational self-governance and to defend or modify her judg-ment-sensitive attitudes goes some way towards distinguishing moral blame from mere negative grading. Similarly, the kind of significance

[22] See Scanlon (1998), 268–72, 275–6.
[23] Scanlon (1998), 271–2.   [24] See Smart (1961).

agents' moral faults have for their relationships with others distinguishes moral blame from other forms of rational criticism and explains what, for most of us, is moral blame's particular sting. Despite this, the two features of moral blame that Scanlon cites seem not fully to capture the special force of moral criticism. They certainly do not capture the sort of force that proponents of an ultimate responsibility requirement have in mind when they claim that, absent ultimate responsibility, appraisals involving the attribution of defects of character would not be *moral* appraisals—that they would lack moral force.

The easiest way to see that Scanlon's account leaves something out—and, just as importantly, what that thing is—is by looking more closely at what Scanlon has and does not have in mind when he speaks of moral appraisal's 'calling for' or 'calling upon the agent to engage in' certain kinds of response, including 'justification, explanation, or admission of fault'. In this connection, he makes four points.[25] The first and least important of these points for present purposes is that in expressing negative moral appraisal or blame to an agent's face, a person 'is often literally asking for or demanding an explanation, justification or apology' from the agent for what she has done.[26] Second, and more importantly, insofar as moral blame concerns an agent's judgment-sensitive attitudes, it concerns features of the agent with regard to which it is appropriate in principle for the agent and others to raise questions concerning rational justification. An agent's attitudes are things for which 'requests for reasons are in principle relevant'.[27] It makes sense to request reasons for them, in a way in which

---

[25] The first, second, and fourth points are ones that Scanlon enumerates in his (1988). The third point is one that he makes in his (1998) and further emphasizes in his replies to critics. See, e.g., his (2002).

[26] Scanlon (1988), 367. It is because it relates to what a person might be doing in outwardly expressing negative moral appraisal that I consider this point the least important for present purposes.

[27] Scanlon (1988), 366. It is the 'in-principle-appropriateness' of asking the agent for normative reasons—i.e., the fact that it *makes sense* to ask for such reasons—that Scanlon has in mind when he speaks of agents' being 'accountable' or 'answerable' for their judgment-sensitive attitudes. A different way of expressing my main objection to Scanlon's account of the force of moral blame is that the notion of answerability that it involves is too weak. This weakness may explain Scanlon's belief that an agent needn't possess the capacity to understand moral reasons in order to be morally answerable for her actions or potentially deserving of moral blame. If, as I shall argue, the force of moral blame is bound up with the force of moral obligation, then any account of blame that does not include minimal moral capacity among the necessary conditions of moral blame's desert will be unable to capture moral blame's force.

'[i]t makes no sense to request such a response for something that is not even in principle sensitive to [the agent's] judgment'.[28] Third, in the event that an agent's judgment-sensitive attitudes are morally faulty, the correct response on the part of the agent is to acknowledge fault and to revise her judgment-sensitive attitudes accordingly. According to Scanlon, this response is 'called for' or 'in order' whether or not the agent 'is capable of making it, or of seeing why, in a particular case, revision is called for'.[29] Fourth, to the extent that the person being blamed cares about being able to justify her actions to others, she will want to respond to the calls in question, 'will want to be able to respond positively (i.e., with a justification), and will want to carry out the kind of first-person reflection . . . that makes such a response possible'.[30] 'For such a person', Scanlon concludes, 'moral blame differs from mere unwelcome description not only because of its seriousness but also because it engages in this way with an agent's own process of critical reflection, thus raising the questions, Why did I do that? Do I still endorse those reasons? Can I defend the judgment that they were adequate grounds for acting?'.[31] Yet, of course, as Scanlon acknowledges, as long as we speak of 'admission of fault' rather than 'apology', parallel points apply to all forms of criticism involving charges of faulty rational self-governance. All forms of criticism involving charges of faulty rational self-governance 'call for' the responses in question in the four senses just described.

In the case of moral criticism, something stronger can be said than what was said above and than can be said in relation to other forms of criticism. The responses that Scanlon describes are called for in a stronger sense. Indeed, that these responses are called for in a stronger sense in the case of moral criticism than in the case of other forms of criticism is part of our ordinary understanding of the special force of moral criticism. The nature of the defects that moral criticism picks out impacts the normative force of the call. Remember: in the case of moral criticism, the principles that the agent is alleged to have violated are ones that specify what she, as a moral agent, owes to others. They are principles specifying moral obligations—obligations that apply to all moral agents unconditionally. Thus, in the event that the allegation is true, the modification of attitudes that moral blame calls for will not just be appropriate or in order. Nor will the

[28] Scanlon (1998), 272.   [29] Scanlon (2002), 512.
[30] Scanlon (1998), 367.   [31] Scanlon (1988), 367.

modification simply be one that an agent who cares about being able to justify her actions to others will want to undertake. It will be one that an agent is unconditionally obligated to undertake, i.e., regardless of whether she cares about being able to justify her actions to others. This is the aspect of the special force of negative moral appraisal that Scanlon's account leaves out: its connection to unconditional obligation. In leaving this out, the account leaves out what Kant and his followers rightly regard as the distinctively moral force of such criticism. Moral force is the force of unconditional obligation.

If I care about being a good chess player, then I will want to eliminate my defects as a chess player. Similarly, if I care about being a good mathematician, I will want to eliminate whatever defects I might possess as a mathematician. My defects as a moral agent, by contrast, are ones that I am morally required to eliminate even if I do not care about being a good moral agent. (Looked at slightly differently, *qua* moral agent, I am obligated to care about being a good moral agent.) *Qua* moral agent, I am obligated (to care about being a good moral agent and) to eliminate my moral defects simply because I am obligated *to be* a good moral agent. Moreover, unlike my identity as a chess player or mathematician, my identity as a moral agent is neither contingent, nor optional. It is given to me with my capacities and not something I can simply opt out of. The obligations it generates are therefore unconditional and inescapable.

This is what renders moral defects categorially different from other types of defects and negative moral appraisal categorially different from other types of negative appraisal: the defects with which moral appraisal is concerned are ones that the agent is—and, at the time of action, already was—unconditionally obligated to eliminate in herself. This difference also explains why one might think that unless character was ultimately self-chosen, there could be no moral defects. To paraphrase Nagel: to claim that an agent possesses a moral defect is to claim that she ought (unconditionally) not to be like that, not just that it is unfortunate that she is.[32] And, one might argue, unless character were ultimately self-chosen, there could be no unconditional obligations to have a certain character (or to be or do anything else, for that matter).[33] For there to be unconditional obligations

[32] See Nagel (1979). He writes: 'Condemnation implies that you should not be like that, not that it is unfortunate that you are' (181).

[33] As we shall see, all moral obligations pertain in the first instance to character.

to have a certain character—obligations that apply to all persons (for immediate purposes, all normal adult human beings) merely as such—all persons would have to be (or have once been) capable of having the required character (i.e., of being morally good persons), no matter what their character up to that point. Unconditional oughts imply unconditional cans. Good character would have to be (or have once been) accessible to all. For this to be the case, either agents' present choices with respect to their character would have to not be determined by the conjunction of their circumstances and their already existing character, or their initial (or perhaps even their entire, temporally unfolding) empirical character would have to have ultimately been chosen by them and them alone.[34]

Note that if the argument outlined in the preceding paragraph is correct, then an absence of ultimate responsibility would undermine not just desert of moral blame on the present account of moral blame, but moral desert and moral responsibility across the board. (This includes desert of moral praise and reward for what we would ordinarily think of as morally good or morally exemplary action.) Absent ultimate responsibility, there would be no unconditional obligations. And without unconditional obligations, there would be no moral anything, properly speaking. To reiterate, the mark of the moral is unconditional obligation.

But is the argument that I sketched two paragraphs back correct? Does the possibility of being unconditionally obligated to have a certain character depend on persons' being ultimately responsible for the characters they have? I am not going to challenge the claim that for there to be unconditional obligations to have a certain character, all persons would have to be (or have once been) capable of having that character (of being morally good persons) no matter what their character up to that point. Frankfurt-style counterexamples to the Principle of Alternative Possibilities notwithstanding, it seems clear that the 'ought' of moral obligation implies some sense of 'can' (or 'could').[35] At the very least, a person cannot be morally

---

[34] On one interpretation, Kant requires an agent's entire empirical character to have been self-chosen in a single noumenal choice if the agent is to be capable of being morally good or evil. I do not subscribe to this interpretation.

[35] There may be philosophers who would deny that 'ought' implies some sense of 'can'; however, they are unlikely to be among those who maintain that without ultimate responsibility, there could be no unconditional obligations. It is the arguments of those in the latter group that are my present concern. It is worth noting that Frankfurt did not view his counterexamples to the Principle of Alternate Possibilities as undermining 'ought implies can'. See his (1983).

obligated to do something that is (and always was) beyond her general capacities to do, such that even if she exercised her capacities to their fullest, she still would not succeed in doing it. Although perhaps more controversial in the present context, to me it seems equally clear that for a person presently to stand under a moral obligation, it is not enough for her to have once been capable of doing what she is putatively morally obligated to do; she must *now* be capable.[36] That is, her general capacities in their present condition must be such as would, under normal circumstances, enable her to do what she is obligated to do if she exercised them to their fullest. What I want to challenge is the idea that for all persons, irrespective of their character up to that point, to be capable of being good persons, they would have to be ultimately responsible for their own characters.

Before taking the discussion further, we need a more precise account of character and of agents' obligations to have a certain character. Since the position we are discussing is associated with Kant, I have decided to adopt a Kantian model of character rather than the more familiar Aristotelian model.[37] On the Kantian model, an agent's character is constituted by her subjective practical principles (i.e., her maxims). These are the practical judgments upon which the agent acts and in accordance with which she wills. As practical judgments, they express the agent's conception of value and determine which considerations she counts as reason-giving.

---

[36] Some proponents of ultimate responsibility requirements might deny this. They might argue that if an agent is ultimately responsible for her present lack of capacity to do something that she would otherwise be morally obligated to do, then her lack of capacity does not exempt her from the moral obligation in question. If moral obligations governed outer actions or the securing of certain outcomes, rather than willings, this might be right. If, however, they are will-governing, as I shall argue that they are, then it cannot be right. The pertinent lack of capacity would be a lack of capacity on the part of the agent to govern her will in accordance with moral reasons. An agent who lacked this capacity would no longer be a moral agent. She would no longer be the sort of agent capable of standing under moral obligations.

[37] On the Aristotelian model of character, an agent's character is constituted by her dispositions towards thought, feeling, and action. These dispositions reflect the agent's conception of the good. For a helpful discussion of Aristotle's conception of character, and his views concerning responsibility for character, see Meyer (1993). I suspect that, in the end, there is no deep conflict between the Aristotelian and Kantian models of character—that the differences between Aristotle and Kant reflect different points of focus rather than different understandings. While Aristotle focuses on dispositions reflecting the agent's conception of the good or, in Kantian terms, dispositions reflecting the agent's principles, Kant focuses on the principles that such dispositions reflect.

At the same time, they are practically efficacious, involving a commitment on the part of the agent to do what she can to promote the end specified in the principle. In adopting a principle, an agent sets herself to be the cause of some end that she judges to be good. A defect of character is a morally defective subjective practical principle—one that fails to accord with morality's requirements on willing. For Kant, it is a principle that lacks the form of universality and thus fails to accord with the Categorical Imperative. More broadly, it is a principle that fails to give proper weight to the moral standing of others (or of the agent herself, *qua* rational being). The obligation to be a morally good person or good moral agent is an obligation to have as one's principles only principles that meet morality's requirements on willing and to reject any principle that fails to meet these requirements. The claim that for there to be unconditional obligations to have a certain character, all persons would have to be capable of having that character no matter what their character up to that point can thus be reformulated as the claim that all persons would have to be capable of having as principles only principles that meet morality's requirements, no matter what their principles up to that point. The claim that I want to challenge is that for all persons to be so capable, their choices of principles would have to not be determined by the conjunction of their circumstances and their already existing principles.

Why think that for all persons to be capable of having only principles that meet morality's requirements, their choices of principles would have to not be determined by the conjunction of their circumstances and their already existing principles? The worry, I take it, is that a person's existing principles might systematically be morally faulty. In this case, not only might it be impossible for her correctly to identify, by use of her existing principles, which principles she is in fact morally obligated to reject, but even if she were capable of identifying them, her existing principles might not afford her a motive to act on the identification. For her existing principles to afford her a motive, they would have to include a commitment to morality. If they do not include such a commitment, and yet they completely determine all further choices that the agent might make with respect to her principles, then the recognition that she is morally required to reject a given principle would lack access to her will. The only possibility of such an agent's rejecting the principles that she is required to reject might then seem to lie in her having a power to choose independently of, and in a way not determined by, her existing principles, just as an agent's only possibility of doing what she ought to do in the absence of any natural inclination to do so depends on her possessing a power to choose independently of, and in a way not determined by, her natural inclinations.[38]

I shall not explore what a power to choose independently of one's existing principles might look like or whether positing such a power might help to resolve the worry described. I do not need to. The worry itself is misguided. What traction it has stems from failing to keep in mind the type of agents we are discussing—viz., normal adult human beings—and what such agents are like. *Ex hypothesi*, the normal adult human being is not a psychopath. She is not someone altogether lacking in moral sense or, as Kant refers to it, 'moral feeling' ('a *susceptibility* on the part of free choice' to be moved by moral requirements).[39] As Kant emphasizes, moral feeling is something that every normal human being has within her originally. It is part of her first nature: her nature logically prior to, and underlying the possibility of, moral character. For the normal adult human being, the recognition that she is morally obligated to reject a given principle is thus necessarily a sufficient determining ground of the will—not in the sense that she will necessarily act on its basis, but in the sense that the recognition needn't first be backed up by some other desire or purpose to serve as a possible motive. It has direct access to the will. The normal human being might be bad, but no matter how bad she is, she is not completely dead or entirely indifferent to moral considerations.[40] Were an agent truly dead or indifferent to moral considerations, she, like the psychopath, would fall outside the class of normal adult human beings and, hence, outside the class of beings who would be subject to moral obligations were they to exist. As Kant might say, the moral ought is only addressed to those whose recognition of it implies that they can: those for whom the recognition of moral requirements is a sufficient determining ground of the will.

Equally, the normal adult human being is not an agent whose formative circumstances were so unfortunate that she never developed the ability to distinguish right from wrong and govern herself accordingly. As Herman

---

[38] For the idea that an agent's ability to do what she ought to do depends on her possessing a power to choose independently of, and in a way not determined by, her natural inclinations, see Wallace (2000) and, of course, Kant (1997). My formulation is modeled on Wallace's.

[39] Kant (1996), 529.

[40] Kant writes: 'So when it is said a certain human being *has* no conscience, what is meant is that he pays no heed to its verdict' ((1996), 529).

emphasizes, the character of the normal human being is built on top of what she terms 'moral literacy': a minimal moral capacity that enables its possessor to 'read and respond to the basic elements of a moral world'.[41] As articulated by Herman, moral literacy 'begins with the primitive and necessary acknowledgement of the difference between persons and things and the practically effective understanding of what it means for moral claims to be attached to persons'. These claims are 'elaborated through a culturally based lexicon of basic moral wrongs and injuries that are more or less fixed and easily recognized by a morally literate person'.[42] It follows that, when a normal adult human being violates a moral requirement, she typically knows that she is violating a moral requirement—or she would know, if only she reflected more seriously, or more carefully, or more honestly, about what she was doing. (It is for precisely this reason that normal adult human beings sometimes go to such great lengths to avoid having to think more seriously, or more carefully, or more honestly, about what they are doing.) Even if her upbringing was far from good, even if she enters adulthood having already adopted some seriously defective principles, still the normal adult human being enters adulthood equipped with a practically effective understanding of the difference between right and wrong, and the ability (and if there are obligations, an obligation) to critically examine her existing principles and revise them if defective. While her capacities as they stand might not be perfect, while they might not be sufficient as they stand for full virtue, they are sufficient to enable her under normal circumstances to recognize whether a principle is one that she is obligated to reject, and to reject it, if it is.[43]

Hence, we may dismiss the idea that if all persons are to be capable of having as principles only principles that meet moral requirements, their choices of principles must not be determined by the conjunction of their circumstances and their already existing principles. Their nature as persons—as normal adult human beings—already guarantees their capability. On reflection, this is just as it should (and must) be. If moral obligations are to bind all persons, all normal adult human beings, merely as such, then the powers that they need to possess to be capable of fulfilling these obligations had better be powers that they possess simply as persons, as normal adult human beings. In fact, this point can be extended to all moral agents, i.e., to all rational agents with developed moral capacity. It is to this possibly larger class of agents that moral obligations are often thought to apply. If moral obligations are to bind all moral agents merely as such, then the powers that moral agents need to possess in order to be capable of fulfilling such obligations had better be powers that they possess merely as moral agents, as rational agents with developed moral capacity. These powers are precisely the powers of moral reflection, recognition, and self-governance (governance of the will) that are bound up with moral literacy. I emphasize this point because it has significant implications for how we are to understand the content of moral obligations.

The capacities that moral agents possess simply as moral agents are not specific physical capacities. They are not capacities to move their bodies in specific ways or capacities to perform particular external acts—much less capacities to secure certain results. They are not powers to make changes in the external world at all.[44] They are powers of moral agents to make changes in themselves—powers that extend only as far as governance of the will. Hence, if possession of these powers is sufficient to render moral agents capable of fulfilling their moral obligations, moral obligations must likewise extend only as far as governance of the will. Moral obligations, in other words, are will-governing, not act-governing.[45] They bind agents not to performing specific external acts, but to adopting only principles that meet specific requirements as the laws of their will.[46] In this sense, all moral obligations are obligations to have a certain character or to be a certain type of person: a morally good person.

---

[44] This is not to deny that moral agents must have some ability to make changes in the external world. They must, if they are to be capable of willing at all. The point is that there is not a specific form that this ability must take, or a specific physical ability that it must include, for those possessing it to qualify as moral agents.

[45] In her (1990), Herman marks the distinction between obligations that govern outer action and obligations that govern willing in terms of a distinction between performance obligations and non-performance obligations. She argues that Kantian obligations are of the latter type. My understanding of the nature of moral obligations owes much to her discussion.

[46] The obligation to adopt only principles that meet certain requirements does entail an obligation *not* to act on principles that fail to meet these requirements. Thus while moral obligations do not bind agents to performing specific acts, they do bind agents to *not* performing certain types of action, viz., those based on principles that fail to meet morality's requirements on willing.

At this point, those who believe that there can be no unconditional obligations to have a certain character unless agents are ultimately responsible for their characters are likely to respond that although possession of the general capacities bound up with moral literacy might be a necessary condition of an agent's standing under moral obligations, it is not a sufficient condition. After all, if determinism holds, then whether an agent reflects upon her existing principles (and if she does, then how conscientiously and what she decides) will still be determined by the conjunction of her already existing principles and her circumstances. And, the objection continues, why should we think that it is sufficient that she would be able to recognize and reject the relevant principles if she exercised her capacities to their fullest, if the conjunction of her existing principles and her circumstances determine that she will not exercise them to their fullest? It will not satisfy those who raise this objection to point out that the principles that determine a normal adult agent's decisions are ones that she as a morally literate adult chose to adopt or to retain as the laws of her will. For, of course, if determinism holds, then the agent's choice to adopt or to retain those principles will have been determined by earlier exercises of her capacities which will themselves have been determined by the conjunction of her circumstances and her earlier existing principles, the choice to adopt or to retain which will have been determined by still earlier exercises of her capacities . . . and so on. If we go back far enough, inevitably we arrive at principles that the agent adopted prior to becoming a full adult (and so for which she cannot be considered fully morally responsible) and ultimately at principles that the agent did not choose at all (and so for which she cannot be considered even partly responsible) but which instead derive from her first nature. For this reason, objectors will insist, the fact that the principles that immediately determine the agent's current choices are principles that she as a morally literate adult decided to adopt or retain as the laws of her will is of little consequence. The deterministic sequence leading up to the decision still ultimately traces back to factors for which the agent is not morally responsible.

It is true that human beings start to adopt principles at a point in their lives prior to that at which they could potentially be considered fully morally accountable for their choices. If determinism holds, then it is also true that their earliest choices of principles will have been determined by a conjunction of their temperament, their environment, and the principles that form part of their first nature as human beings.[47] It follows that by the time normal human beings reach adult-hood, they will already have in place a set of existing principles for which they are not ultimately responsible. Finally, it is true, as Galen Strawson reminds us, that adult human beings cannot, hope to accede to ultimate responsibility for their principles moving forward by making changes to their existing principles.[48] If determinism holds, then any decision that a person makes to reject an old principle or to adopt a new one will be determined by (some subset of) her already existing principles. Still, this is not to tell us anything new. It is just to reiterate that if determinism holds, then no agent ever is, or can become, ultimately responsible for her character. However, what is at issue is not whether normal human beings can accede to this sort of backtracking responsibility for character once they are adults. At issue are the necessary conditions of what is sometimes referred to as 'prospective' responsibility and which Hart refers to as 'role-responsibility'.[49] To be responsible for something (or someone) in the prospective or role-responsibility sense is to have a duty of care or oversight with respect to it (or him or her). This is the sense of responsibility on which one can speak of a person's responsibilities (plural) and of an agent's having a responsibility *to do* something (and not just being responsible *for* something). To have a prospective (moral) responsibility to do something is to be (morally) obligated to do it. I mention this other way of referring to obligations as it reminds us that, unlike the concepts of blame, punishment, and desert (all of which are backwards-looking concepts associated with 'retrospective' responsibility) the concept of obligation is essentially forward-looking. It relates not to what has been done, but to what is to be done. In line with the forward-looking nature of obligation, when it comes to determining whether an agent stands under moral obligations, how she came to have the principles that she has is largely irrelevant. (Indeed, that she has the principles that she has rather than other principles is largely irrelevant.[50])

---

[47] As part of human first nature, these principles are the same in all normal human beings. If we follow Kant, there are two such principles: the principle of self-love and the moral law (expressed in moral feeling). Together they account for normal adult human beings' being subject to moral imperatives.

[48] See G. Strawson (1994), 213–14.

[49] See, e.g., Duff (2008) and Hart (1967), respectively.

[50] How an agent came to have the principles she has and that she has them may be relevant to assigning blame, and to the degree of blame, to be assigned. However, they are not relevant to whether an agent is one who stands under moral obligations.

All that is relevant is whether she can ensure that her principles meet morality's requirements moving forward. If she can, then she stands under moral obligations.

As Strawson admits, normal adults do have a choice going forward as to whether to retain their existing principles or to adopt new ones. As adults with developed moral capacity, they have an ongoing opportunity—and if moral obligations exist, an ongoing obligation—to reassess their existing principles. This represents an ongoing opportunity to bring their now more fully developed capacities to bear on principles that they might have adopted when their capacities were less developed. While an agent might not have been capable of recognizing that a certain principle was morally defective when she first adopted it, as a normal adult human being she is capable of recognizing it now. And she is capable of acting on this recognition, rejecting any principle that she deems morally defective. Together, these facts suffice to render normal adult human beings prospectively responsible for their characters whether or not they are ultimately responsible for them. They suffice for the existence of unconditional obligations to have a certain character.

Those who believe that without ultimate responsibility for character there can be no unconditional obligations may respond that I've missed a crucial part of their objection. Returning to the possibility of an agent's being determined by the conjunction of her circumstances and her existing principles not to re-examine her principles or not to reject a principle that even she acknowledges is morally defective, they may argue that if determinism holds, then, contrary to what I've suggested, normal adult human beings are not always able to recognize and reject the principles that they are said to be required to reject—at least not in the sense of 'able' required for the existence of unconditional obligations. unconditional obligations. (Perhaps this inability would have been un-problematic, proponents of an ultimate responsibility requirement might add, if the agents affected had been ultimately responsible for their inability. But, of course, if determinism holds, then the agents concerned will not be ultimately responsible for their inability.) For there to be unconditional obligations to have a certain character, it is not enough for all normal adult human beings to possess the general capacities needed to recognize and reject morally defective principles. Absent ultimate responsibility, it must further be the case that all normal adult human beings faced with normal circumstances possess the 'specific ability' to do so—where possession of a specific ability at a given time requires not just that the agent possess the relevant general capacities at the time, but that she be able to exercise them.[51] (The inability of a normal adult human being under abnormal circumstances to do what normal adult human beings are purportedly unconditionally obligated to would not call into question the existence or unconditional nature of the obligation any more than the inability of an abnormal or non-adult human being would. Hence the limitation to normal circumstances.) Short of this, the objectors might argue, there can be no unconditional obligations to have a certain character.

There is a way of understanding the requirement that agents be able to exercise their capacities under normal circumstances on which the requirement literally goes without saying. It is the traditional compatibilist understanding, on which an agent's being able to exercise her capacities at a time is principally a matter of her not being prevented from doing so by abnormal interferences such as being under extreme stress, or overwhelmed with grief, or paralyzed with fear, or the victim of brainwashing or some other form of mind-control or manipulation.[52] This is clearly not the way in which incompatibilists intend the requirement to be understood. In any case, absence of such abnormal interferences is already guaranteed by the restriction to normal circumstances.

When incompatibilists claim that all normal adult human beings must be able to exercise their capacities (and, indeed, to exercise them properly) under normal circumstances, they mean that it must be physically possible that they do so, holding constant the laws of nature and the state of the universe just prior to the time in question. Provided that the circumstances are normal, their properly exercising their capacities at time t must be compatible with the conjunction of the laws of nature and the total state of the universe at the just prior t_{-1}. However, if determinism holds, then only the actual is physically possible. The only thing that can happen at a time is that which does happen at the time. Any occasion on which an agent does not exercise her capacities properly is an occasion on which she could not exercise her capacities properly. Yet, of course, such occasions are far from uncommon. Even under normal circumstances, normal adult human beings often fail to exercise their

---

[51] Specific ability is always ability at a specific time. The term 'specific ability' comes from Mele (2003).

[52] For a classic presentation of the traditional compatibilist understanding, see Ayer (1954).

capacities properly. Hence, if determinism holds and the incompatibilist understanding of 'can' is the correct understanding, then normal adult human beings are often unable to exercise their capacities properly even under normal circumstances. If this is the case, then there can be no unconditional obligations to have a certain character.

I shall not dispute that there is a sense of 'can' with respect to which the incompatibilist understanding is the correct understanding. There is. It is the theoretical sense of 'can': the sense that we employ when, from the theoretical standpoint or standpoint of an observer, we try to explain some past happening or to predict some future happening. It is the 'can' of what might happen, the 'can' of possible occurrences. What I dispute is that the theoretical 'can' is the 'can' implied by moral oughts. Although human choices and actions are among the occurrences that can be explained and predicted from the theoretical standpoint (albeit not a purely theoretical standpoint),[53] it is not as occurrences per se that human choices are regulated by moral oughts, but as members of a particular subclass of occurrences: that comprising the doings of agents with developed moral capacity. The 'can' that applies to human choices as such doings is not the theoretical 'can' or 'can' of possible occurrences. It is an essentially agential 'can'—a 'can' that only applies to agents with wills and only in relation to those acts brought about through the exercise of will. (Indeed, this must be the case if the 'can' in question is to capture agential ability and not just pure possibility.) The 'can' implied by moral oughts is the practical 'can', i.e., the 'can' that an agent herself employs when, from the practical or deliberative standpoint, she is trying to decide what to do or what principles to adopt as the laws of her will.[54] The relevant form of possibility is possibility from within the deliberative standpoint—the standpoint of the agent facing the decision—and designates the options between which the agent must choose.[55] From the deliberative standpoint, what an agent can do is what falls within the limits of her general capacities to do and what she wouldn't be blocked from doing (in the case of outer actions, by external obstacles, or) by forces that interfere with the control that she

---

[53] Whenever we explain or predict another agent's action by appeal to rational considerations, we appeal to the agent's point of view.

[54] If moral oughts are to regulate deliberation about what to do, then what we ought to do must be something that, from the deliberative standpoint, we can do because of the recognition that we ought to do it.

[55] On the practical or deliberative perspective and practical possibility, see Bok (1998).

normally has over her will. Where what is in question is whether to adopt or reject a given principle, the agent can decide in whatever way she sees fit. It is a presupposition of deliberation that this is the case. In fact, from the deliberative standpoint, with respect to the decision currently under consideration, the 'can' of physical possibility cannot so much as appear.

It is sometimes said that from the deliberative standpoint an agent cannot view her choices as determined. From this it is inferred that from the deliberative standpoint an agent must believe indeterminism to hold. The truth is more complicated than this. From the deliberative standpoint, the agent can no more view her choices as governed by non-deterministic causal laws than by deterministic ones. Either would involve the agent's viewing her own choices from the theoretical standpoint—the standpoint appropriate to a spectator. While deliberating, this is not something that the agent can do. Similar remarks apply to the deliberative standpoint and the theoretical 'can'. From the deliberative standpoint—the standpoint of an agent trying to decide whether to reject a certain principle—whether it is physically possible that she reject a particular principle given the conjunction of her circumstances and her already existing principles is not a question that the agent can ask. Not at the very same time as trying to decide whether to reject the principle. The agent's asking the question would involve her adopting a spectator's stance towards her own decision. It would involve her adopting towards the decision the stance of an individual who either has no control over what is going to be decided or is not planning to exercise the control that she has. This is not a stance an individual can take towards a decision she is in the process of trying to make. Not at the very same time as trying to make it. Trying to make a decision necessarily involves planning to exercise control over what is decided.

This is not to say that it is impossible for an agent to move outside the deliberative standpoint and, from this external vantage point, try to predict what she will decide. It is certainly possible for an agent to ask herself what a person holding the principles that she presently holds and facing the circumstances that she presently faces would decide to do. Or she might attempt to draw inferences from her previous decisions. Still, no answer that the agent arrived at in this way could by itself answer the deliberative question of what to decide. The answer to the deliberative question must be based on practical reasons, not theoretical ones. Nor, upon reentering the deliberative standpoint, could the agent continue to view her now past prediction as definitively answering the theoretical question of what she will decide. Not as long as she believes that she retains her basic moral capacities and that nothing is going to interfere with her exercising them. And provided that she is deliberating in good faith, this is something that she must believe.

To clarify: our agent can continue to believe that a person who holds the principles that she held at the time of making the prediction and who faces the circumstances she then faced will decide this way rather than that. What she cannot do is regard this as binding her to decide this way rather than that. For, she cannot regard herself as bound by her pre-existing principles. Not merely as such. She might decide to retain a pre-existing principle based on a continued belief in its merits. Or, in theory, she might have made it one of her principles always to decide in accordance with her pre-existing principles—though from the deliberative perspective, even this principle would have to be regarded as open to possible revision or rejection. The point is that *qua* deliberator, the agent cannot regard her principles as if they were fixed external laws to which she is passively subject. Whether to retain her pre-existing principles is directly up to her. It is under the direct control of her will. For the agent to say to herself, on the basis of her earlier prediction, that the conjunction of her circumstances and her existing principles determine that she will decide not to reject a given principle even if she recognizes that it is morally defective, and so there is no point to her deliberating or to her attempting to reject it, would be for her to fall victim to confusion or to act in bad faith. If she recognizes that a principle is morally defective, then she ought to reject it. Indeed, to recognize that it is morally defective *is* to recognize that she ought to reject it. It is a presupposition of the recognition and of deliberation itself that she can.[56] Bad faith cannot free her from her obligation.[57]

---

[56] This is the way in which Kant understands the entailment between 'ought' and 'can': to recognize that you ought to adopt (or reject) some principle is to view that principle as to-be-adopted-by-you (or to-be-rejected-by-you). Viewing a principle in this way already involves the understanding that you can adopt (or reject) it. I owe my appreciation of this point and many of the other points in this chapter to Stephen Engstrom.

[57] Nor, for the reasons cited, would the fact that an agent's pre-existing principles in conjunction with her circumstances determine that she will act in bad faith at *t* free her from her obligations to reject the principle in question. From the perspective of morality, that an agent's pre-existing principles in conjunction with her circumstances determine that she will behave in this way despite the circumstances being normal merely reinforces the verdict that

Thus, we can reject the Kantian claim that unless agents are ultimately responsible for their characters, neither they nor their characters could be *morally* good or bad. Agents need not be ultimately responsible for their characters in order to be unconditionally obligated to eliminate their defects of character. Nor does determinism pose any other obstacle to agents' being under unconditional obligations to eliminate their defects of character. And it is the fact that persons are so obligated that renders defects of character distinctively *moral* defects and appraisals involving the attribution of such defects distinctively *moral* appraisals with moral force.

As a final move, proponents of an ultimate responsibility requirement for desert of moral blame might return to what I earlier described as their first option for responding to the claim that an absence of ultimate responsibility would not undermine desert of the judgment that an agent's action reflects a moral defect or defect of character. The option was to admit that an absence of ultimate responsibility would not undermine desert of such a judgment, but argue that the judgment falls short of 'true' moral blame.[58] While this first option might have seemed promising when I initially described it, the arguments that I've adduced in the interim undermine its promise. They close off both of the two routes by which one might have attempted to show that the judgment in question falls short of genuine moral blame.

The first route by which one might have attempted to show that the judgment that an agent's action reflects a defect of character falls short of genuine moral blame would have involved arguing that to identify moral blame with this type of judgment is to reduce moral blame to what, if spoken, would be mere Smartian dispraise. To judge that an agent's action reflects a defect of character is merely to negatively grade the action or its agent. It is just to report that the action or the agent fares badly against some standard of excellence. It is not yet to blame. Scanlon already

---

her character is morally defective. In no way does it undermine this verdict or her obligation to eliminate the defect. The same applies to the absence of ultimate responsibility that determinism would entail. In no way would it undermine the verdict that an agent's character is morally defective or her obligation to eliminate its defects. As a colleague of mine remarked, 'Ought implies can, not will'.

[58] For this option to be of use to proponents of an ultimate responsibility requirement, they would also have to show that, on the proper understanding of moral blame, desert of moral blame requires ultimate responsibility. Whether there is some other understanding of moral blame on which desert of moral blame would require ultimate responsibility will be investigated in Chapters 3 and 5.

provides a partial response to this objection. Our having established what distinguishes moral defects or defects of character from other types of defect places us in a position to complete the response. As we've seen, in attributing a defect of character to an agent we are not merely attributing to her an imperfection or an unfortunate feature or a feature that we (or she) would prefer that she did not have. We are attributing to her a feature that she is unconditionally obligated to not have and to eliminate no matter what her preferences. This renders the judgment that an agent's action reflects a defect of character very different from mere dispraise.

The second route by which one might have attempted to show that the judgment that an agent's action reflects a defect of character falls short of genuine moral blame would have been to argue that in morally blaming an agent for an action, we trace her action not simply to a moral defect, but to a moral defect for which she is herself morally to blame.[59] The problem with this argument is that on the account that I've provided, agents whose actions reflect defects of character are morally to blame for the defects in question. The obligation to reject principles that do not meet morality's requirements is an obligation that all normal adult humans beings are under from the time that they enter adulthood until the end of their normal adult lives. From this, it follows that any defective principle to which a normal adult human being's action might be traced will be a principle that she was already under an unconditional obligation to reject at the time of the action. That the agent failed to meet this obligation means that she was morally to blame for having the defective principle at the time of her action. Moreover, she was morally to blame for having it irrespective of whether she was ultimately responsible for having initially acquired it. Hence, the second route by which one might have attempted to show that the judgment that an agent's action reflects a defect of character falls short of genuine moral blame is also closed off to proponents of an ultimate responsibility requirement for desert of moral blame. With this, they seem to have run out of avenues by which to attempt to show that where moral blame is understood in terms of the judgment that an agent's action reflects a defect of character.

---

[59] For this type of objection, see Levy (2005).

3

The Moral Reactive Attitudes

This chapter explores desert of moral blame where such blame is under-stood in terms of the negative moral reactive attitudes.[1] The main task of the chapter is to determine whether, on this understanding of moral blame, an agent would have to be ultimately responsible for an action to be deserving of moral blame for it. Inspired by P. F. Strawson, those who hold this conception of moral blame reject the idea that moral blame can adequately be understood in purely cognitive terms, or in purely behav-ioral terms, or through some admixture of the two. To limit ourselves to such things is, as Strawson sees it, to 'overintellectualize the facts'.[2] To morally blame an agent for an action is not to form a negative moral judgment of her on the basis of the action. It is not to judge that her action reflects in her a moral defect or defect of character. Nor is it to outwardly express such a judgment or otherwise admonish the agent. It is to experience a certain type of emotional response to what is perceived as the agent's lack of goodwill, respect, or regard for ourselves or others. Our susceptibility to this type of emotional response reflects what Strawson takes to be a fundamental feature of human nature and human engagement, viz., 'the very great importance we attach to the attitudes and intentions . . . of other human beings' both towards our-selves and others.[3]

As Strawson emphasizes, it matters to us what other people, 'and particularly . . . *some* other people', think and feel about us, and hence whether their actions 'reflect attitudes towards us of goodwill, affection,

[1] Among those who understand moral blame in terms of the reactive attitudes are Wallace (1994), Fischer and Ravizza (1998), Rosen (2004), and Hieronymi (2004).

[2] P. F. Strawson (1962), 78. Throughout this chapter, references to Strawson should be assumed to be references to P. F. Strawson (and not references to G. Strawson) unless otherwise noted.

[3] P. F. Strawson (1962), 75.

or esteem on the one hand or contempt, indifference or malevolence on the other'.[4] That we care in this way about the attitudes of others is part and parcel of participation in normal adult interpersonal relationships. It is interpersonally part and parcel of caring about and respecting those with whom one is involved as *persons*, i.e., as beings whose attitudes and opinions matter. How much we care, and the type and amount of regard we consider adequate or inadequate, insulting or not insulting, varies with the nature of our relationship with the person in question. But we demand some degree of good will and respect from all normal adult human beings merely as such—merely as fellow members of the ordinary adult community. Moreover, to the extent that we care about and respect other people—or care about and respect morality—we demand that other people be shown some degree of good will and respect as well. It is failures to meet this basic demand for good will, concern, and respect that give rise to negative reactive attitudes.

In the personal (or non-detached) case, where what is in question is another's attitudes toward, or treatment of, oneself, considered personally, the most prominent negative reactive attitudes are resentment and hurt feelings. In the impersonal (or depersonalized or vicarious) case, where what is in question is another's attitudes towards others or towards oneself considered impersonally (i.e., as merely one among many), the most prominent negative reactive attitudes are moral indignation and disapprobation. For Strawson, it is the generalized character of the demand for good will and respect in its impersonal form—the fact that it is a demand that others manifest a reasonable degree of good will and respect not merely towards oneself but, as Strawson puts it, 'towards all those on whose behalf moral indignation may be felt; i.e. as we now think, all men'—that makes it a specifically moral demand, and the indignation and disapprobation occasioned by the failure to satisfy it, specifically moral attitudes.[5] Insofar as our concern in this chapter is the desert of moral

---

[4] P. F. Strawson (1962), 76.

[5] P. F. Strawson (1962), 84. In response to Bennett (1980), Strawson acknowledges that attitudes in the third class of reactive attitudes that he distinguishes—viz., the self-reactive attitudes—likewise have a claim to being considered moral attitudes. See P. F. Strawson (1980), 206. (Among the attitudes in this class, Strawson includes 'feeling bound or obliged; feeling compunction; feeling guilty or remorseful or at least responsible; and the more complicated phenomenon of shame' ((1962), 84–5). Wallace and others, criticize Strawson for not similarly acknowledging moral instances of personal reactive attitudes like resentment. See Wallace (1994), 35–6. I take it that Strawson has a principled reason for not

blame for moral wrongdoing, I shall focus in what follows on the basic demand, and negative reactive attitudes, in their impersonal (i.e., moral) forms—and shall have these forms in mind when I speak of them.[6] Moreover, I shall focus exclusively on (and have exclusively in mind) actual violations or transgressions of the demand—i.e., failures to afford another even the minimum degree of good will, concern, or respect she is owed—as opposed to less serious failures—i.e., failures to afford another the full degree of good will or concern one ideally ought to afford to her. It is only in the case of transgressions of the basic demand in its impersonal form that moral blame would potentially be deserved.[7] Finally, to

acknowledging moral instances of the personal reactive attitudes. For Strawson, what distinguishes moral indignation and moral disapprobation from personal reactive attitudes like resentment and hurt feelings—qualifying the former but not the latter as moral—is precisely that the former are impersonal while the latter are not. What Strawson has in mind here is not that the former are reactions to another agent's failure to treat some third party with the respect he or she is due, while the latter are responses to another agent's disrespectful treatment of oneself. To the contrary, Strawson emphasizes that moral indignation can be felt on behalf of oneself. The distinction Strawson is pointing to is rather a distinction between two different ways of conceiving of the treatment in question. Whether one's reaction to disrespectful treatment qualifies as moral indignation, on one hand, or resentment, on the other, depends on which of the two conceptions underlies one's reaction: whether one is reacting to the mistreatment as mistreatment of oneself merely as 'one among many', or whether one is reacting to the mistreatment as mistreatment of oneself in particular. (Compare 'How dare you treat another human being that way!' with 'How dare you treat *me* that way!') A reaction to mistreatment of oneself, considered as one among many, automatically qualifies as indignation (or disapprobation) rather than resentment. Thus, the very thing that distinguishes resentment from indignation also prevents resentment from counting as a moral reactive attitude. As soon as it takes on the impersonal character of a moral reactive attitude, it is no longer resentment. At first glance, this account of what qualifies an attitude or demand as moral might seem at odds with the account that I provided in Chapter 2 of what qualifies a defect or form of appraisal as moral. In fact, they are not at odds. Rather they are two sides of the same coin or two sides of the one categorical imperative.

    [6] Although my focus throughout the discussion will be the reactive attitudes and basic demand in their impersonal forms, much of what I say will equally apply to the attitudes and demand in their personal forms. A possible exception relates to the content of the retributive sentiments that are bound up with the reactive attitudes, where strong. See n. 73. If the content of the retributive sentiments bound up with resentment differs from the content of the sentiments bound up with moral indignation and disapprobation, then the connection between the reactive attitudes, where strong, and the retributive sentiments may be more problematic in the case of resentment than in the case of moral indignation and disapprobation.
    [7] There is a further distinction that can be made here: that between the demand in its generic form (i.e., the form that applies to one merely as a member of the moral community and that governs relationships between members of the moral community, merely as such) and non-generic versions of the demand that apply to one only insofar as one stands to another in some more intimate relationship such as that of friend or colleague or lover. Like the distinction between actual transgressions of the basic demand and less serious failures, the

distinguish it from other forms of moral disapprobation, I shall refer to moral disapprobation occasioned specifically by transgressions of the basic demand in its impersonal form as 'moral reprobation'.[8] My primary aim in this chapter is to show that an agent need not be ultimately responsible for her actions in order to be deserving of moral indignation or reprobation for an action.

The argument that I shall provide will take the form of a reconstruction and defense of what I see as Strawson's own core argument for the claim that the truth of the thesis of determinism would not imperil the moral reactive attitudes or their desert.[9] To some this statement might seem odd. After all, Strawson himself never speaks of 'desert' of the reactive attitudes. Indeed, in the eyes of many of his critics (and even some of his supporters) the principal problem with Strawson's defense of compatibilism is that its central arguments no more speak to incompatibilists' worries about desert than did the utility-based arguments of earlier compatibilists (or 'optimists', as Strawson calls them), whom Strawson criticizes on that very count. As I see it, such criticisms of Strawson are based on a misunderstanding of his defense. The criticisms take as primary two arguments never intended to serve as a stand-alone reply to incompatibilist worries and which, in fact, are inessential to Strawson's core defense of compatibilism.[10] A subsidiary aim of this chapter is to remove this and other misunderstandings of Strawson's argument.

distinction between the generic and non-generic forms of the demand is orthogonal to that between the personal and impersonal forms. Whereas the distinction between the generic and non-generic forms of the demand has to do with the particular relationship the demand governs, the distinction between the personal and impersonal forms of the demand relates to the way in which the person making the demand conceives of the treatment she is demanding—as owed merely to herself (or her own) viewed personally or to all who stand in the pertinent relationship. The distinction between the generic version of the demand and non-generic versions of the demand will be relevant when we come to discuss punishment. It is only in the case of transgressions of the generic version of the demand that punishment is potentially at issue.

[8] As I understand the attitudes, the principal difference between moral indignation and moral reprobation is that moral indignation essentially involves anger while moral reprobation does not. Cf., Stern (1974). I return to this point in Chapter 5.

[9] Those who have doubts as to whether the argument I defend is already to be found in Strawson are free to view the argument as Strawsonian rather than Strawson's.

[10] The two arguments are, first, that it is senseless to ask whether it would be rational for us to relinquish the reactive attitudes if determinism holds since it is not in our nature to be able to relinquish them; and second, that even if we were able to relinquish them, we would have to consider 'the gains and losses to human life', with the losses outweighing the gains. See P. F. Strawson (1962), 82–3, 87.

As I understand Strawson, his core defense of compatibilism is based on the three following claims. First, the reactive attitudes, including the moral reactive attitudes, are governed by their own internal standards of appropriateness, which are conditioned by the nature of their respective objects. Second, the truth of the thesis of determinism would not undermine the appropriateness of the moral reactive attitudes as judged by these internal standards. It would not entail the universal presence of what, given the attitudes' own internal standards, might be considered a valid excusing or exempting condition. Third, these internal standards fully and independently determine the conditions an agent must satisfy to be morally responsible, or morally blameworthy or praiseworthy, for her actions. There are no prior facts of moral responsibility that these standards track.[11] Nor are there further standards of appropriateness to which to appeal in determining whether an agent is 'truly' morally responsible or 'truly' deserving of moral blame for what she has done.[12] The relevant standards are fully internal to the attitudes themselves. And, crucially, to say the moral reactive attitudes would be appropriate by their own internal standards is to say that the moral reactive attitudes would be deserved. This follows from the nature of desert—from the fact that desert is a matter of what is *intrinsically* just or fitting. To say that a person is deserving of a certain reactive attitude is to say that it would be intrinsically just or fitting to hold that attitude towards the person in question—that the attitude in question is an intrinsically just or fitting response to the person in virtue of her actions. Whether an attitude is an intrinsically just or fitting response is necessarily determined by appeal to the standards of appropriateness internal to the attitude itself. The central question for our purposes thus becomes whether, in the absence of ultimate responsibility, the negative moral reactive attitudes would be universally inappropriate by their own internal standards.

---

[11] Cf., Watson (1987): 'In Strawson's view there is no such independent notion of responsibility that explains the propriety of the reactive attitudes. The explanatory priority is the other way around' (121). My appreciation of this point owes much to Watson's discussion.

[12] Importantly, to say that a standard is internal to morality or to our moral practices is not the same as to say that it is internal to the reactive attitudes. That Wallace, in attempting to determine the necessary conditions of moral responsibility, does not limit himself to standards internal to the reactive attitudes (i.e., standards of their desert), but instead appeals to standards of fairness more generally is a serious flaw in his account. See Wallace (1994), 103–9.

As a way of clarifying the type of internal standards I have in mind when I speak of the reactive attitudes' internal standards of appropriateness, it may be helpful to recall Philippa Foot's remarks concerning pride and the way in which pride is 'internally related' to its object.[13] Though Foot does not discuss the moral reactive attitudes, they too are examples of attitudes that possess an internal relation to their respective objects. As Foot observes, there are 'limits to the things a man can be proud of': the object of pride must be 'something seen (a) as in some way a man's own, and (b) as some sort of achievement or advantage; without this object pride cannot be [a]scribed . . . not because no one could psychologically feel pride in such a case, but because whatever he did feel could not logically be pride'.[14] It is the fact that there are such limits that Foot means to point to when she says pride possesses an internal relation to its object. Where an attitude is in this way internally related to its object, there are certain conditions the subject of the attitude must believe its object to meet for the attitude to be the attitude in question. (In the case of pride, the relevant conditions are those specified in (a) and (b).) These conditions in turn give rise to internal standards of appropriateness for the attitude. For the attitude to be appropriate by its own internal standards, the conditions that the subject of the attitude must believe its object to meet for the attitude to be the attitude in question must in fact be met. That is, the beliefs constitutive of the attitude must be true. To determine whether an absence of ultimate responsibility would render the negative moral react-ive attitudes (moral indignation and moral reprobation) universally in-appropriate by their own internal standards, we need to determine the beliefs constitutive of them. To bring these into relief, Strawson directs our attention to the sorts of circumstance that might ordinarily be expected to give rise to moral indignation or reprobation, and the types of consider-ations that would ordinarily be expected to dispel or temper or inhibit such attitudes.[15] If we can come to understand just how and why the

---

[13] See Foot (1959), 113–18.

[14] Foot (1959), 113–14.

[15] In fact, Strawson first directs our attention to the sorts of circumstance that might ordinarily be expected to give rise to resentment, and the types of considerations that would ordinarily be expected to dispel or temper or inhibit resentment. Part of his strategy for defending compatibilism is to show that the attitudes constitutive of moral blame are impersonal or generalized analogues of resentment.

considerations in question affect our attitudes, we will have pinpointed the beliefs constitutive of them.

We've already discussed the general sorts of circumstance that might ordinarily be expected to give rise to moral indignation or reprobation: those in which an agent is perceived to have violated the basic demand for interpersonal regard and concern in its impersonal form. We've now to discuss the considerations that would normally be expected to temper or remove or inhibit such attitudes. Strawson divides these considerations into two groups, the first of which encompasses considerations that would ordinarily be seen as excusing an agent from blame for his behavior, while the second encompasses considerations that would ordinarily be seen as exempting an agent from responsibility-ascriptions altogether. My discussion of the considerations in the first group will be brief. Strawson's account of the way in which these considerations function is both well understood and widely accepted. The discussion of the second group will be more extended.

Among the considerations belonging to the first group, Strawson lists those expressed in the pleas 'He didn't mean to', 'He hadn't realized', 'He didn't know', and 'He couldn't help it', where this last plea must be supported by such further pleas as 'He was pushed', 'He had to do it', 'It was the only way', 'They left him no alternative'.[16] As Strawson emphasizes, what these pleas have in common is that each suggests that, contrary to appearances, the agent's behavior did not in fact violate the basic demand. It is this feature that accounts for their exculpatory force. They show to be false what reflection confirms to be one of the beliefs constitutive of moral indignation and reprobation—viz., that the agent violated the basic demand in its impersonal (i.e., moral) form. Hence they reveal the attitudes to be inappropriate by one of their own internal standards. However, as Strawson argues, it would hardly follow from the truth of determinism—or, I would add, from the absence of ultimate responsibility that determinism would entail—that agents never violate the basic demand. As such, neither determinism nor an absence of ultimate responsibility would render moral indignation and reprobation universally inappropriate by the standard in question.

---

[16] P. F. Strawson (1962), 77.

Strawson divides the exempting considerations into two subgroups. Like Strawson, I will focus on the second subgroup. Among the considerations falling within the second subgroup are those expressed in such pleas as 'He's only a child', 'He's a hopeless schizophrenic', 'His mind has been systematically perverted', 'That's purely compulsive behavior on his part', and 'He was peculiarly unfortunate in his formative circumstances'.[17] Where considerations from this subgroup are operative, the agent is viewed as psychologically abnormal or morally undeveloped, and so incapable of participating in ordinary adult interpersonal relationships.[18] Unlike the pleas discussed in connection with excuses, these pleas tend to remove or inhibit not merely a particular reactive attitude, but the moral reactive attitudes in general, and to promote instead what Strawson refers to as the 'objective' attitude or attitudes. Rather than 'invite us to see the agent's action in a way consistent with the full retention of ordinary interpersonal reactive attitudes and merely inconsistent with one particular attitude', the pleas associated with this subclass of exemptions 'invite us to view the agent [her]self in a different light', viz., as one towards whom all ordinary moral reactive attitudes and the demand that they involve are to be suspended.[19] To the extent that the agent 'is seen in this light, [s]he is not seen as one on whom demands and expectations lie in that particular way in which we think of them as lying when we speak of moral obligations; [s]he is not, to that extent, seen as a morally responsible

---

[17] See P. F. Strawson (1962), 78–9. Among the considerations falling within the first subgroup are those expressed in such pleas as 'He wasn't himself', 'He's been under very great strain recently', and 'He was acting under post-hypnotic suggestion'. Of these, Strawson simply states the following:

Though they perhaps raise, in the short term, questions akin to those raised, in the long term, by the second subgroup, we may dismiss them without considering those questions by taking that admirably suggestive phrase, 'He wasn't himself', with the seriousness—for all its being logically comic—it deserves. We shall not feel resentment against the man he is for the action done by the man he is not; or at least we shall feel less. We normally have to deal with him under normal stresses; so we shall not feel towards him, when he acts as he does under abnormal stresses, as we should have felt towards him had he acted as he did under normal stresses' ((1962), 78).

What distinguishes these short-term exempting considerations from the excusing considerations discussed earlier is that the short-term exempting considerations, like the longer-term exempting considerations, invite us to suspend for the duration of the exemption not just one particular reactive attitude, but all ordinary reactive attitudes and the demand upon which they rest.
[18] See P. F. Strawson (1962), 79.
[19] P. F. Strawson (1962), 78.

agent, as a term of moral relationships, as a member of the moral community'.[20] Rather she is viewed 'as an object of social policy; as a subject for what, in a wide range of sense, might be called treatment; as something certainly to be taken account, perhaps precautionary account, of; to be managed or handled or cured or trained'.[21]

Strawson's account of the (long-term) exemptions strikes many as incomplete in a way in which his account of the excusing conditions does not.[22] To their minds, we still need to know what it is about seeing an agent 'as warped or deranged [or] neurotic or just a child . . . or peculiarly unfortunate in formative circumstances' and, hence, incapable of ordinary adult interpersonal engagement that leads us to suspend our ordinary moral reactive attitudes and the demand that underlies them. What is it about someone's being subject to one of these conditions that renders the moral reactive attitudes and the demand that they involve inappropriate? It is here that proponents of an ultimate responsibility condition, and incompatibilists more generally, believe they can gain a foothold. For on one very natural interpretation, what accounts for the suspension of our reactive attitudes in such cases—as well as in cases where we purposefully step back from ordinary adult interpersonal interaction and try to look at the behavior of the 'normal' and 'mature' with the same objective eye as we look at the behavior of the 'abnormal' and 'immature'—is the realization that the agent is not ultimately responsible for being the way she is and thus for doing the things she does. According to this interpretation, when we are not actively involved with an agent on an ordinary adult interpersonal level, we are able to attain a clearer and more complete perspective on her and her actions—one that reveals the full extent to which her actions are caused by factors beyond her ultimate control.[23] When actively

---

[20] P. F. Strawson (1962), 86.

[21] P. F. Strawson (1962), 79.

[22] See, e.g., Watson (1987), Russell (1992), and McKenna (1998).

[23] Although Strawson, in speaking of the 'objective' attitude and viewing agents in a purely 'objective' light is referring to viewing agents as *objects*—i.e., as items 'whose behavior . . . we may seek to understand, predict and perhaps control in just such a sense as that in which we may seek to understand, predict and control the behavior of nonpersonal objects' ((1985), 34)—ambiguities in the term 'objective' can encourage the thought that in coming to view agents in an 'objective' light, we come to see them as they 'really' are and not as we subjectively mistakenly take them to be. In his (1985), Strawson warns against thinking that the objective view (in his sense) is more real or more veridical than the non-objective one.

engaged with another person on an ordinary adult interpersonal level, we tend not to think about the full chain of causes leading the other person to act as she does. Even if we are aware of the more proximate causes of an agent's behavior, we typically do not pause to reflect upon her lack of ultimate responsibility for these causes and, hence, for the behavior itself. The exempting conditions, both through their salience as causal factors for which the agent is in no way responsible and through the distance that the impossibility of interpersonal engagement creates, encourage such reflection. This reflection leads us to abandon our ordinary reactive attitudes. For it reveals the agent not to be ultimately responsible for her actions in the strong sense in which we pre-reflectively take agents to be and which the moral reactive attitudes presuppose.[24]

Indeed, incompatibilists will continue, as even Strawson admits, we experience the same dissolution of our moral reactive attitudes in relation to 'normal' human beings when we deliberately stand back from our ordinary participatory perspective and try to look at their behavior in the same objective way in which we look at the behavior of the abnormal.[25] As Strawson points out, '[b]eing human, we cannot, in the normal case, do this [i.e., stand back from the ordinary participatory perspective] for long, or altogether'.[26] We are naturally drawn back into the participatory perspective. Once we are, the fact that the agent is not ultimately responsible for her actions recedes from view and our ordinary reactive attitudes naturally return. Yet this does not change the fact that, if determinism is true, then no agent is ever ultimately responsible for her actions. Accordingly, it does not alter what, on the current interpretation of the way the exemptions function, would be the universal inappropriateness of the moral reactive attitudes by their own internal standards.[27]

As Strawson is often read, his primary response to what one incompatibilist charges is the moral reactive attitudes' 'demonstrabl[e] inappropriate[ness] given their essential dependence on a belief that is demonstrably

[24] For the claim that the reactive attitudes presuppose a belief in ultimate responsibility, see G. Strawson (1986), Honderich (1988), Pereboom (2001), and Kelly (2002).

[25] P. F. Strawson (1962), 82.

[26] P. F. Strawson (1962), 80.

[27] G. Strawson speaks in this connection of the reactive attitudes' being 'demonstrably inappropriate given their essential dependence on a belief that is demonstrably false' ((1986), 72). The belief he is referring to is the belief that we bear the sort of 'true' (i.e., ultimate) responsibility for our actions that he views as logically impossible. Hence his claim that the belief is demonstrably false.

false' is to insist, first, that it is not in our nature to be able to relinquish the reactive attitudes and, second, that, even if we were to relinquish them, it would not be rational for us to do so. According to Strawson, our commitment to the reactive attitudes is 'part of the general framework of human life' and human relationships.[28] Indeed, 'being involved in inter-personal relationships as we normally understand them precisely is being exposed to the range of reactive attitudes and feelings that is in question.'[29] To rid ourselves of the reactive attitudes, we first would have to relinquish ordinary adult interpersonal engagement and relationships as we normally understand them. In the end, '[a] sustained objectivity of inter-personal attitude, and the human isolation which that would entail, does not seem to be something of which human beings would be capable, even if some general truth were a theoretical ground for it'.[30] Moreover, even if a sustained objectivity of interpersonal attitude were something of which human beings were capable, then, Strawson argues, 'we could choose rationally only in light of an assessment of the gains and losses to human life, its enrichment or impoverishment'.[31] As Strawson sees it, not only would the losses outweigh the gains, but, in relation to such a choice, the truth or falsity of determinism would be 'simply irrelevant'.[32]

If Strawson's primary response to incompatibilists did consist of the two claims just mentioned—first, that it is not in our nature to be able to relinquish the reactive attitudes and, second, that it would not necessarily be rational for us to relinquish them even if we could—then his response would clearly be inadequate. Let us assume a maximally concessive in-compatibilist challenger. Let her concede that we would not be able to rid ourselves of the reactive attitudes even if we subscribed to some general theoretical doctrine that provided us with clear grounds for doing so— though many of Strawson's critics would be reluctant to concede even this much.[33] Still, let her concede that, given our nature, it would be impossible for us to rid ourselves completely of the reactive attitudes without (first) relinquishing the normal adult interpersonal relationships within which the attitudes naturally arise. Surely she we would have to agree that our commitment to such relationships is 'too thoroughgoing and deeply rooted for us to take seriously the thought' that we could or

---

[28] P. F. Strawson (1962), 83.   [29] P. F. Strawson (1962), 81.
[30] P. F. Strawson (1962), 81.   [31] P. F. Strawson (1962), 83.
[32] P. F. Strawson (1962), 87.   [33] See, e.g., G. Strawson (1986) and Pereboom (2001).

would relinquish such relationships completely.[34] Let her further concede that, given the above, there is a sense in which it is pointless to ask 'whether it would not be rational, given a general theoretical conviction of the truth of determinism, so to change our world that in it these attitudes were wholly suspended': we would not be willing or able to undertake such a change even if we discovered that it would be rational, so the discovery would not affect our actual behavior.[35] Still, it is far from clear that a question's being pointless to ask in this sense should deter a philosopher from asking it in the form of a hypothetical question—particularly if she is pursuing a line of enquiry to its logical conclusion. Certainly she might question whether, if such a choice were possible, it would not be rational to choose to rid ourselves of the reactive attitudes if we discovered that we were not ultimately responsible for our actions in the strong sense that our reactive attitudes presuppose. Let our incompatibilist challenger further concede that if a philosopher did decide to pursue the question, then to accurately assess the all-things-considered rationality of choosing to rid ourselves of the reactive attitudes, she would have to consider, among other things, 'the gains and losses to human life'. Finally, let her concede that, if the reactive attitudes are as tightly bound up with ordinary adult interpersonal relationships as Strawson suggests, then the losses would outweigh the gains. Still, it would not follow from this that the truth or falsity of determinism was 'simply irrelevant' to the rationality of choosing in the one way rather than the other (unless, perhaps, all Strawson means by this is that, in relation to moral responsibility, indeterminism is no better than determinism).[36]

---

[34] P. F. Strawson (1962), 81. As I understand Strawson, his claim is not that the reactive attitudes are required for the sustenance of good interpersonal relationships, such that if we first eliminated the reactive attitudes, this would damage our relationships. His claim is that susceptibility to the reactive attitudes is an inevitable concomitant of involvement in ordinary interpersonal relationships as we ordinarily understand them, such that we could only eliminate the reactive attitudes by first ceasing to be involved in such relationships. For the suggestion that Strawson claims the former, see Pereboom (2001), 199–204.

[35] The question whether we ought to give up the reactive attitudes even though we are incapable of doing so is pointless or, better, senseless, in another way: 'ought implies can'; hence, if it is beyond human psychological capacities to be able to give up the reactive attitudes, then it cannot be the case that we ought to give them up.

[36] That part of what Strawson has in mind when he asserts that the truth or falsity of determinism would be 'simply irrelevant' to deciding whether to give up the reactive attitudes is that, with respect to moral responsibility, indeterminism is no better or worse than determinism is suggested by the comment that immediately follows the claim of irrelevance. Referring back to this claim, Strawson writes 'this becomes ironically clear when we remember that for those convinced that the truth of determinism would make the one choice

Surely we ought to attach *some* weight to 'living in accordance with the facts'.[37] And if the foregoing interpretation of the exemptions is correct, then the fact is that without ultimate responsibility the moral reactive attitudes are universally inappropriate by their own internal standards. Admittedly, when the value of living in accordance with the facts is weighed against the costs such living would impose on human relationships, 'it would not necessarily be rational to choose to be more purely rational than we are'.[38] Still, the fact that, for this reason, it would not be rational to give up the moral reactive attitudes will come as little comfort to those who believe that if determinism is true (and arguably even if it is not), then the moral reactive attitudes are grounded in beliefs that are demonstrably false. It will as little console them as arguments concerning punishment's continued or enhanced efficacy under determinism did to console previous generations of incompatibilists.

As Strawson acknowledges, the principal concern of incompatibilists is desert. The reason that incompatibilists had rejected earlier compatibilist accounts of moral responsibility that, like Moritz Schlick's, were based entirely on considerations of efficacy was not that they doubted that blame or punishment would be efficacious under determinism.[39] It was that efficacy has nothing to do with desert. On this count, Strawson and incompatibilists are in complete agreement. As Strawson himself empha-sizes, not only is the efficacy of blame and punishment 'not a sufficient basis' for justified blame and punishment; 'it is not even the right *sort* of basis . . . for these practices as we understand them'.[40] Yet, of course, the two claims that we have been discussing have no more to do with desert than claims concerning efficacy do. As was true of efficacy, the type of considerations to which these two claims point—viz., our inability to relinquish the reactive attitudes and the would-be irrationality of doing

---

rational, there has always been the insuperable difficulty of explaining in intelligible terms how its falsity would make the opposite choice rational' ((1962), 87–8).

[37] I borrow the phrase 'living in accordance with the facts' from Wolf. See her (1981), 107.

[38] P. F. Strawson (1962), 84, n. 4.

[39] See Schlick (1939). According to Schlick, the question 'Who is responsible?' is identical to the question 'Who, in a given case, is to be punished?'. It is a question concerning 'the correct point of application of the motive' of punishment if punishment is to achieve its goals of education, reformation, and 'intimidation' (153, 152). Strawson cites P. H. Nowell-Smith (1948) a compatibilist who holds this type of account. See P. F. Strawson (1962), 73–4.

[40] P. F. Strawson (1962), 74.

so, given the costs, even if we could—are not even the right *sort* of basis for our practices of blame and punishment as we ordinarily understand them. That the type of considerations to which these two claims point are so obviously not the right sort should render us skeptical of the idea that Strawson, having seconded incompatibilists' desert-related objections to accounts of moral responsibility based on efficacy several pages earlier, now intends the two claims to serve as his primary response to the original incompatibilist objection.

In the end, I conclude that those who press the original incompatibilist objection—viz., that under determinism, the moral reactive attitudes would be universally inappropriate by their own internal standards—as well as those who regard the two claims that we have been discussing as Strawson's primary response to the original objection, fail to grasp his argument. The objection presupposes precisely what Strawson rightly denies, viz, that in those cases in which we naturally abandon the moral reactive attitudes, our abandoning them results from our coming to recognize the truth of some metaphysical proposition that might, 'consistently with the facts as we know them', hold true of every human action.[41] Strawson explicitly rejects this interpretation, viewing it as another instance of our over-intellectualizing the facts.[42] As he emphasizes, 'neither in the case of the normal . . . nor in the case of the abnormal is it true that, when we adopt an objective attitude, we do so *because* we hold such a [metaphysical] belief'.[43] Having already adopted the objective attitude for some other reason, we might come to believe that the agent's actions are determined, or, in any event, actions for which she is not ultimately responsible. But neither in the case of the normal nor in the case of the abnormal is our abandonment of the reactive attitudes 'the result of prior embracing of . . . such a belief'.[44]

---

[41] The phrase 'consistent with the facts as we know them' is Strawson's. See, e.g., P. F. Strawson (1962), 82.

[42] The over-intellectualization is merely compounded when accompanied by the thought that the reason that we abandon our ordinary reactive attitudes when we thereby discover that the agent is not ultimately responsible for her actions is that we thereby discover that she is not morally responsible for her actions and, hence, that the reactive attitudes are inappropriate. This ignores one of Strawson's fundamental insights—that, as Watson puts it, 'there is no such independent notion of responsibility that explains the propriety of the reactive attitudes. The explanatory priority is the other way around' ((1987), 121).

[43] P. F. Strawson (1962), 82.

[44] P. F. Strawson (1962), 82.

Still, this seems to bring us back to the question with which we began: What is it about seeing an agent 'as warped or deranged [or] neurotic or just a child . . . or peculiarly unfortunate in formative circumstances', and hence as incapable of participation in ordinary adult interpersonal relationships, that leads us to abandon the reactive attitudes and adopt the objective attitude? Why does seeing an agent in this light lead us to view her as not a term in moral relationships, not a member of the moral community? Similarly, what accounts for the dissolution of our ordinary reactive attitudes towards even a person capable of ordinary adult interpersonal involvement when we intentionally step back from such involvement and instead concentrate, as Strawson puts it, 'on understanding "how he works" '?[45] The most basic answer is that the reactive attitudes and underlying demand are bound up with involvement in ordinary adult interpersonal relationships. (The most general of these relationships is the relationship in which two normally functioning adults stand merely as such—as fellow members of the ordinary adult interpersonal community and so potential 'parties to an enormous range of [ordinary adult interpersonal] transactions and encounters', extending from the most intimate to the most casual.[46]) For this reason, the reactive attitudes and the basic demand tend not to arise where ordinary adult interpersonal relationships are believed to be impossible or have otherwise been suspended.

Less summarily, the demand for regard and respect underlying the reactive attitudes is made from inside the participatory stance and is directed specifically towards those with whom we are engaged (or project ourselves as being engaged) on an ordinary adult interpersonal level. To address the basic demand to an agent is, for one's own part, to engage with that agent on an ordinary adult interpersonal level. It is to view and treat her as a member of the ordinary adult interpersonal community. And for Strawson, to view and treat an agent as a member of the ordinary adult interpersonal community is to view and treat her as a fellow member of the moral community—as 'one on whom demands and expectations lie in that particular way in which we think of them as lying when we speak of moral obligation'.[47] Seeing an agent as incapable of ordinary adult

[45] P. F. Strawson (1962), 82.   [46] P. F. Strawson (1962), 76.
[47] See P. F. Strawson (1962), 86. For Strawson, the moral community just is the community of those capable of ordinary adult interpersonal engagement, the community comprised of all normal adult human beings.

interpersonal engagement—or simply being unable to relate to her on an ordinary adult interpersonal level—tends to lead to the abandonment of the participatory stance. Once we leave this stance, the demand for regard and respect that conditions the reactive attitudes does not arise. It is not that having left the participatory stance, we come to recognize some fact that renders the reactive attitudes inappropriate, with this recognition in turn leading to the dissolution of the reactive attitudes. To the contrary, the dissolution of our ordinary reactive attitudes is the direct unmediated result of our having abandoned the participatory stance for some other reason or due to some other cause.[48]

Note that this explanation of the dissolution of our reactive attitudes when we intentionally step outside the ordinary participant perspective and concentrate on understanding how a person works explains what Jonathan Bennett and others insist that an adequate Strawsonian account must explain: viz., how an intellectual operation could 'dispel' the ordinary reactive attitudes without 'disqualifying' them.[49] It also explains why reflection on an agent's formative circumstances and on the ways in which they impacted her tends temporarily to inhibit or dissolve our ordinary reactive attitudes regardless whether the circumstances were particularly unfortunate or operated deterministically. To reflect on an agent's formative circumstances and the ways in which they impacted her is to step outside the participatory perspective. Once outside the participatory perspective, the demand underlying the reactive attitudes does not arise. Far from presenting difficulties for Strawson's account, such dissolution is exactly what one would expect.

In arguing as I have, I do not mean to deny that it is inappropriate to direct the moral reactive attitudes at those whose peculiarly unfortunate formative circumstances, or mental illness, or young age incapacitates them in some or all respects for ordinary adult interpersonal relationships. Nor do I mean to deny that Strawson regards it as inappropriate.[50] Strawson

---

[48] In not every case is our abandonment of the participant perspective intentional or something we decide upon. In certain cases unable to relate to the other on an ordinary adult interpersonal level.

[49] See Bennett (1980), 28–9.

[50] What makes it inappropriate to direct the reactive attitudes at those whose formative circumstances were so peculiarly unfortunate as to incapacitate them, in some or all respects for ordinary interpersonal relationships is not that the individuals in question are a product of their circumstances, but that they are incapacitated. It is only when and to the extent that an agent's peculiarly unfortunate formative circumstances have rendered her incapable of

speaks of seeing an agent as psychologically abnormal or undeveloped and so incapacitated for ordinary adult interpersonal engagement as not just tending to inhibit the reactive attitudes and basic demand, but as representing the agent as one towards whom the reactive attitudes and basic demand are to be suspended.[51] Thus it would be a mistake to view Strawson's claims as 'merely' psychological. However, it is equally a mistake to think that we need to look to some further (e.g., moral) standard to explain the inappropriateness of subjecting the agents in question to the moral reactive attitudes and the demand underlying them.[52] We need only appeal to the standards internal to the moral reactive attitudes themselves. By these standards, it is inappropriate to direct the moral reactive attitudes and underlying demand towards those whose psychological abnormality or lack of development incapacitates them in some or all respects for ordinary adult interpersonal relationships. What makes it inappropriate is that the agents in question are incapacitated in some or all respects for ordinary adult interpersonal relationships as we normally understand them. There is no need to look to some distinct moral or metaphysical incapacity, or even an incapacity for some distinctively moral form of relationship, to explain the inappropriateness.[53]

---

ordinary interpersonal relationships that she is to be considered an inappropriate object of ordinary reactive attitudes.

[51] See, e.g., P. F. Strawson (1962), 82.

[52] Thinking that we need to look to an external moral standard to explain the inappropriateness of subjecting the psychologically abnormal and morally undeveloped to the reactive attitudes is a mistake made by Wallace in his (1994). There he appeals to standards of fairness and, more specifically, standards of reasonableness to explain the inappropriateness of subjecting such agents to the reactive attitudes. I do not deny that there are external moral standards—including, arguably, Wallace's standard of reasonableness—that make it morally inappropriate to subject the psychologically abnormal and morally undeveloped to the reactive attitudes. My point is that there is no need to appeal to external moral standards to explain the inappropriateness of subjecting the agents in question to the reactive attitudes; the standards internal to the reactive attitudes provide sufficient explanation. Moreover, the standards internal to the reactive attitudes are the only standards that bear on their desert.

[53] Thinking that one needs to appeal to a further, distinctively moral, incapacity or an incapacity for some special, distinctively moral form of relationship to explain the inappropriateness of subjecting the psychologically abnormal and morally undeveloped to the reactive attitudes is a second mistake that Wallace makes in his (1994). Wallace maintains that '[w]hat matters for accountability is not merely one's capacity for ordinary or normal interpersonal relationships, since immoral but culpable behavior may disqualify one from these; it is rather one's suitability for a certain kind of moral relationship. The relevant kind of moral relationship is a relationship defined by the successful exchange of moral criticism or justification' (164). I do not deny that one must possess the capacity for the successful (or, at least, meaningful) exchange of moral criticism or justification for one to be an appropriate target of the reactive attitudes. I deny that this capacity is distinct from the capacity to participate in

The relevant incapacity is precisely the one that Strawson has been emphasizing from the start, viz., the incapacity for participation in ordinary adult
interpersonal relationships as we normally understand them.

Why is the incapacity for participating in ordinary adult interpersonal
relationships the relevant incapacity? Why is it appropriate to direct the
moral reactive attitudes and demand underlying them towards those
capable of participating in ordinary adult interpersonal relationships, but
not towards those incapable? Because only those capable of participating in
ordinary adult interpersonal relationships are capable of understanding
and, based on their understanding, responding appropriately to the
demand. Unlike the psychopath or the individual with severe autism,
both of whom lack the affective capacities and emotional intelligence
necessary for relating to others on an ordinary adult interpersonal level,
those capable of participating in ordinary adult interpersonal relationships
'get it'. They get the basic human needs and desires that animate ordinary
adult interpersonal relationships and that account for our imposing the
demand and our reacting as we do when we believe that the demand has
been violated. Unlike the psychopath or the individual with severe autism,
those capable of involvement in ordinary adult interpersonal relationships
share these needs and desires. And sharing these needs and desires, they are
in a position to understand and respond to the demand in a way in which
those incapable of ordinary adult interpersonal involvement are not. The
necessary form of understanding is insider understanding—understanding
only possessed by those who know what it is like to be a term in ordinary
adult interpersonal relationships, and who, out of the same human needs
and desires as their fellow participants, impose the same demand on others
(and, out of empathy or respect for others, impose the same demand on
themselves) as others do on them.[54] In imposing the demand on an agent,
we assume that she 'gets' ordinary adult interpersonal matters. We assume

ordinary adult interpersonal relationships as we normally understand them, and so deny that it
is a problem for Strawson's account that he ties moral accountability to the latter. Even if
culpable immoral conduct disqualifies one from certain normal adult interpersonal relationships—and I'm not sure that it does—it does not disqualify one from possessing the capacity
for such relationships. It is the capacity that is required.

[54] The ordinary human capacity to empathize with others and to put oneself in others'
shoes is itself crucial to being able to understand what is being demanded and why it is being
demanded and what would fulfill it in a given case.

that she is a normal adult human being capable of participating in normal adult interpersonal relationships and of understanding the demand that arises from, and regulates, just these relationships.[55] We further assume that she possesses the capacity to act in accordance with this understanding. (This capacity is another constituent of the capacity for ordinary adult interpersonal engagement.) The assumption of these capacities is a precondition of the intelligibility of imposing the demand.[56] Where the assumption is or would be false, the moral reactive attitudes and the demand underlying them are inappropriate by their own internal standards.

In arguing that the capacity an agent must possess to be an appropriate target of the moral reactive attitudes and underlying demand is the capacity for ordinary adult interpersonal relationships as we normally understand them, I do not mean to deny that an agent must possess the capacity for specific types of moral interaction—e.g., Wallace singles out 'the successful exchange of moral criticism or justification'— to be an appropriate target. Nor do I mean to deny that a person must be morally literate, or possess the type of developed moral capacity that we discussed in Chapter 2, if she is to be an appropriate target of the moral reactive attitudes.[57] Without these capacities, a person would not be capable of

---

[55] The demand underlying the reactive attitudes is a demand that those with whom we (or others) are involved in ordinary adult interpersonal relationships treat us (and them) with a certain degree of regard and respect during the conduct of precisely these relationships.

[56] For the idea that 'understanding is a precondition of intelligible demand', see Watson (1987).

[57] In her (2004) and perhaps also her (2007), Hieronymi seems to deny that the capacity to understand and properly respond to moral reasons is a necessary condition of the appropriateness of the reactive attitudes in terms of which she understands moral blame. There are passages in her (2007) that suggest that the lack of capacity that Hieronymi views as not disqualifying is not a complete lack of moral capacity, but some more localized lack of capacity that the agent could overcome through greater effort on her part.) Hieronymi's reasoning seems to be much the same as Scanlon's reasoning in his (1998): the fact that an agent is incapable of understanding moral reasons does not alter whether her actions manifest disregard for others, nor the significance of the disregard for her interpersonal relationships with others. It does not, Hieronymi writes, alter the 'importance or standing of the will that was ill' ((2004), 132). As such, Hieronymi concludes, it neither does nor should affect the reactive attitudes. I strongly disagree with Hieronymi and Scanlon on this point. Discovering that an agent lacks the capacity to understand and respond to moral reasons has, and should have, the same sort of undermining effect on our reactive attitudes as discovering that an agent is merely a child. It does alter the significance of the disregard or, better, the lack of regard—disregard requires a level of basic moral comprehension that the agent we are considering lacks—as well as the standing of the agent who exhibited the lack of regard. Where an agent is

ordinary adult interpersonal relationships as we normally understand them.[58] What I deny—and Strawson denies—is that developed moral capacity is distinct from the capacity to participate in ordinary adult interpersonal relationships as we normally understand them. The capacity for moral understanding just is the capacity for understanding the ordinary interpersonal demand for regard and respect, and for understanding it from the inside, as an agent must, if she is to be capable of seeing what would count as adequate regard or concern in this particular case, or under this or that novel set of circumstances.[59] The understanding needed is not understanding that can be acquired from the outside by learning some formal set of rules that might then formulaically be applied case by case. The rules that exist are formulated in terms only fully accessible to those with the requisite insider understanding. And it is this same insider understanding that is necessary for the 'successful exchange of moral criticism or justification' of which Wallace speaks.

That the capacity to engage in ordinary adult interpersonal relationships as we normally understand them is the capacity crucial to an agent's being an appropriate target of the moral reactive attitudes and the demand underlying them means that we can be confident that no metaphysical thesis 'consistent with the facts as we know them' would render the moral

---

incapable of understanding why she should have such regard for anyone, and equally, why anyone should have such regard for her, her lack of regard for you in particular is not personally insulting in the way in which it would otherwise have been. Similarly, the agent's lack of regard for human beings in general does not smack of the same sort of claim to lordship over others as it would otherwise do. The agent is not claiming special prerogative for herself. (On the claim to lordship normally implicit in wrongdoing, see Hampton (1992a) and (1992b).) As long as we keep the inability of such an agent firmly in focus, we come to look upon her (and her behavior) in much the same way as we would look upon (that of) a dangerous animal, albeit perhaps with a sadness that we would not feel in the case of a non-human animal and with greater compunction about treating her in certain ways insofar as she remains a member of our species and, in many ways, very much like us. As for the standing of such an agent, she is not a potential term in human interpersonal relationships, not a member of the normal adult human being interpersonal community, and so not 'one on whom demands and expectations lie in that particular way in which we think of them as lying when we speak of moral obligations' (P. F. Strawson (1962), 86). She is not a person.

[58] Nor do I deny that it is possible to explain the inappropriateness of subjecting the agents under discussion to the negative moral reactive attitudes and underlying demand by direct appeal to their lack of developed moral capacity. What is important is not to lose the insight that developed moral capacity and the capacity for ordinary adult interpersonal engagement are one and the same capacity.

[59] Cf., Watson (1987) and, in particular, his discussion of the developing moral understanding of children.

reactive attitudes universally inappropriate by their own internal standards. This includes any thesis concerning an absence of ultimate responsibility that might hold true of us as we are. Among the facts as we know them is that many of us are capable of participating in ordinary adult interpersonal relationships as we normally understand them. For many of us do participate in such relationships. In speaking of 'ordinary adult interpersonal relationships as we normally understand them', Strawson is expressly referring to the relationships in which we actually participate. It is this—and not the thought that we would be unable to give up the reactive attitudes even if we believed that some metaphysical thesis provided us with reason to do so, nor an equivocation, on Strawson's part, between abnormality and incapacity—that explains Strawson's confidence that the thesis of determinism poses no threat to desert of the moral reactive attitudes.[60] We can be equally confident that no thesis concerning the absence of ultimate responsibility that might be true of us as we are would pose such a threat.

At this point, some may accuse me of having provided an overly sanitized account of the moral reactive attitudes. I have yet to mention what many regard as the most troubling feature of the negative reactive attitudes in even their moral form: the connection that Strawson and others posit between such attitudes, on the one hand, and certain retributive sentiments, on the other. Strawson describes the connection as follows:

Indignation, disapprobation, like resentment, tend to inhibit or at least to limit our goodwill towards the object of these attitudes, tend to promote an at least partial and temporary withdrawal of goodwill: they do so in proportion as they are strong; and their strength is in general proportioned to what is felt to be the magnitude of the injury and to the degree to which the agent's will is identified with, or indifferent to, it . . . But these attitudes of disapprobation and indignation are precisely the correlates of the moral demand in the case where the demand is felt to be disregarded. The making of the demand *is* the proneness to such attitudes. The holding of them does not, as the holding of objective attitudes does, involve as a part of itself viewing their object other than as a member of the moral community. The partial withdrawal of goodwill which *these* attitudes entail, the modification *they* entail of the general demand that another should, if possible, be spared suffering, is, rather, the consequence of *continuing* to view him as a member of the moral community; only as one who has offended against its demands. So the

---

[60] In his (1992), Russell charges that Strawson's argument against determinism's rendering the reactive attitudes universally inappropriate 'turns (repeatedly) on a conflation or equivocation between being "abnormal" and being "incapacitated"' (299). In light of our discussion, Russell's charge is easily be dismissed.

preparedness to acquiesce in that infliction of suffering on the offender which is an essential part of punishment is all of a piece with this whole range of attitudes of which I have been speaking.[61]

Many find the idea of such a connection between moral indignation and reprobation and a readiness to acquiesce in the infliction of suffering on wrongdoers morally disturbing.[62]

Of those who are disturbed by such a connection, some question whether it actually exists. Others accept that the connection exists—at least in the case of certain reactive attitudes—and see it as a definitive reason to abandon these attitudes and the associated concept of moral responsibility even apart from concerns about determinism. Still others accept the connection and view it as grounds for endorsing some sort of ultimate responsibility condition for desert of the moral reactive attitudes, reasoning that only if wrongdoers are ultimately responsible for their actions could such a willingness to acquiesce in the infliction of suffering ever be appropriate.[63] All three reactions seem to me misguided. They appear to be based on a more extreme interpretation of Strawson's remarks and the

---

[61] P. F. Strawson (1962), 90.

[62] See, e.g., Watson (1987) and Scanlon (1998), (2008). Watson writes:

This passage is troubling. Some have aspired to rid themselves of the readiness to limit goodwill and to acquiesce in the suffering of others not in order to relieve the strains of involvement, nor out of a conviction in determinism, but out of a certain ideal of human relationships, which they see as poisoned by the retributive sentiments. It is an ideal of human fellowship or love which embodies values that are arguably as important to our civilization as the notion of moral responsibility itself. ((1987), 148)

If I am right, there is no tension between the ideal of human fellowship or love of which Watson speaks and the particular retributive sentiments that are bound up with moral indignation and reprobation. One can punish at the same time as continuing to love the wrongdoer and with sadness at the suffering punishment will cause. In a footnote, Watson suggests that the possibility of harmonizing retribution and good will is worth exploring.

[63] Watson (1987) and Scanlon (1998), (2008) question the connection that Strawson posits between the reactive attitudes and a willingness to acquiesce in the infliction of suffering, as does Stern (1974) in the case of moral disapprobation. While Scanlon seems to think that the existence of such a connection would constitute a decisive objection to the reactive attitudes, Watson suggests that it might be possible to reconcile good will and retribution. Kelly (2002) suggests that the connection between the negative reactive attitudes and the retributive sentiments is both a reason to believe their desert requires ultimate responsibility and a reason for trying to rid ourselves of such attitudes irrespective of concerns about ultimate responsibility. Honderich (1988) maintains that the connection between the type of moral disapproval that we have been discussing and a desire to see the wrongdoer suffer distress is undeniable and also clear grounds for believing that desert of this type of disapproval would require a form of self-origination inconsistent with determinism.

nature of the retributive sentiments in question than is warranted.[64] For the moment, however, I shall leave this point to one side. Even on a less extreme interpretation, it seems clear that moral indignation and reprobation, where strong, and the wrong occasioning them public rather than private, involve some desire or willingness to see the wrongdoer punished and, so, some modification of the general demand that another be spared suffering if possible. Some might argue that this is enough to render the attitudes in question morally suspect, even 'barbarous': certainly not attitudes a 'civilized' person would hold towards others in the absence of ultimate responsibility, and perhaps not even in its presence.

There are agents with respect to whom the link between moral indignation and reprobation and a desire or willingness to punish would render it uncivilized to hold the former attitudes. The agents I have in mind are the same agents as we've been discussing: those whose psychological abnormality or lack of moral development incapacitates them for ordinary adult interpersonal relationships, as a result of which they are already exempt from the moral reactive attitudes. That the link with the retributive sentiments renders it uncivilized to hold the moral reactive attitudes towards such agents is particularly clear in the case of those incapacitated for ordinary adult interpersonal relationships by deep-rooted psychological abnormality (e.g., 'by the fact that [their] picture of reality is pure fantasy'; or by the fact that their behavior 'is unintelligible to us, perhaps even to

---

[64] It seems undeniable that moral indignation and reprobation, where strong, involve some inhibition or withdrawal of good will—some degree of estrangement from, and loss of solidarity with, the wrongdoer, at least in the pursuit of her ends. Similarly, it seems undeniable that, where it is strong and the wrong occasioning it public, moral indignation involves some desire to see the wrongdoer punished or some thought that punishment is called for or deserved, even if only as a vehicle for communicating to the offender the moral indignation or reprobation she deserves. In such cases, moral indignation will involve some 'readiness to acquiesce in the infliction of suffering on an offender, within the 'institution' of punishment . . .', some modification of the general demand that another not deliberately be made to suffer. Insofar as moral reprobation, where strong and where the wrong occasioning it is public, can motivate the same demand for punishment as can moral indignation, it will also involve in certain cases a willingness to acquiesce in the infliction of suffering on a wrongdoer as part of punishment, and so some modification of the basic demand that another not deliberately be made to suffer. (The idea that moral reprobation can motivate the same demand for punishment as moral indignation will be discussed in Chapter 5.) This said, anyone who thinks that we are sometimes morally justified in punishing intentional wrongdoers other than out of concern for their own welfare—and that we are not similarly justified in punishing innocents—must acknowledge that intentional wrongdoing can effect some modification of the general demand in question.

[them] in terms of conscious purposes, and intelligible only in terms of unconscious purposes'; or by the fact that they are 'wholly impervious to the self-reactive attitudes . . . wholly lacking, as we say, in moral sense'[65]. To the extent that such agents are incapable of participating in ordinary adult interpersonal relationships, their lives are already significantly impoverished by the standards of human flourishing. In relation to such agents, punishment seems, as Feinberg urges, 'a kind of "pouring it on"'. As he continues, 'we might well say of such people what the more forgiving Epictetus said of all wrongdoers, that they are sufficiently punished simply to be the sorts of persons they are'.[66] Moreover, unlike in the case of 'normal' wrongdoers—of whom we are morally obligated to believe that there is at least a chance that the moral condemnation expressed in punishment might serve as an impetus to genuine moral remorse and reform—in the case of the agents currently under consideration, punishment can have no such effect.[67] On the contrary, as Feinberg observes, for those who lack insight into their own motives, or who are completely out of touch with reality, or too deranged to understand the force of moral criticism, or too compulsive to control their impulses in accordance with their understanding, moral condemnation will often only lead to despair.[68] The civilized response to these agents is not a desire to condemn or punish, but a determination to help them (re)gain the capacities required for participation in ordinary adult interpersonal relationships where this is possible, and to treat them as painlessly as is compatible with the protection

---

[65] The examples are Strawson's. See his (1962), 82, 86. In the case of children, matters are perhaps less clear-cut. The fact that children are not yet capable of participation in ordinary adult interpersonal relationships does not entail that their lives are impoverished by the standards of human flourishing. Moreover, in the case of children, we are, as Strawson emphasizes:

dealing with creatures who are potentially and increasingly capable of both holding, and being objects of, the full range of human and moral attitudes, but are not yet truly capable of either. The treatment of such creatures must therefore represent a kind of compromise, constantly shifting in one direction, between objectivity of attitude and developed human attitudes. Rehearsals insensibly modulate towards true performances. ((1962), 88)

(Perhaps something similar could be said of those recovering from certain types of mental illness, though here I am less sure.) Still, to the extent that children are not yet fully capable of understanding the demand underlying the reactive attitudes, or of controlling their own impulses, it would be uncivilized, even barbarous, to hold the negative reactive attitudes towards them in unqualified forms. The further a child is from possessing the requisite capacities, the more barbarous it would be.

[66] Feinberg (1970), 287.
[67] On this moral obligation, see Margalit (1996).
[68] See Feinberg (1970), 291.

of others where it is not. To paraphrase Strawson, to view someone as outside the reach of ordinary interpersonal relationships is already, for the civilized, to be committed to treating her in this way.

Incompatibilists might argue that the connection between moral indignation and reprobation and the desire (or willingness) to overtly condemn and punish renders it uncivilized to bear such attitudes not just towards the psychologically abnormal or morally undeveloped, but towards any agent who lacks ultimate responsibility for what she does, irrespective of whether she is capable of participating in ordinary adult interpersonal relationships.[69] Others (including some compatibilists) might go a step further and argue that the connection between such attitudes and the desire (or willingness) to acquiesce in the infliction of suffering on wrongdoers renders it uncivilized or barbarous to hold the moral reactive attitudes towards any agent, irrespective of concerns about freedom and responsibility. Given the connection, the civilized thing to do is to abandon such attitudes altogether to the extent that we can.

I have three responses to such arguments. The first two are primarily directed at those who believe that the connection between the moral reactive attitudes and the desire (or willingness) to acquiesce in the infliction of suffering renders it uncivilized or even barbarous to hold the moral reactive attitudes towards any agent, irrespective of concerns about freedom and responsibility. The third is directed specifically at incompatibilists. First, if the link between our proneness to moral indignation and reprobation and our involvement in ordinary interpersonal relationships is as tight as Strawson describes—if, as Strawson argues, and as I believe we have reason to accept, 'being involved in inter-personal relationships as we normally understand them precisely is being exposed to the range of reactive attitudes and feelings that is in question', such that the only way of ridding ourselves entirely of these attitudes and our susceptibility to them would be by abandoning ordinary adult interpersonal relationships as we normally understand them—then trying to rid ourselves of our susceptibility to these attitudes could not be the more civilized option.[70] Surely it could

[69] Note: unless the claim that (a) it is uncivilized to hold the reactive attitudes towards anyone in the absence of ultimate responsibility is based on the claim that (b) in the absence of ultimate responsibility, the reactive attitudes would be universally inappropriate by their own internal standards, establishing claim (a) would not establish the claim that (c) in the absence of ultimate responsibility, moral blame could never be deserved. It would establish that, in the absence of ultimate responsibility, it is uncivilized to blame whether or not blame is deserved.

[70] P. F. Strawson (1962), 81.

not be more civilized to try to rid ourselves of these attitudes than to retain them, if trying to rid ourselves of them would require us to so distance ourselves from others on an ordinary interpersonal level as to be able to view their behavior with the studied detachment of a Freudian analyst or through the clinical lens of a physician thinking exclusively in terms of symptoms, causes, and cures.[71] Indeed, the latter option would, as Strawson might put it, offend against the humanity of the wrongdoer herself.

Second, and more importantly, we need to question whether there is anything uncivilized about directing moral indignation or reprobation towards those who are capable of participating in the relationships that give these attitudes meaning and with respect to whom the condemnation expressed through punishment might occasion genuine remorse and reform of the sort required for the restoration of good standing within such relationships.[72] Here, it is crucial to distinguish between a partial (and often temporary) withdrawal of good will and ill will; between modification of the general demand that another, if possible, be spared suffering and wholesale abrogation of the right not to be harmed or killed; between a conditional 'readiness to acquiesce in the infliction of suffering, on an offender, within the "institution" of punishment', if necessary to communicate to the wrongdoer the moral indignation or reprobation she deserves and a readiness to acquiesce in the infliction of suffering on wrongdoers 'in a fashion we saw to be quite indiscriminate or in accordance with procedures which we knew to be wholly useless'; and finally, between a desire to see those who engage in certain forms of moral wrongdoing suffer punishment and a desire to see them suffer *simpliciter*.[73] Moral indignation and

---

[71] Although many have questioned whether the connection between involvement in ordinary interpersonal relationships and susceptibility to negative reactive attitudes is as strong as Strawson alleges it is, I agree with Strawson on this point. For most, if not all, human beings, it seems that distancing ourselves from others on an ordinary interpersonal level would be the only way to rid ourselves entirely of such attitudes.

[72] Thus, even if the harm that 'normal' wrongdoers do to themselves through their wrongdoing exceeds the harm they do to others, still punishing them is not a kind of 'pouring it on'. Punishment addresses the wrongdoer as a normal adult human being capable of understanding the force of the condemnation underlying punishment and of behaving differently in the future. To exempt an agent altogether from punishment and the attitudes underlying it would signal a loss of faith in the agent's ability to improve her behavior. As such, it would be a sign of disrespect. On this last point, see Margalit (1996).

[73] The claim that punishment may be necessary, in the case of serious pubic moral wrongdoing, to communicate to the wrongdoer the moral indignation or reprobation she deserves is defended in Chapter 5. I do not deny that moral indignation and perhaps even

reprobation, where strong and the wrong occasioning them public, may well entail the first member of each of the pairs listed; however, there is no reason to assume that they entail the second.[74]

Even where strong, moral indignation and reprobation are compatible with continuing compassion and concern for their targets and with will-ingnesses to forgive and to show mercy.[75] They are also compatible with the recognition that, had we been in the wrongdoer's place or grown up under circumstances similar to hers, we might have committed similar wrongs. In practice, the recognition that this is the case has a tendency to take some of the anger out of indignation; sometimes it dispels it altogether. However, as we have seen, not every mental operation that dispels a reactive attitude reveals it to be inappropriate. What the recogni-tion does reveal to be inappropriate is the sort of smug self-righteousness that sometimes surfaces alongside moral indignation or reprobation, although it is not a proper part of either, and that tells us that we need not pity the wrongdoer insofar as her suffering is simply her 'just deserts'.

It is true that moral indignation in particular, while not itself incompat-ible with a willingness to forgive or to show mercy, can sometimes overwhelm these willingnesses, especially where the person on whose behalf indignation is felt is oneself. It is also true that what we tell ourselves is justified moral indignation or reprobation is sometimes a cover for

reprobation may sometimes be contaminated by a desire to see the wrongdoer suffer *simpliciter*. However, such a desire is not a proper part of either moral indignation or moral reprobation. Whether the same is true of resentment is unclear. A desire to see the target of one's resentment suffer *simpliciter* might be internal to resentment.

[74] Nor is there reason to assume that Strawson takes strong moral indignation or reproba-tion to involve the second member of any of the four pairs that I mentioned. In the case of the third pair, he explicitly denies it:

I am not in least suggesting that these readinesses to acquiesce . . . are always accompanied or preceded by indignant boilings . . . [nor] that it belongs to this continuum of attitudes and feelings that we should be ready to acquiesce in the infliction of injury on offenders in a fashion we saw to be quite indiscriminate or in accordance with procedures which we knew to be wholly useless. On the contrary, savage or civilized, we have some belief in the utility of practices of condemnation and punishment. ((1962), 91)

[75] To forgive an agent is to renounce towards her negative reactive attitudes despite acknowledging that such attitudes would be deserved. To show mercy to an agent is to treat her, out of compassion, in a manner less (outwardly) severe than she deserves. The two are independent of one another. One might forgive an agent, relinquishing all resentment or indignation, but still insist on punishing her to the full extent that she deserves. On this point, see Murphy in Murphy and Hampton (1988).

less palatable attitudes: for envy, insecurity, malice, self-righteousness, guilt-transference, and unconscious sadism.[76] However, these truths do not enjoin a wholesale rejection of moral indignation or reprobation as themselves necessarily cruel or uncivilized. Rather they suggest that we be prepared to scrutinize what underlies our own moral indignation and reprobation when we experience them and remain cognizant that these attitudes are, as Strawson acknowledges, 'a prime realm of self-deception'.[77]

Thus, we can dismiss the charge that the connection between the negative moral reactive attitudes and the desire (or willingness) to punish renders it uncivilized to direct the attitudes towards normal adult human beings, whether in the absence of ultimate responsibility or more generally. For it to be uncivilized to do so, moral indignation and reprobation would have to involve the sort of ill-will or desire to see the wrongdoer suffer *simpliciter* that I have denied that they involve. But—and this brings me to my third response—there is a further point that can be made here. If moral indignation or reprobation did involve ill will or a desire to see the wrongdoer suffer *simpliciter*, then, I would argue, it would be uncivilized to hold moral indignation and reprobation towards wrongdoers irrespective of whether they were ultimately responsible for their wrongdoing. The presence or absence of ultimate responsibility would not make a difference.[78]

There is, however, another move that incompatibilists might make. They might argue that the fact that moral indignation and reprobation, where strong and the wrong occasioning them public, involve a not purely instrumental desire to see the wrongdoer suffer punishment or a belief that punishment would be deserved, while not enough to render the attitudes uncivilized, is enough to generate an ultimate responsibility requirement for their desert. For, incompatibilists might argue, to the extent that it is of the nature of moral indignation and reprobation to involve such a desire or belief, these attitudes can only be fully appropriate by their own internal standards if it is possible for punishment to be morally deserved. And, incompatibilists might argue, for a wrongdoer to be morally deserving of punishment for her wrongdoing, she must be ultimately responsible for her wrongdoing. Moral desert of punishment presupposes ultimate responsibility. Whether

---

[76] The last two descriptions are Strawson's. See his (1962), 93.

[77] P. F. Strawson (1962), 93.

[78] We shall return to such claims in the next chapter and again in the book's conclusion.

incompatibilists can make good on this argument concerning the moral desert of punishment is the focus of the book's remaining chapters. A final verdict as to whether desert of the moral reactive attitudes requires agents to be ultimately responsible for their actions will have to await a verdict concerning punishment.

4

Moral Desert of Punishment

This chapter and the next discuss the moral desert of punishment. Their aim is to determine whether, to be morally deserving of punishment, wrongdoers must be ultimately responsible for their actions. Though questions regarding the moral desert of punishment were once prominent in discussions of free will and moral responsibility, they are often sidelined—particularly by compatibilists—in contemporary discussions. This is a mistake. As we saw in Chapter 1, worries concerning the moral desert of punishment feature centrally in some incompatibilists' thinking concerning the need for ultimate responsibility. Beyond this, the idea of desert of punishment continues to feature centrally in ordinary thinking concerning moral responsibility. It seems to be built into our ordinary understanding of moral responsibility that those who culpably engage in more serious forms of moral wrongdoing morally deserve not just blame, but punishment. Any account of moral liability-responsibility that does not speak to such desert will to that extent be deflationary or, at least, incomplete. But there is another reason why even compatibilists should be concerned with the moral desert of punishment. As we discussed in Chapter 3, moral indignation and reprobation, where strong and the wrong occasioning them is public rather than private, involve some desire to see the wrongdoer punished or some thought that punishment is called for or deserved. To the extent that it is the nature of these attitudes to involve some such thought or desire (and the desire is not a purely instrumental one), it will only be possible for the attitudes themselves to be deserved if it is possible for punishment to be deserved. As such, anyone who wants to show that desert of the negative moral reactive attitudes is compatible with determinism—and with the absence of ultimate responsibility that determinism would entail—must first show that desert of punishment is similarly compatible.

There has been much discussion of the proper definition of punishment. Though I do not intend to discuss the matter at length, it will
become necessary to say something about it later in the chapter. In the
interim, I shall provisionally define punishment as the deliberate imposition of 'hard' (i.e., unwelcome or unpleasant) treatment or deprivation
upon an alleged wrongdoer for her alleged wrongdoing. This will enable
us to focus initially on the concept of desert as it relates to overt treatment.
Before turning to desert, however, there is one matter concerning my
treatment of punishment that I should mention.

Although the concern of this chapter is with *moral* wrongdoers' *moral*
desert of punishment for *moral* wrongdoing (and not with the *legal* desert of
legal wrongdoers for *legal* wrongdoing), I do not intend to focus on some
special, exclusively moral, form of punishment. Many of the consequences
of wrongdoing sometimes referred to as 'moral punishment'—e.g., the
damage wrongdoers do to their relationships with others or to their souls;
loss of others' respect and esteem; estrangement from God or from 'the
Good'—are not consequences that are deliberately imposed upon wrongdoers for their wrongdoing. As such, they do not qualify as punishment
other than, perhaps, metaphorically. Nor do I intend to discuss divine
punishment, with the special difficulties raised by a single being's simultaneously occupying the roles of omniscient, omnipotent creator, on the
one hand, and judge and punisher, on the other. Whether divine retribution is what most ordinary people have in mind when they think of moral
wrongdoers morally deserving to be punished for their wrongdoing, I will
not speculate. Fortunately, there is another way in which thoughts about
the moral desert of punishment enter into ordinary discourse: through the
thought that in receiving a specific punishment from the state for what
would independently be considered a moral offense, a particular wrongdoer received the (level of) punishment that she morally 'had coming to
her', or morally deserved, given the moral seriousness of her offense. That
the desert in question in this context is moral rather than legal is suggested
by the fact that, even after it has been established that the relevant legal
procedures were followed and the wrongdoer assigned precisely the
punishment prescribed by law, it can still be asked whether the wrongdoer
received the punishment she deserved. For many, the extent to which the
punishments that the state metes out correspond to wrongdoers' moral
deserts is one of the primary benchmarks against which the justice of a
state's institutions of punishment is to be measured. While I do not

necessarily mean to endorse this thought, it suggests that one way to bring the ordinary understanding of the moral desert of punishment into view is to focus not on some special, exclusively moral form of punishment—let alone divine punishment—but on the types of treatment that we ordinarily consider forms of punishment (or perhaps intentional hard treatment or deprivation considered generically) and to try to figure out what we mean when we say of someone who has committed what would independently be considered a moral offense, that she morally deserves to be punished or did or did not receive the punishment she morally deserved. This is how I shall proceed. It is worth emphasizing that, in proceeding in this way, I do not mean to suggest that the 'general justifying aim' of state institutions of punishment is to see to it that wrongdoers receive their moral deserts.[1] Nothing I say in this chapter or the next should be construed as an endorsement of this or any other view concerning the primary aim or justification of state institutions of punishment. This is not my topic.[2] My aim is to figure out how we should understand claims concerning the moral desert of punishment with an eye to determining whether, to be morally deserving of punishment, wrongdoers must be ultimately responsible for their actions.

What do we mean when we say that a wrongdoer received the punishment that she morally deserved? Or, to start with the more basic question, what do we mean when we claim that a wrongdoer morally deserves to be punished? It seems clear that the claim is a claim about justice. The precise nature and force of the claim are less clear. Two questions must be addressed immediately. First, in claiming that a person deserves to be punished, are we making a claim about what would be just, all things considered, or is the claim narrower than this? Second, in claiming that a

---

[1] Talk of the 'general justifying aim' of punishment traces to Hart (1959). Hart distinguishes three questions concerning the justification of punishment: the question of the 'general justifying aim of punishment' or the aim that justifies the creation and maintenance of formal institutions of punishment; the question of 'distribution' or who may be punished; and the question of 'amount' or how severely to punish. Hart argues that if we are not to oversimplify matters concerning the justification of punishment, then what is necessary 'is *not* the simple admission that . . . a plurality of values and aims should be given as a conjunctive answer to some *single* question concerning the justification of punishment, [but] the realization that different principles (each of which may in a sense be called a 'justification') are relevant at different points in any morally acceptable account of punishment' (3).

[2] Nor do I mean to suggest that anyone apart from the state has authority to impose on wrongdoers the sorts of hard treatment that the state imposes on offenders on the basis of their legal desert. I also do not mean to deny it. It is not my topic.

person morally deserves to be punished, are we merely claiming that she lacks (a certain) ground for complaint of being treated unjustly if she is punished or are we pointing to a possible ground for punishing her or for wanting her to be punished, i.e., a ground for believing that, by one measure of justice, justice would be promoted by her being punished?

In addressing both questions, I suggest that we follow Feinberg's analysis of personal desert claims more generally.[3] According to Feinberg, desert is a ' "natural" moral notion' the demands of which represent 'only a part, and not necessarily the most important part, of the domain of justice'.[4] While the claim that a person morally deserves to be punished, or morally deserves to be treated in some other fashion, thus implies that there is 'a certain sort of propriety' in her being treated in this fashion, it does not imply that treating her this way would be just overall, much less that justice as a whole demands such treatment.[5] Still, as Feinberg emphasizes, this last point applies equally to other justice-related claims, including claims of rights and entitlements. What distinguishes desert claims from these other claims is the pre-institutional nature of the propriety involved.[6] (This is what Feinberg means when he refers to desert as a *natural* moral notion.) To claim that, in virtue of some action (or personal characteristic), an agent is morally deserving of a particular form of treatment is to claim that such treatment is an (or the) intrinsically morally fitting response to the agent in virtue of the action (or personal characteristic) in question. In affording an agent the treatment she morally deserves, we give her the treatment that she morally 'has coming' to her, or that it would be morally fitting for her to receive, whether or not any institution or formal set of

[3] See Feinberg (1963). Although there has been some controversy as to whether all desert claims are pre-institutional, where the claims are claims of moral desert, there is no such controversy. What distinguishes moral desert claims from other personal desert claims (in connection with which there is controversy) is the moral nature of the desert base in claims of moral desert. What a person deserves is always deserved in virtue of some possessed characteristic or past action that is generally disapproved of or admired. In the case of moral desert, the disapproval or admiration must be *moral* disapproval or admiration.

[4] Feinberg (1963), 56. Importantly, acknowledging that desert is 'only a part, and not necessarily the most important part, of the domain of justice' is perfectly compatible with maintaining that considerations of desert are fully determinative of the causal and capacity conditions of moral responsibility.

[5] Feinberg (1963), 56.

[6] See Feinberg (1963), 56–8.

rules assigns her such treatment or gives her an entitlement to receive it. Such treatment is what prior to and apart from any institution would constitute a just requital for what she has done.

As for the second question, Feinberg clearly thinks that a person's moral desert of a certain form of treatment provides a positive ground for affording her such treatment—even where (as is normally the case with punishment) the treatment in question is one the potential recipient would prefer not to receive.[7] Thus Feinberg writes 'a person's desert of X is always a reason for giving X to [her]', albeit, as he emphasizes, 'not always a conclusive reason'.[8] The idea that a person's desert of a certain type of treatment provides a positive ground for affording her such treatment or for wanting her to receive it certainly seems to accord with ordinary thinking about desert, including the desert of punishment. While there may be everyday contexts in which the claim that an agent deserves to be punished is merely intended to convey that the agent lacks (a certain type of) ground for complaint of unjust treatment if she is punished, the claim is more often intended to convey that the agent has punishment positively coming to her, where this is seen as a *pro tanto* reason for wanting her to be punished: a reason for believing that, by one measure of justice, justice would be promoted by her receiving punishment.[9]

Whether, within the context of philosophical discussions of free will and moral responsibility, claims concerning desert of punishment are intended to be understood as providing a *pro tanto* ground for punishment is less clear. Wallace, the most prominent recent compatibilist to devote separate attention to desert of punishment, makes it clear that when he claims a wrongdoer deserves to be punished, what he has in mind is simply that she cannot complain of being treating unfairly if she is punished.[10] I suspect that this is the strongest claim concerning desert of punishment that, prior to further argument, many compatibilists would be willing to

---

[7] This was already implied by what was said above.

[8] Feinberg (1963), 60.

[9] More formally, the consideration that those who culpably engage in certain types of conduct morally deserve to be punished constitutes a *pro tanto* reason for creating (and supporting) institutions with the authority to punish those duly found to have culpably engaged in such conduct.

[10] See Wallace (1994). Wallace recognizes that restricting claims of desert to claims concerning the absence of grounds for complaint might seem deflationary. For expression of this recognition, see his (1994), 226–8.

accept.[11] However, at least one compatibilist seems willing to commit himself not just to the claim that desert of punishment entails a positive ground for punishing, but to the even stronger claim that desert entails a positive duty to punish.[12] This stronger claim seems to be one that even many incompatibilists would reject.[13] At the same time, the majority of incompatibilists never distinguish between the two other claims that we have been considering. Much of the language they employ is ambiguous between the two. Even the seemingly unambiguous claim that, in the absence of ultimate responsibility, all punishment is (in one way) unjust does not establish that incompatibilists understand the force of desert claims in one way or the other.[14] Rather than indicating that incompatibilists understand the claim that an agent morally deserves to be punished as not implying anything beyond her lacking a certain type of ground for complaint of being treated unjustly if she is punished, it might simply reflect the assumption that an agent's having punishment positively coming to her on desert-based grounds is a necessary condition of her lacking ground for complaint.

Despite the ambiguity, I suggest that when incompatibilists question whether in the absence of ultimate responsibility wrongdoers could truly deserve to be punished, they are not simply questioning whether wrong-doers could be punished without having grounds for complaint of unjust treatment. For incompatibilists, desert of punishment constitutes a *pro tanto* ground in favor of punishment. Even if this is not the way in which the majority of incompatibilists understand claims concerning the moral desert of punishment, it is the way in which they (as well as compatibilists) should understand claims concerning the moral desert of punishment. Anything short of this would fail to capture the ordinary understanding of what it is to morally deserve punishment: as I indicated above, on the ordinary

---

[11] The reluctance of many compatibilists to embrace any claim concerning desert of punishment stronger than the claim concerning the absence of grounds for complaint may reflect a failure to distinguish between a consideration's supplying a *pro tanto* ground for punishment and its giving rise to sufficient ground for punishment or even a duty to punish.

[12] The compatibilist I have in mind is Michael Moore. See his (1987). Moore's arguments will be discussed in the concluding chapter of the book.

[13] If Feinberg's analysis of desert claims is correct, incompatibilists do well to reject the claim that desert of punishment entails a duty to punish.

[14] Smilansky speaks of punishment's being 'in one way' unjust in the absence of ultimate responsibility or libertarian free will. See his (2003a). Hence, the qualification. I will return to Smilansky's claims in the book's final chapter.

understanding, that an agent morally deserves to be punished constitutes a *pro tanto* reason for punishing her or for wanting her to be punished.

Bearing these points in mind, perhaps the following might be a way of filling out the incompatibilist claim that in the absence of ultimate responsibility, no one would ever 'truly' deserve to be punished: even if in the absence of ultimate responsibility compatibilistically-free wrongdoers could not complain of being treated unfairly simply in being punished, still they would not 'truly' deserve to be punished in the sense of having punishment *pro tanto* positively coming to them as what, apart from any institution, would constitute a just requital for what they had done. The only positive reasons we might have for punishing wrongdoers, some incompatibilists would add, would be utilitarian ones.[15] The claim that, absent ultimate responsibility, compatibilistically-free wrongdoers would not truly deserve to be punished in the sense specified is, I believe, one that the majority of incompatibilists would be willing to endorse—though prior to further argument, many would undoubtedly add that, absent ultimate responsibility, all punishment is (in one way) unjust. Still, it is unclear that the claim is one that incompatibilists should endorse even without the supplement. For it is unclear that there are not pre-institutional considerations of justice that a compatibilist might cite as providing *pro tanto* reason for punishing compatibilistically-free wrongdoers even in the absence of ultimate responsibility.[16]

In this connection, I want to consider Herbert Morris's idea that in the face of wrongdoing punishment may be required to reinstate a fair distribution of the basic benefits and burdens of non-interference.[17] Although Morris does not introduce the idea as a way of explicating wrongdoers' moral desert of punishment, George Sher attempts to put the idea to this

[15] See, e.g., Kane (1996). He there writes: 'To be sure, there would remain utilitarian reasons for punishment even if UR [the Ultimate Responsibility condition] were not satisfied . . . But utilitarian justifications circumvent rather than address issues of blame*worthiness* for past actions, or *desert* of punishment, which is the issue that leads to UR-related questions about whether actions or circumstances were ultimately within the agent's control' (83). See, also, G. Strawson (1994) and Parfit (2011).

[16] Although the considerations that I am about to cite in connection with Morris's argument turn out not to provide a *pro tanto* reason for punishment proper, the considerations that I point to in Chapter 5 in connection with the communicative understanding of the moral desert of punishment do provide such a reason and, moreover, a reason that would obtain even in the absence of ultimate responsibility.

[17] Morris (1968).

use.[18] To anticipate: after an extended discussion I shall conclude that the attempt fails—that although the considerations that Morris points to might give rise to a *pro tanto* reason for imposing some form of hard treatment or deprivation on intentional wrongdoers, the reason would not be one of desert. More interestingly, the hard treatment or deprivation for which such considerations would provide *pro tanto* support would lack certain essential features of punishment properly understood. I include this extended discussion of morris's argument because of what it reveals about the nature of desert and the nature of punishment.

Applying to the conduct of all agents, Morris asks us to suppose, is a set of 'primary' rules prohibiting violence and deception, and compliance with which provides benefits for all. More specifically, compliance with the rules affords each agent a sphere free from interference and manipulation by others. At the same time, and as a necessary condition of the enjoyment of this benefit, compliance involves the voluntary assumption of what might be thought of as a 'burden' of self-restraint. Individuals must forgo the use of means and the pursuit of ends that 'directly interfere or create a substantial risk of interference with others in the proscribed ways'.[19] Provided that every agent complies with rules, the resulting distribution of the basic benefits and burdens of non-interference is equal and fair. Each agent enjoys the same sphere of freedom and faces the same constraints on permissible action. Intentional wrongdoing disrupts this equilibrium, creating a disparity between those who have restrained themselves and those who have not. In exercising her will in a proscribed way, an intentional wrongdoer 'renounces a burden', a constraint on her liberty, 'which others have voluntarily assumed and thus gains an advantage', a further liberty or indulgence, 'which others, who have restrained themselves, do not possess'.[20] As Morris emphasizes, '[m]atters are not even until this

---

[18] See Sher (1987). Jeffrie Murphy, in his (1971), (1972), and (1973), articulates a similar understanding of the moral desert of punishment to Sher and also attributes such an understanding to Kant. He later comes to view both the understanding and the attribution as problematic. See Murphy (1987). Several others have considered using Morris's idea to explicate the moral desert of punishment or assumed that this is how Morris intends it to be used. See, e.g., Wasserstrom (1980), Burgh (1982), and Duff (1986). Unlike Sher, the others conclude that the idea cannot be used to explicate the moral desert of punishment, though their reasons differ from mine. They seem not to see that the hard treatment or deprivation that Morris's argument would sanction could not properly be considered punishment.

[19] Morris (1968), 33.

[20] Morris (1968), 33.

advantage is somehow erased'.[21] Punishment, Morris argues, erases this advantage, thereby restoring an equal distribution of the benefits and burdens of non-interference. *Qua* forced deprivation or imposition of something (normally) unwelcome, punishment 'disindulges' the will, taking away from the wrongdoer 'that which does not rightfully belong to [her] . . . exacting the debt'.[22] Insofar as it is a basic requirement of justice that, other things being equal, the benefits and burdens of non-interference be distributed equally among agents, considerations of justice provide us with a *pro tanto* reason for 'punishing' (i.e., imposing some form of hard treatment or deprivation upon) intentional wrongdoers, a reason that seemingly would apply even in the absence of ultimate responsibility.

How should incompatibilists respond to this argument (hereafter, the 'benefits-and-burdens argument')? They might challenge the argument's soundness *qua* argument purporting to adduce a pre-institutional, justice-based reason for imposing hard treatment or deprivation on intentional wrongdoers, either in the absence of ultimate responsibility or more generally. I shall refer to such challenges as challenges to the argument in its less ambitious form. But there is a second option. They might concede that the considerations the argument cites could give rise to such a reason for imposing hard treatment or deprivation on intentional wrongdoers—a reason that might hold in the absence of ultimate responsibility—but deny that this reason would be one of moral desert. Since the second option strikes me as more promising and more illuminative of the natures of moral desert and punishment it is the option that I shall ultimately pursue. Before doing so, however, there are three challenges to the argument in its less ambitious form that we ought to consider. The first two challenges are based on misunderstandings of the argument that I hope, by considering, to pre-empt; the third intersects with incompatibilists' concerns about ultimate responsibility and moral luck.

As for the first challenge: it is sometimes assumed that the unfair benefit or advantage that punishment is intended to remove from the wrongdoer is whatever gain in material goods or subjective satisfaction the wrongdoer managed to achieve as a result of renouncing her burden of self-restraint. Based on this assumption, it is objected that the benefits-and-burdens argument fails to provide a general reason for punishing

---

intentional wrongdoers, since not every case of intentional wrongdoing yields such a benefit or advantage. The problem with the objection is that its way of understanding the unfair advantage to be removed by punishment is not the only way of understanding it. Nor, given the nature of the benefits and burdens that the argument has as its more general focus—viz. those of non-interference, understood as various liberties and restrictions on liberty—is it a particularly plausible understanding. There is a type of advantage that, in addition to being of the same 'currency' as the benefits and burdens that the argument has as its general focus, is intrinsic to wrongdoing: that of not bearing the burden of self-restraint, where this involves taking a liberty that one is not entitled to take.[23] On this alternative interpretation, it is not that the wrongdoer's self-indulgence or lack of restraint enables her to acquire some further benefit to which she is not entitled. It is that the self-indulgence or lack of restraint, involving as it does a prohibited liberty, itself constitutes a benefit to which she is not entitled. As a benefit intrinsic to intentional wrongdoing, this benefit accrues to all wrongdoers.[24]

---

[23] For the idea that there is such an 'intrinsic advantage' to wrongdoing, see Murphy (1973). For a similar understanding of the unfair advantage that punishment is designed to remove, see Honderich (1984/1989), Duff (1986), and Sher (1987). Certain of Morris's claims suggest that he understands the unfair benefit that the wrongdoer acquires through her wrongdoing not in terms of a proscribed liberty per se, but in terms of the wrongdoer's enjoying the core benefits of non-interference without having 'paid' for them. On this interpretation, the wrongdoer is viewed as a free rider. Although she benefits from the larger system—i.e., from other people's voluntary assumption of the burdens of self-restraint without which the benefits of non-interference would be impossible—she does not contribute to the system herself. Her failure to contribute to the system results in an inequitable distribution of the basic benefits and burdens of maintaining the system. Punishment corrects the inequity by taking from the wrongdoer a benefit that she has not earned. Though there may be something to this interpretation, I would want to resist any suggestion that the right to non-interference is conferred originally by society.

[24] Interpreting the unfair benefit acquired through intentional wrongdoing as a proscribed indulgence or liberty also enables us to respond to several other objections to the benefits-and-burdens argument. On this interpretation, not only is the benefit that punishment is intended to remove of the same 'currency' as the benefits and burdens of non-interference; it is also of the same currency as punishment (*qua* forcible imposition upon the will). That it is of the same currency as punishment answers Wasserstrom's query 'how it is that *punishing* the wrongdoer constitutes a taking of the wrongfully appropriated benefit away from him or her' ((1980), 145). Moreover, *pace* Burgh (1982), understanding the wrongfully appropriated benefit as a proscribed liberty or indulgence enables us to explain why, other things being equal, those who commit more serious wrongs morally deserve more severe punishments than those who commit less serious wrongs: as Sher emphasizes, the more serious the wrong, the greater the liberty taken and hence the greater the imposition required to counterbalance it. Or, rather,

The second challenge to the benefits-and-burdens argument in its less ambitious form is that the argument commits its adherents to a problematic explanation of why it is morally wrong to engage in the actions prohibited by the primary rules: that it suggests that what makes rape, for example, wrong is that it involves assuming for oneself 'an unfair advantage over those who do restrain themselves' and not that 'it is a grievous assault on its victim's interests and integrity'.[25] The problem with the objection is that it is wrong to think that the benefits-and-burdens argument commits its advocates to this or any other particular account of why it is morally wrong to rape or kill or deceive. This is not its purpose. The purpose of the argument is not to explain what makes certain acts unjust and so ones that the primary rules ought to prohibit. It is to explain why, against the backdrop of the primary rules and the benefits and burdens to which the rules gives rise, justice provides a *pro tanto* reason for imposing some form of hard treatment or deprivation on those who violate the rules. Someone might counter that any attempt to explain the justice of imposing some form of hard treatment or deprivation on those who violate the primary rules that does not appeal to the moral wrongness of the acts that the rules prohibit will, for this very reason, fail to capture the moral desert of punishment: where punishment is morally deserved, it is deserved because of the moral quality of the agent's action.[26] I agree. But this is a different kind of objection from the one that we are presently considering. It calls into question not the soundness of the benefits-and-burdens argument *qua* argument designed to adduce a *pro tanto* reason for imposing hard treatment or deprivation upon those who violate the primary rules, but the argument's ability to explicate the moral desert of punishment. Discussion of this further objection will therefore be postponed until later.

Given its link to concerns about ultimate responsibility and moral luck, the third challenge to the benefits-and-burdens argument in its less ambitious form warrants closer consideration than the previous two did. The challenge relates to a central assumption underlying the argument—viz., that the distribution of the basic benefits and burdens of non-interference

---

understanding the wrongfully appropriated benefit as a proscribed liberty or indulgence would enable us to explain such things if the benefits-and-burdens argument were not for other reasons incapable of explicating the moral desert of punishment.

[25] Duff (1986), 212.

[26] For this type of objection, see Hampton in Murphy and Hampton (1988), 116–17.

that obtains pre-wrongdoing, and that punishment is intended to restore, is an equitable one, or at least more equitable than the distribution that obtains post-wrongdoing but prior to punishment. Were it not for this assumption, considerations of justice would afford no reason to attempt to restore the initial distribution. However, the assumption is one that many theorists question and that those concerned about ultimate responsibility and moral luck are particularly likely to find problematic. Admittedly, the primary rules guarantee every agent the same freedoms from interference and require each agent to observe the same limits on permissible action. Yet, objectors argue, how burdensome it is for a particular agent to refrain from performing a certain action depends in large part on the strength of her inclinations to perform it and on the range of other options and opportunities realistically open to her—neither of which is subject to her ultimate control.[27] Not everyone is inclined to rape, steal, or kill. Moreover, not all those who are inclined to perform these actions are as strongly inclined as those who eventually perform them. For those strongly inclined to engage in the prohibited behaviors, the burdens of self-restraint seem far heavier than they do for those less strongly inclined or not inclined at all. Once we take these differential burdens into account, we see that those who violate the primary rules do not renounce a burden assumed by all the others; they renounce a burden many of the others do not face. Insofar as the additional burden is one for which the violators are not ultimately responsible, it is, according to objectors, not a burden that they should have to bear.[28] From this perspective, far from restoring a fair equilibrium of the benefits and burdens of non-interference, punishing those who break the primary rules reinstates an equilibrium that was never fair to begin with.[29]

How much, if anything, there is to this objection depends on the legitimacy of its construal of the burdens of self-restraint. Rather than equating the burdens of self-restraint with the limits on permissible action,

---

[27] Commenting on the burdens imposed by the criminal law, Honderich (1984/1989) remarks that 'one cannot avoid the thought that the burdens of self-restraint or dissatis-factions-in-not-acting defined by the law are lighter for the man who has everything as against the man who has nothing' (230).

[28] Or, at least, the additional burden is not one that they should have to bear without some form of compensation. For the idea that those whose wrongdoing results from childhood deprivation deserve compensation, see Klein (1990).

[29] For objections of this sort, see Murphy (1973) and Honderich (1984/1989).

the objection assimilates them to the effects of the limits, to how subjectively burdensome the objective burdens are. To the extent that this construal constitutes a departure from that assumed as background to the argument, it would at least require defense. Even with such a defense, however, it is unclear that the objection would be capable of undermining the benefits-and-burdens argument *qua* argument designed to adduce a pre-institutional justice-based reason for imposing some form of hard treatment or deprivation upon wrongdoers that might obtain in the absence of ultimate responsibility. Even if, in the real world, the burdens of self-restraint imposed by the moral law are so distributed that an attempt to reinstate the distribution disrupted by wrongdoing would constitute a move away from equality rather than towards it, we can imagine a world in which this would not be the case—a world in which all agents possess roughly the same propensities towards wrongful behavior and enjoy the same range of opportunities. In such a world, the objection we are considering would hold no weight. (Granted, we would still have appeal to factors beyond agents' ultimate control to explain why, when faced with substantially the same burdens of self-restraint, some agents choose to keep to the primary rules while others do not. However, as long as these factors do not affect the equality of the initial distribution of burdens and that the net effect of imposing hard treatment or deprivation upon intentional wrongdoers is merely to reinstate the initial distribution, the presence of such factors as part of the explanation of wrongful behavior would not undermine the argument's rationale for imposing such treatment; for, it would not undermine hard treatment's claim to restore an equitable distribution of benefits and burdens.) Someone who opposed the benefits-and-burdens argument solely on the basis of worries about inequalities in the initial distribution of benefits and burdens would have to concede that, in our imagined world, considerations of justice might well support imposing hard treatment or deprivation on intentional wrongdoers as a means of restoring a fair equilibrium of benefits and burdens.[30] To concede this, however, is to concede that pre-institutional considerations of justice could give rise to a *pro tanto* reason for imposing hard treatment or

---

[30] One might still have other objections to the benefits-and-burdens argument. For instance, one might argue that considerations of fairness can never provide even a *pro tanto* reason for 'leveling down'. In this strong form, the leveling down objection is implausible.

deprivation upon intentional wrongdoers even in the absence of ultimate responsibility.

There might be incompatibilists willing to concede this much. That is, there might be incompatibilists willing to concede that although in the real world, with its substantially unequal distribution of opportunities and inclinations, considerations of justice would not support the imposition of hard treatment on intentional wrongdoers in the absence of ultimate responsibility, in a world without such inequalities ultimate responsibility might not be necessary. Some incompatibilists might even be willing to make the same concession in connection with the moral desert of punishment. However—and this brings us to the second possible incompatibilist response to the benefits-and-burdens argument—it is not a concession that incompatibilists should make in connection with the moral desert of punishment. Or, at least, it is not a concession that they should make on the basis of the benefits-and-burdens argument. Even on the assumption of an equal distribution of opportunities and inclinations, the situations in which the benefits-and-burdens argument would provide *pro tanto* support for some form of imposition would fail to line up with the situations in which we would ordinarily see punishment as morally deserved.

As a means to bringing out the discrepancies between the benefits-and-burdens argument and ordinary thinking concerning the moral desert of punishment, consider the following scenario. (Although fanciful, the scenario will bring to the fore features of the benefits-and-burdens argument that we might otherwise miss.) Imagine a community of agents whose members share similar tastes, values, interests, and opportunities, and for whom the burdens of self-restraint are, therefore, roughly equally burdensome. One evening, every member of the community happens to watch a particular talk show on television. The topic of the evening is pleasure. The principal guest is a psychologist hypothesizing that the most pleasurable experience a person could ever have would be to kill another person just for sport—an experience so pleasurable as to outweigh the risks of punishment. The psychologist goes on and on, describing the pleasure so vividly that by the end of the program every member of the community, including the speaker himself, is thoroughly convinced. Each member realizes it would be wrong to kill another person just for sport, but this thought only increases the imagined titillation. Deeming his or her own personal pleasure more important than any other consideration (including the rights of his or her potential victim), each member of the community resolves on his or her own and in complete ignorance of the decisions of the other members that the next morning this is exactly what he or she will do: go out and kill (or at least try to kill) another person 'just for sport'. And in fact each member goes out and attempts to do just this, still in total ignorance of the fact that every other member of the community is attempting the same thing. By the end of the next day, half of the members of the community are dead; the remaining half of the community is composed entirely of killers whose lives, we may suppose, are not worsened by the loss of those killed. Regardless of his or her fate, each member of the community failed to uphold one of the essential burdens of self-restraint imposed by morality. Each member attempted to kill another person for sport. Hence, each member equally put down the burden in question. Insofar as this is the case, rather than yielding a *pro tanto* reason for punishing every member of the community, the benefits-and-burdens argument fails to provide a reason for punishing anyone. Yet provided he or she satisfies the causal and capacity conditions for moral responsibility, surely a person who attempts to kill another person just for sport deserves to be punished—this even if every other member of his or her community happens to do the same.

Why does the benefits-and-burdens argument fail to yield the intuitively correct result? Here it is important to recall a point mentioned earlier, but discussion of which I postponed: the reason that the benefits-and-burdens argument adduces for imposing hard treatment on those who violate the primary rules does not appeal to the moral wrongness of the acts prohibited by those rules. Indeed, the argument does not depend on the agent's having done something morally wrong at all: a structurally identical argument can be applied to cases in which there is no question of wrongdoing. For example, suppose that what is in question is not the burdens of non-interference, but rather the financial burden imposed by mandatory contributions to a town fund for the construction of a much-needed lighthouse. Jones, being conscientious, puts a cheque for the required amount in the post as soon as he receives a notice that it is due. Despite this, and through no fault of his own, his cheque fails to reach the town treasurer. As a result, the required sum is never deducted from his bank account, although the proper amount is deducted from every other townsperson's bank account in short order. Due to an innocent error in bookkeeping, Jones never notices the discrepancy. Nor is it noticed by the then-treasurer. In fact, the discrepancy is only detected a decade later, by which time the lighthouse has been built. (By a stroke of good fortune, the town had enough money to build it even without Jones's contribution.) Owing to the increase in tax revenue generated by the lighthouse, there is, we may suppose, no question of the town's *needing* Jones's money for any other purpose. Nor, to reiterate, is there a feasible way of dividing up the money so as to offer a partial refund to every other townsperson. Nor, finally, is there any question of wrongdoing on Jones's part. However, there is an unequal distribution of the benefits and burdens associated with the town's construction of the lighthouse. Jones enjoys the same benefits from the lighthouse as every other townsperson despite his not having contributed the same funds to its construction. As such, provided (1) an otherwise equal distribution of the basic benefits and burdens associated with the town's provision of shared public goods, and (2) that it is a basic principle of justice that, other things being equal, the burdens associated with the provision of shared public goods be borne equally by the members of the community, an argument structurally identical to the original benefits-and-burdens argument would have the town treasurer belatedly deduct the sum in question (plus interest) from Jones's bank account—or else find some other way to remove his unfair advantage—just as the original argument instructed us to remove from the intentional wrongdoer her unfair advantage.

The above reasoning is not meant to be a *reductio ad absurdum* of the benefits-and-burdens argument. To my mind, it is not absurd to suppose that considerations of fairness supply a *pro tanto* reason for deducting the sum in question from Jones's account.[31] The point of introducing the example is simply to highlight the extent to which the concern underlying the benefits-and-burdens argument is purely distributional. The justification the argument provides for imposing some form of hard treatment or deprivation upon wrongdoers is not intrinsically tied to the moral character of what they have done. The central concern is not the redress of wrongdoing, but the redress of inequality. This is why a structurally identical argument applies to a case in which an agent fails to bear his assigned share of some other societal burden through no fault of his

---

[31] There may be other considerations that weigh against deducting the sum from Jones's bank account, e.g., considerations of charity or benevolence. Still, this would not undermine the claim that considerations of fairness provide a *pro tanto* reason to deduct the sum in question.

own (and without a whiff of any other type of wrongdoing). Similarly, it is why the benefits-and-burdens argument fails to provide even a *pro tanto* reason for imposing some form of hard treatment or deprivation on those in our imagined community of killers. Insofar as all equally failed to sustain their burden, there is no inequality that needs to be removed; yet the removal of inequality is the primary concern underlying the argument. And it is one of the main reasons why the benefits-and-burdens argument fails as an elucidation of the moral desert of punishment.[32] To repeat: any attempt to explain the fairness of punishing a wrongdoer that does not appeal to the moral wrongness of her action will fail to capture the moral desert of punishment as it is ordinarily understood. When punishment is morally deserved, it is precisely in virtue of the moral quality of the act committed. It is the moral wrongness of a responsible agent's act, and this alone, that renders her morally deserving of punishment.

There is another respect in which the benefits-and-burdens argument fails to do justice to ordinary thinking about desert of punishment: even in cases of heinous wrongdoing, all that the benefits-and-burdens argument calls for, and can call for, is the imposition upon the wrongdoer of a deprivation or disadvantage just large enough to offset the unfair advantage she acquired in renouncing her burden of self-restraint. The wrongdoer is not to be brought to enjoy a net balance of the benefits and burdens of non-interference lower than that enjoyed by those who observed the rules. She is not to be made to sustain a net loss, either in comparison with others or in comparison with herself prior to having engaged in wrongdoing. On the contrary, she is to enjoy precisely the same balance of benefits and burdens as everyone else—precisely the same balance she would have enjoyed had she never engaged in wrongdoing in the first place. The question is whether such leveling exhausts the negative treatment we take wrongdoers to deserve when we speak of their morally deserving punishment.

When we say that a wrongdoer morally deserves to be punished, we seem to have more in mind than the mere leveling of advantages. It is not that we think that morally culpable wrongdoers—i.e., those who

---

[32] For those who view the concept of desert as irreducible, it will come as no surprise that the benefits-and-burdens argument fails to elucidate the moral desert of punishment. To the extent that it attempts to explicate the idea of desert of punishment, it attempts to explicate it in terms of other justice-related concepts.

engage in moral wrongdoing without excuse or exemption—have received all they deserve by way of punishment as soon as whatever advantage they acquired through their wrongdoing has been eliminated. We think that they ought to pay for their wrongdoing by suffering a net loss. Indeed, where the treatment deliberately meted out to wrongdoers is not such as would normally render wrongdoers worse off in the short term than they would have been had they not engaged in wrongdoing, it starts to look less like punishment and more like a retroactively imposed licensing fee or tax on consumption.[33] Not only does such treatment fail to convey the sort of moral reprobation that punishment is normally taken to convey and that many, since Feinberg, have come to regard as the distinguishing mark of punishment 'in the strict and narrow sense that interests the moralist' as opposed to mere penalization. It does not even convey the rejection of certain behavior as 'not allowed' or 'against the rules' that distinguishes punishments and penalties alike from licensing fees and taxes on forms of conduct that, although perhaps viewed as undesirable if practiced widely, are nevertheless permitted.[34] In this respect, too, the benefits-and-burdens argument fails to capture what we have in mind when we speak of wrongdoers morally deserving to be punished.[35]

In arguing in this manner, I do not mean to commit myself to the view that the general justifying aim of punishment is to convey to wrongdoers

[33] I include the qualification 'in the short term' so as not to rule out, simply by definition, any attempt to justify punishment by appeal to the wrongdoer's own long-term best interests. For one such attempt, see Moberly (1968). The qualification 'normally' is included to acknowledge the possibility of cases in which the punishment imposed upon a wrongdoer incidentally renders her better off, even in the short term, than she would have been had she not been punished.

[34] For the distinction between punishment 'in the strict and narrow sense that concerns the moralist' and 'mere' penalties, as well as the distinction between punishment and mere penalties, on the one hand, and licensing fees, consumption taxes, and permit charges, on the other, see Feinberg (1965). In connection with the former distinction, Feinberg writes, 'Even floggings and imposed fastings do not constitute punishment . . . [where] they do not express public censure . . . ' ((1965), 114).

[35] Fingarette (1977) offers a similar criticism of the benefits-and-burdens argument as an account of desert of punishment:

On this view, provided that the books are ultimately balanced, I would seem to have two equally legitimate options—paying my debts earlier in cash, or paying later in punishment. But surely that's not the intent of the law *prohibiting* stealing. The intent is precisely to *deny* us a legitimate alternative to paying the storekeeper for what we take . . . So Morris' kind of view—the economic view, one might call it—fails to account for law as prohibition, and . . . fails to make intelligible the question of punishment as something over and above the equitable distribution of burdens and benefits. (502)

our moral reprobation. Again, the general justifying aim of punishment is not my topic. Nor do I mean to commit myself to the view, entertained by Feinberg, that 'responsive attitudes are the basic things persons deserve', with punishment being deserved by wrongdoers 'in only a derivative way . . . [as] the customary way of expressing the resentment or reprobation [the wrongdoer] "has coming"' to her.[36] The latter is perhaps one way of understanding the moral desert of punishment. However it is not the only way. The point I am presently making is the weaker but more basic one that there is an essential reprobative element to punishment that distinguishes punishment from mere penalization. This is the case whether or not the primary purpose of punishment is to express to wrongdoers the moral reprobation that they have coming to them or anything at all.[37] At the same time, it is only where the treatment meted out to wrongdoers is meant to penalize them for their wrongdoing—i.e., to render them worse off in the short term than they would have been had they not engaged in culpable wrongdoing—that it is capable of expressing reprobation. Both elements—the reprobative element and the penalization element—must be in place for hard treatment or deprivation imposed upon wrongdoers for their wrongdoing to constitute the imposition of punishment.

The argument of the preceding paragraphs suggests that we ought to revise our initial definition of punishment (as the deliberate imposition of hard treatment or deprivation upon an alleged wrongdoer for her alleged wrongdoing) so as to include two further conditions. First, the deprivation or hard treatment imposed upon the wrongdoer for her wrongdoing must be of such a type and magnitude as would normally render a wrongdoer worse off (result in her suffering a net loss of some good) in the short term relative to the position that she would have been in had she not engaged in wrongdoing. Second, the imposition of the treatment or deprivation in question must express moral reprobation of the wrongdoer for culpably engaging in moral wrongdoing. The first of the new conditions is intended to capture the penalization element of punishment, while the

---

[36] Feinberg (1963), 82.

[37] In fact, I view the communication of moral indignation and reprobation and the judgments underlying such attitudes to be a constitutive aim of punishment. For articulation and defense of the idea that the communication of censure is to be regarded as a constitutive aim of punishment rather than its general justifying aim, see Tasioulas (2006).

second is intended to capture the essential reprobative element. Once the new conditions are taken into account, the benefits-and-burdens argument, far from explicating the moral desert of punishment, turns out not to be an argument about punishment at all.

How, then, are we to understand the moral desert of punishment? One possibility was mentioned above: we might take moral desert of punishment to derive from desert of the negative moral reactive attitudes, with punishment's being seen as a vehicle for expressing or, to use a better term, communicating to the wrongdoer the moral indignation or reprobation that she deserves.[38] (I prefer 'communicate' to 'express' as it underscores that what is in question is not the pure venting of emotions but rather a form of address.[39]) On this understanding of the moral desert of punishment, it is *pro tanto* (and pre-institutionally) just deliberately to impose upon wrongdoers some type of loss, as a vehicle for communicating to them the moral indignation or reprobation they deserve. As communication, the deliberate imposition of some type of loss is the intrinsically morally fitting response to wrongdoers in return for their wrongdoing. (Both here and below, I use 'the deliberate imposition of some type of loss' as shorthand for 'the deliberate imposition of hard treatment or deprivation of such a type and magnitude as would normally render a wrongdoer worse off, or result in her suffering a net loss of some good, in the short term, relative to the position that she would have been in had she not engaged in wrongdoing'.) The alternative would be to try to understand the moral desert of punishment in non-communicative terms. On this

---

[38] More broadly, we might take desert of punishment to derive from desert of moral blame, with punishment serving as a vehicle for communicating to the wrongdoer the moral blame she deserves. Although no part of the communicative account that I develop in Chapter 5 depends on casting the account in terms of the negative moral reactive attitudes rather than blame more generally—on the account that I provide, it is the judgments underlying the reactive attitudes that do the real work—I shall nevertheless continue to focus on the negative moral reactive attitudes when discussing the communicative understanding. Since there are outstanding issues concerning the negative moral reactive attitudes' desert that the communicative understanding has the potential to resolve. Note that on the communicative account that I develop in Chapter 5, it would be wrong to think of the moral desert of punishment as *merely* derivative from desert of the negative moral reactive attitudes or blame more generally. It is deserved as rebuke, where 'rebuke' is intended to retain its original Old French sense of beating back or checking or thwarting. Punishment is the thwarting of the wrongdoer's will. For a similar understanding of punishment, see Fingarette (1977).

[39] Cf., Duff (1996).

alternative understanding, it is pre-institutionally *pro tanto* just, in and of itself, for those who culpably engage in moral wrongdoing to be deliberately made to suffer some type of loss in return for their wrongdoing. Being deliberately made to suffer a loss is deserved by wrongdoers in and of itself—i.e., simply as the deliberate imposition of some type of loss—as what, prior to any institution, constitutes a just requital for moral wrongdoing. It is what moral wrongdoers positively have coming to them in return for their wrongdoing. I shall refer to the first way of understanding desert of punishment as the 'communicative' understanding and to the second, for the time being, as the 'non-communicative' understanding.

Note that even on the non-communicative understanding, the behavior for which the agent deserves to be punished is necessarily morally condemnable behavior and behavior for which the agent herself is deserving of moral condemnation or reprobation. To punish an agent on the basis of her morally deserving to be punished is to punish her precisely because she culpably engaged in morally condemnable behavior. As such, the act of punishing an agent on this basis reflects—and, in this sense, expresses—the recognition that she culpably engaged in morally condemnable behavior. Moreover, it is built into the understanding of what it is to culpably engage in morally condemnable behavior that, in so behaving, the agent renders herself deserving of moral indignation or reprobation. Accordingly, punishing a wrongdoer because she non-communicatively deserves to be punished reflects and expresses the recognition that she is deserving of such attitudes. Nevertheless, the hard treatment or deprivation imposed upon the wrongdoer is deserved, and is imposed because it is deserved, in itself and not as a vehicle for communicating to her the negative moral reactive attitudes she deserves. It is for this reason that, on the non-communicative understanding, a wrongdoer's desert of punishment remains non-communicative even though it entails desert of the negative reactive attitudes and even though punishing a wrongdoer on the basis of her non-communicatively deserving to be punished expresses recognition of her desert of these attitudes.

For the moment, I want to set to one side the question which of the two understandings—the communicative or the non-communicative—more accurately reflects the ordinary understanding of the moral desert of punishment. I also want to set aside the question which of the understandings stands a better chance of providing adequate grounds for incompatibilism. With these two issues set to the side, I suspect that the

majority of philosophers—incompatibilists and compatibilists alike—
would find the communicative understanding prima facie more attractive
than the non-communicative. On reflection, there seems to be little
difference between saying that morally culpable wrongdoers deserve, in
and of itself, to have imposed upon them hard treatment or deprivation of
the kind here in question—i.e., of such a type and magnitude as would
normally render a wrongdoer worse off (result in her suffering a net loss of
some good) relative to the position that she would have been in had she
not engaged in wrongdoing—and saying that morally culpable wrongdoers deserve to be made to suffer *simpliciter*. As such, the non-communicative understanding seems to commit its proponents to the type of
traditional moral retributivist understanding of desert of punishment that
many philosophers, both inside and outside of the debate concerning
determinism, have been anxious to avoid.[40] By the traditional moral

[40] For recent disavowals of traditional moral retributivism from inside the debate concerning the compatibility of moral responsibility and determinism, see Wallace (1994) and Scanlon
(1998) and (2008). (Wallace and Scanlon are both compatibilists.) Wallace warns against 'the
cruel and discredited thought that it would be an intrinsically good thing if those who have
done wrong should suffer harm', and also against the thought that wrongdoers 'have
"personally earned" the harmful consequences that may redound to them as a result of
their wrongdoing' (59, 60). Scanlon in his (1998) insists that what he there terms the 'Desert
Thesis'—viz., 'the idea that when a person has done something that is morally wrong it is
morally better that he or she should suffer some loss in consequence'—is 'morally indefensible' (274). Scanlon later steps back from this nomenclature, but not from the sentiment.
Thus, in his (2008), he tells us that while he continues to reject the thesis that it is morally
better that moral wrongdoers should suffer some loss as a consequence of their wrongdoing,
'it no longer seems to [him] helpful, or fair, to the idea of desert, to identify desert with this
thesis' (189). For disavowals of traditional moral retributivism from outside of the debate
concerning moral responsibility and determinism, see, e.g., Feinberg (1965a), Fingarette
(1977), Mackie (1982), Árdal (1984), Dolinko (1991), and Murphy (1999) and (2007). Murphy
is a particularly interesting example as he formerly defended traditional moral retributivism.
See, e.g., his contribution to Murphy and Hampton (1988). After having been widely written
off in the first half of the twentieth century as barbaric, retributivism (broadly construed) has
since enjoyed revival among those working on the justification of state punishment. Prior to
the revival Mabbot speaks of the 'deep suspicion and hostility' with which retributivist
accounts are viewed by philosophers, 'who must have felt that the retributive view is the
only moral theory except perhaps psychological hedonism which has been definitely des-
troyed by criticism' (1939(152)). However, the retributivism that emerged from the revival is
very different from traditional moral retributivism and consists, in the main, of attempts to
explain retributivism without having to commit to the morally problematic idea that wrongdoers deserve to suffer *simpliciter*. For discussion of the new retributivism—or new retributi-
visms: there is more than one type—see Honderich (1984/1989). Cottingham (1979)
distinguishes nine varieties of new or old retributivism. The most prominent form of new
retributivism at present 'expressive retributivism'; the view receives its fullest development in

retributivist understanding of the moral desert of punishment, I have in mind the view that those who deliberately (and perhaps those who negligently) make others suffer ought to be made to suffer themselves.[41] Granted, the wording of the non-communicative understanding makes clear that the suffering to be imposed need not be physical or psychological suffering in a narrow sense—let alone the everlasting torment in hell that Galen Strawson mentions in his discussion of ultimate responsibility—though the treatment imposed must be such as would ordinarily be unwelcome, involving a loss of something of value).[42] Moreover, the fact that desert claims are claims about justice should make clear that what is being claimed is not that the *suffering* of wrongdoers or the loss that they experience or their experiencing of it is itself intrinsically good or less bad than the suffering or losses experienced by others. One can acknowledge that the suffering of wrongdoers or their experiencing of loss is just as bad, and just as much a cause for pity and sorrow, as the suffering or experiencing of loss by anyone else at the same time maintaining that considerations of justice provide *pro tanto* reason for imposing some type of loss on wrongdoers in return for their wrongdoing. Having said this, we are still talking about deliberately, and pointedly, imposing some type of loss on wrongdoers. Their being made to suffer a loss is not a mere regrettable side effect of their being punished or of justice being done, but a deliberate aim of punishment. Moreover, on the understanding of desert of punishment presently under consideration, being made to suffer a loss is something that wrongdoers deserve in and of itself and not for the sake of its symbolic or communicative value. In the eyes of many, this is enough to render the traditional moral retributivist understanding of the moral desert of punishment morally problematic.[43]

Hampton (1992a) and (1992b). Prior to it, the most prominent new retributivism was that attributed to Morris in connection with the benefits-and-burdens argument. Two notable exceptions to the move away from traditional moral retributivism are Davis (1972) and Moore (1987) and (1993).

[41] For an attempt to elucidate traditional moral retributivism, see Manser (1962).

[42] See, e.g., G. Strawson (1994), 9.

[43] Whether as many find the traditional moral retributivist understanding (as) morally problematic when the position is formulated in terms of the imposition of suffering upon wrongdoers being just, in and of itself, as when the position is formulated in terms of the suffering of wrongdoers being intrinsically good is unclear. And, of course, not everyone finds the understanding morally problematic. For an endorsement of the view that the suffering of wrongdoers is itself (*pro tanto*) intrinsically good, see Davis (1972). Davis argues that the proposition that the guilty deserve to suffer, or what he regards as the equivalent proposition, viz., that there is some intrinsic value in the suffering of the guilty is ' "very likely true' on the

There are contemporary incompatibilists (and at least one compatibilist) who seem to understand the moral desert of punishment along traditional moral retributivist lines.[44] This appears to be an important part of what prompts the incompatibilists in question to think that moral responsibility requires ultimate responsibility.[45] On both counts, such incompatibilists might appear to be in good stead. I suspect that, pre-reflectively, the vast majority of Westerners would assent to the claim that morally culpable wrongdoers deserve, in and of itself, to be made worse off (i.e., to suffer a loss) in return for their wrongdoing. (Whether they would reflectively assent to the claim is another matter.) Given the influence that Judeo-Christianity—with its ideas of divine judgment and retribution and in the case of Christianity eternal damnation—has had on Western moral thought, it would hardly be surprising if the traditional moral retributivist view were built into our ordinary understanding of the moral desert of wrongdoers. Moreover, against the backdrop of Judeo-Christian doctrine, the demand for ultimate responsibility becomes perfectly understandable.[46] There would seem to be 'something perfectly repellent' about God's condemning an agent to an eternity, or even an hour, of suffering,

grounds (a) that there is no convincing argument against it, and (b) that inclination to believe it seems very widespread among the people whose moral intuitions constitute the main data we have for settling questions of value' (139).

[44] G. Strawson and Latham are among the incompatibilists who explicitly understand moral responsibility and desert of punishment along traditional moral retributivist lines; the compatibilist whom I have in mind as sharing this understanding is Moore. See G. Strawson (1994), (1998), (2000), (2001); Latham (2004); and Moore (1987), respectively. Though Smilansky never explicitly commits himself to the traditional moral retributivist understanding, various things he says, particularly in his (1991), suggest that he too understands moral responsibility and desert of punishment along traditional moral retributivist lines.

[45] The two contemporary compatibilists most vociferous in their rejection of the traditional moral retributivist understanding of desert, viz., Wallace and Scanlon, also associate the demand for ultimate responsibility with this understanding of desert. See Wallace (1994), 200 and Scanlon (2008), 182-9.

[46] This is not to say that the demand for ultimate responsibility would prove well-grounded. If, as I believe, it is no more intelligible how wrongdoers could deserve to be punished in the traditional moral retributivist sense if they possessed ultimate responsibility than if they lack it—if no type of amount of freedom would enable us to make moral sense of such desert—then it cannot meaningfully be claimed that ultimate responsibility is a necessary condition of traditional moral retributivist desert. If it turned out that the traditional moral retributivist understanding of the moral desert of punishment alone captured the ordinary understanding, the victor in the debate concerning moral responsibility and determinism would be neither the compatibilist nor the incompatibilist, but rather P. F. Strawson's 'genuine moral sceptic' who maintains that 'the notions of moral guilt, of blame, of moral responsibility are inherently confused . . .' ((1962), 72).

were the agent's actions ultimately to trace back to forces this same God had put into play.[47] Still, I take it that many incompatibilists would not want to accept this picture of desert of punishment—or, for that matter, any picture on which wrongdoers deserve to be made to suffer a loss, simply *qua* loss—in either a secular or non-secular form. I do not merely mean that many incompatibilists would deny the possibility of anyone's possessing the type of freedom or control required for such desert and so deny that anyone deserved to be punished in the sense in question. I mean that that they would be loathe to say that such desert the type of desert at stake in the debate concerning the compatibility of moral responsibility and determinism. For many, the idea that an agent might deserve to have imposed on her some type of loss, merely *qua* loss, as what in and of itself she had coming to her in return for her wrongdoing is morally objectionable.[48]

To the extent that those incompatibilists who seem to understand desert of punishment in traditional moral retributivist terms maintain that the ultimate responsibility required for such desert would be no

---

[47] I borrow the phrase 'something perfectly repellent' from Bennett (1980). Bennett writes:

If God is responsible for every fact about the natural realm, and is also the arbiter and punisher of wrongdoing, then there is something perfectly repellent about the idea of someone's being blameworthy for an action which is truly a natural event, whether fully caused or not. The God of Christianity cannot justly blame us for anything, it seems, unless he has given us some ultimate kind of agency which takes our actions right out of his field of operations. Thus, Christianity puts pressure upon its adherents to base accountability on some ultimate, not-of-this-world kind of autonomy . . . (27).

It is interesting to ask whether there would be the same demand for ultimate responsibility if God were conceived of as occupying the roles of omniscient judge and punisher but not omnipotent creator—although this might give rise to different questions regarding God's authority.

[48] I might be wrong about this. It is possible that the majority of incompatibilists (are happy to) understand the moral desert of punishment in traditional moral retributivist terms. If this is the understanding held by the majority of incompatibilists, then it is crucial that they specify this at the outset, for it would transform the shape of the debate between them and compatibilists. As I Stated in Chapter 1, the vast majority of compatibilists are happy to admit that their accounts do not provide for traditional moral retributivist desert. What they contest is the idea that they need to provide for such desert to capture the ordinary understanding of moral responsibility. Moreover, should it turn out that they did need to provide for such desert to capture the ordinary understanding, then the majority of compatibilists, it seems, would prefer to put forward accounts that are slightly revisionist than to try to capture the ordinary understanding in its entirety. As they see it, the traditional moral retributivist understanding of desert is morally indefensible. To engage with compatibilists, incompatibilists would thus have to argue, first, that the traditional moral retributivist understanding of moral responsibility and desert is built into the ordinary understanding, and, second, that the understanding is morally defensible. The possibility of successfully prosecuting these arguments is explored in the conclusion.

more attainable by human beings under indeterminism than under determinism—that it would require the logically impossible, viz., that finite
beings be *causa sui*—they are happy to concede that no human being could
ever deserve to be punished in the sense in question. Indeed, this is a point
that both Strawson and Smilansky emphasize. Accordingly, there is room
for them to argue that they are no more committed to the reality of the
sort of desert that so many find morally objectionable than are those who
reject the traditional moral retributivist understanding. Strawson goes a
step further, admitting that, despite his own adherence to the traditional
moral retributivist understanding, he too finds the idea of such desert
'morally repugnant'.[49] Nevertheless, he maintains that the idea 'that it
could be just—without any qualification—to punish some of us with
(possibly everlasting) torment in hell and reward others with (possibly
everlasting) bliss in heaven . . . is perfectly intelligible because if we really
have URD [ultimate responsibility and desert] then what we do is wholly
and entirely up to us in some absolute, buck-stopping way'.[50] Still, many
philosophers—including, I believe, the majority of incompatibilists—
would deny that the idea is intelligible no matter how 'wholly and entirely
up to us' our actions. They would certainly deny that it is intelligible in the
case of everlasting torment. Provided that they keep in mind the force of
desert claims—that what is in question is the treatment that wrongdoers
positively have coming to them, and not merely the treatment that they
could be subjected to without having ground for complaint—I suspect
that they would also be inclined to deny the intelligibility of wrongdoers'
deserving to have imposed on them some type of loss, simply *qua* imposition of loss, even in the case of lesser impositions and, again, no matter
how wholly 'up to wrongdoers' their actions.[51] For many philosophers,
the difficulty with this sort of desert has nothing to do with the impossibility of a particular type of freedom or causal responsibility or control.
In their eyes, no type of freedom or causal responsibility or control

[49] G. Strawson (2001), 451. See also the preface to the paperback edition of G. Strawson
(1986).
[50] G. Strawson (2001), 451.
[51] Again, I could be wrong about the position of the majority of incompatibilists have
towards the traditional moral retributivist understanding of the moral desert of punishment.
(See n. 48 above.) If I am wrong, and the majority of incompatibilists (are happy to)
understand the moral desert of punishment along traditional moral retributivist lines, then
they need to state this.

could render it *pro tanto* just deliberately to impose upon wrongdoers some form of loss simply *qua* loss in return for their wrongdoing.[52] To them, this seems little more than 'tit for tat'—certainly not something that justice could recommend even on a *pro tanto* basis. This is not to say that such philosophers completely reject moral retributivism or the idea that moral wrongdoers morally deserve to be punished. It is just to say that they reject, or would be inclined to reject, the particular form of moral retributivism that emerges from understanding the moral desert of punishment in non-communicative terms.

What, then, of the communicative understanding of the moral desert of punishment? Even if viable in its own right, it is unlikely to represent a viable option for incompatibilists. Recall that prior to our noting the connection between moral indignation and reprobation, where strong, and the desire or willingness to acquiesce in the infliction, on wrongdoers of the suffering essential to punishment, it looked as though the desert of moral indignation and reprobation was compatible with determinism. If it turns out that the moral desert of punishment, and the desire or willingness to acquiesce in the infliction of suffering as part of punishment both derive from punishment's role in communicating to wrongdoers the moral indignation or reprobation that, apart from the desire or willingness, they would deserve, then both the moral desert of punishment and the desert of moral indignation and reprobation, including the desire or willingness will turn out to be compatible with determinism. Still, this is only an 'if'. If, on the other hand, the communicative understanding of the moral desert of punishment turns out not to be a viable understanding—or if it smuggles back in the traditional moral retributivist understanding—then, at the very least, incompatibilists will be in no worse of a position than compatibilists. Some might argue that they would be in a better position. Reluctant though the majority of incompatibilists might be to understand the moral desert of punishment along traditional moral retributivist lines, it could be argued that the traditional moral retributivist understanding is still an option for them in a way in which it is not an option for compatibilists: whatever else can be said of the traditional moral retributivist understanding of desert of punishment, it is clear that the freedoms available under

---

[52] Scanlon, for one, is explicit on this point: 'To my mind, no degree of freedom or self-determination could make the Desert Thesis morally acceptable' ((1998), 275).

determinism are insufficient for such desert.[53] And, for some incompatibilists, the absence of a viable alternative to the traditional moral retributivist understanding the moral desert of punishment might go a long way toward easing their reluctance. Faced with a choice between giving up the belief that morally culpable wrongdoers if any existed would deserve to be punished and giving up the belief that, no type or amount of freedom could render it pro tanto just deliberately to impose on wrongdoers some type of loss, simply *qua* loss, some might find that their attachment to the former belief was stronger than their attachment to the latter.

If we are not to get ahead of ourselves, however, then we must first determine whether or not the communicative understanding of the moral desert of punishment is a viable alternative to the traditional moral retributivist understanding. For it to be a viable understanding—and one less morally problematic than the traditional moral retributivist understanding—three conditions must hold. First, for the understanding to be viable, desert of the negative moral reactive attitudes must entail desert of an overt response that serves to communicate to the wrongdoer the negative attitudes she deserves. Where blame is understood as non-overt moral appraisal, it is often argued that to be justified, all things considered, in blaming an agent for an action is not necessarily to be justified, all things considered, in communicating one's appraisal, be it to the agent or anyone else.[54] It has similarly been argued that to be justified, all things considered, in holding a negative reactive attitude towards an agent on account of her action is not necessarily to be justified, all things considered, in communicating that attitude to her or anyone else.[55] For it to be possible to derive desert of punishment from desert of the negative reactive attitudes on the basis of punishment's serving to communicate these attitudes,

---

[53] In fact, I do not believe that incompatibilists are in a better position than compatibilists. For, I do not believe that the traditional moral retributivist understanding is any more an option for incompatibilists than it is for compatibilists. In the end, it is no more intelligible how an agent could be deserving of punishment in the traditional moral retributivist sense if she possessed ultimate responsibility than if she lacked it. One cannot meaningfully claim that ultimate responsibility is a necessary condition of traditional moral retributivist desert if it is unintelligible how anyone, under any set of circumstances, could deserve to be punished in the traditional moral retributivist sense.

[54] See, e.g., Kneale (1967), Scanlon (1998).

[55] See, e.g., Smith (2007).

then moral desert must differ in this respect from all-things-considered justification.

Second, for the derivation to succeed and the desert derived to be less morally objectionable than that afforded by the traditional moral retributivist understanding, punishment must be more than 'the customary way of expressing the resentment or reprobation [the wrongdoer] "has coming"' to her.[56] It must be the case that the resentment or reprobation that those who engage in serious moral wrongdoing deserve cannot be adequately communicated except through punishment. Although a particular community's use of one particular form of hard treatment or deprivation might be mere a matter of custom or convention, the use of hard treatment or deprivation (as a species) and not some other form of treatment to express moral indignation and reprobation cannot itself be purely conventional.[57]

Third, for the communicative understanding to be less morally problematic than the traditional moral retributivist understanding, the reason that the moral indignation or reprobation that wrongdoers deserve can only be adequately communicated through punishment cannot be that the attitudes themselves involve the belief that culpable wrongdoers independently (i.e., non-communicatively) deserve to be made worse off than they would have been had they not engaged in wrongdoing. If this

---

[56] Feinberg (1963), 82.

[57] It is often suggested that Feinberg views the use of hard treatment to express the negative reactive attitudes as merely conventional. See, e.g., Skillen (1980) and Hampton in Murphy and Hampton (1988). The passage typically cited in support of this reading seems not to support it. Having commented that 'the reckless motorist who is sent to prison for six months is thereby inevitably subject to shame and ignominy—the very walls of his cell condemn him . . .', Feinberg goes on to comment:

To say that the very physical treatment itself expresses condemnation is to say simply that certain forms of hard treatment have become the conventional symbols of public reprobation. This is neither more nor less paradoxical than to say that certain words have become conventional vehicles in our language for the expression of certain attitudes, or that champagne is the alcoholic beverage traditionally used in celebration of great events, or that black is the color of mourning. ((1965), 99–100)

What Feinberg is claiming to be conventional in this passage is not the use of hard (as opposed to not-hard) treatment to express public reprobation, but the particular form of hard treatment used for this purpose (e.g., the deprivation of liberty as opposed to limbs). Having said this, there are other passages in which Feinberg seems to suggest that the connection between hard treatment or deprivation and the expression of negative reactive attitudes is purely conventional. In his (1988), Scanlon also seems to suggest that the connection is purely conventional.

were the reason, then the communicative understanding would smuggle back in the traditional moral retributivist understanding to which it was meant to supply an alternative.[58] Nor can the reason be that the negative reactive attitudes incorporate an independent, non-instrumental desire to see their target suffer. Whether these three conditions hold is what we will determine in Chapter 5.

---

[58] For the suspicion that the communicative understanding of desert of punishment smuggles in the traditional moral retributivist understanding, see Árdal (1984).

5

The Communicative Understanding of Desert of Punishment

In the last chapter, I distinguished two ways of understanding the moral desert of punishment. On the first (which I labeled the 'communicative' understanding), the moral desert of punishment is said to derive from desert of the negative moral reactive attitudes. Punishment is viewed as a vehicle for communicating to wrongdoers the moral indignation or moral reprobation they deserve. On the second understanding (the 'non-communicative' understanding), desert of punishment is seen as primary and not derivative. According to this understanding, it is *pro tanto* just, in and of itself, for those who culpably engage in moral wrongdoing to deliberately be made worse off than they would have been if they had not engaged in wrongdoing. The difficulty with the non-communicative understanding of desert of punishment, I suggested, is that there is little to distinguish it from the traditional moral retributivist understanding according to which morally culpable wrongdoers deserve to be made to suffer *simpliciter*.

However, as I also argued, if the communicative understanding is to serve as a viable and less morally problematic alternative to the traditional moral retributivist understanding, then three conditions must hold. First, for the understanding to be viable, desert of moral indignation or reprobation must entail desert of an overt response that serves to communicate to the wrongdoer the indignation or reprobation she deserves. Second, for the derivation to succeed, and the desert thereby derived to be less problematic than that afforded by the traditional moral retributivist understanding, it is not enough for punishment to be 'the customary way of expressing the resentment or reprobation [the wrongdoer] "has coming"' to her.[1] It must be the case that the moral indignation or reprobation that the wrongdoer has coming to her could not adequately be communicated except through punishment. Third, for the communicative understanding to be less morally problematic than the traditional moral retributivist understanding, the reason that punishment is required to communicate to the wrongdoer the moral indignation or reprobation she deserves cannot be that attitudes in question themselves involve the belief that those who culpably engage in moral wrongdoing deserve, to be made to suffer *simpliciter*, nor that they involve a prior and independent desire to see their target suffer. The aim of this chapter is to determine whether it is possible to provide an account that meets these three conditions.

Before turning to the first condition, I want to say something about the way in which I understand the difference between moral indignation and moral reprobation. (Recall, I reserve the term 'moral reprobation' for moral disapprobation occasioned specifically by violations or transgressions of the basic demand for interpersonal regard in its impersonal form.[2]) Some seem to view (what I call) moral reprobation as just a weaker version of moral indignation—i.e., a response to transgressions that we regard as less serious, or care about less deeply, than transgressions that we respond to with moral indignation proper. I do not share this view. As I understand the attitudes and intend them to be understood, the principal difference between moral indignation and moral reprobation is not that the one is stronger than the other, but that moral indignation essentially involves anger while moral reprobation does not. Granted, for most of us, the more deeply we care about something, the more prone we are to respond to perceived threats or insults to it with anger, and the stronger the anger to which we are prone. Nevertheless, there are some who seem not to experience anger even towards those they deem guilty of truly heinous wrongdoing.[3] This need not indicate that they judge the wrongdoing any

---

[1] Feinberg (1963), 82.

[2] The 'basic demand' and the distinctions between the personal and impersonal form of the demand and between violations or transgressions of the demand and less serious failures, were introduced on pp. 63–64. Talk of the 'basic demand', and the distinction between its personal and impersonal forms, trace back to P. F. Strawson (1962).

[3] Skorupski maintains that 'indignation is what people of spirit feel on witnessing a moral (or religious) violation. It impels them to right the wrong, aggressing if necessary against the violator' ((1999), 180). However, as he emphasizes, 'one may blame with regret or sorrow, not indignation' (180). Based on this, Skorupski argues that we ought not to view indignation as

less serious, or the wrongdoer any less responsible or culpable, than do those who experience moral indignation. Nor need it indicate that they care less deeply about morality. They might take the wrongdoer to be just as culpable and her wrongdoing to be just as serious—and so be just as unwilling to accept her behavior and just as determined actively to oppose it—as those who react with indignation. As I shall argue, these further attitudes and dispositions follow simply from imposing and endorsing the basic demand as a minimum requirement on the acceptable behavior of normal adult human beings. As such, those who react to wrongdoing with moral reprobation may be equally disposed to push for punishment, and for punishment of equal severity, as their indignant counterparts.

Thus, as Feinberg remarks, '[i]mportant as Sidgwick's insight [that punishment is resentment "universalized"] is, it is not the whole truth about the "expressive function" of punishment'.[4] Universalized resentment (moral indignation) might well be the attitude 'prototypically ... involved in ... "the urge to punish"'; however, it is not the only attitude that punishment expresses or might be used to communicate.[5] Punishment can also be used to communicate moral reprobation. This is important to keep in mind. Otherwise, it can seem that the connection between the negative moral reactive attitudes and punishment depends on the negative reactive attitudes themselves involving anger and, so, a desire to strike back

the emotional core of blame. Rather we should think of the 'blame-feeling' as closer to what I call reprobation, an attitude that, as Skorupski sees it, disposes an agent not to aggressive restorative action, but to '*withdrawal of recognition, casting out of the community*' (180)—albeit not so far out that the person blamed is no longer thought of as a moral being. Insofar as I view the moral community as the community of all moral agents—i.e., all those who stand under moral obligations. I prefer not to speak of casting out of the community, but instead of placing the wrongdoer's relationship with members of the community in bad standing. I have similar misgivings about 'withdrawal of recognition'; I prefer Strawson's 'withdrawal of good will'. See his (1962), 90. Despite the differences in terminology, I believe that the Skorupski has in mind when he speaks of the 'blame-feeling' is roughly the same attitude as I have in mind when I speak of moral reprobation. Importantly, although, for Skorupski, the blame-feeling is not aggressive, it does dispose to the seeking of punishment.

  [4] Feinberg (1963), 69.
  [5] Feinberg (1963), 68. Feinberg continues: 'If an entire community ... adopted the cold-blooded Kantian attitude toward punishment, approving of it only because it vindicated the moral law and eschewing altogether any personal resentment towards criminals, the result would no doubt still be recognizable as punishment, although in no sense could it be said to "express" public resentment' (68). Elsewhere Feinberg suggests that at its best, punishment would express only reprobation (disapproval). See his (1965), 101. Even in its universalized or impersonal form, resentment strikes Feinberg as vindictive.

at their target or to make their target suffer. Not only can this way of thinking make punishment seem necessarily vindictive; it can make a collapse of the communicative understanding into the traditional moral retributivist understanding of desert of punishment seem virtually inevitable. For this reason, I shall focus throughout the remainder of the discussion on those features common to moral reprobation and moral indignation rather than, as is typical in discussions of the moral reactive attitudes, on moral indignation alone. Specifically, I shall focus on the moral judgments and commitments constitutively bound up with both moral reprobation and moral indignation as responses to violations of the basic demand in its impersonal form. It is these judgments and commitments that give moral indignation and reprobation their distinctive characters, distinguishing them from other forms of anger and disapprobation. Hence, it is these judgments and commitments that must be communicated to culpable wrongdoers to adequately communicate to them the moral indignation or reprobation they deserve. Finally—and here I introduce a distinction that I did not make use of in Chapter 3—I shall assume that we are discussing violations of the generic version of the basic demand—i.e., the version that applies to a person simply as a member of the moral community and that governs relationships between members of the moral community, considered merely as such) rather than violations of some more particularized version of the demand that applies to a person only insofar as she stands to another in some more intimate relationship such as friend or colleague or lover. Like the distinction between actual transgressions of the basic demand and less serious failures, the distinction between the generic version of the demand and non-generic versions is orthogonal to that between the personal and impersonal forms of the demand. Whereas the distinction between the generic and non-generic versions of the demand pertains to the type of relationship the demand governs, the distinction between the personal and impersonal forms pertains to the way in which the person making the demand conceives of the treatment she is demanding—as owed merely to herself, or to her 'own', viewed personally or to all who stand in that type of relationship. It is only in the case of transgressions of the demand in its impersonal, generic, form that punishment is potentially at issue. Only such transgressions constitute public wrongs.

I now turn to the first of the three conditions that must hold for the communicative understanding of desert of punishment to be a viable, less morally problematic, alternative to the traditional moral retributivist understanding. Desert of the negative moral reactive attitudes must entail desert of an overt response that serves to communicate to the wrongdoer the attitudes that she deserves. The entailment holds. The same behavior as gives rise to desert of moral reprobation or indignation—viz., violation of the basic moral demand by a member of the moral community—also gives rise to desert of an overt response intended to communicate to the wrongdoer the reprobation or indignation she deserves. The intrinsically fitting response to such an agent *qua* continuing member of the moral community who violated the basic demand in its impersonal, generic form is some type of moral address that, first, seeks to communicate to the agent that, in treating another as she did, she violated a demand which she, merely as a member of the moral community, is obligated to keep—along with the reprobation and opposition to her and her actions that this implies—and, second, readdresses the original demand to her by calling on her to repudiate the offending behavior and to forswear such behavior for the future. In slightly more detail, the deserved response is a form of moral address that communicates to the wrongdoer: (1) that in behaving as she did, she violated a minimum requirement on the respect and regard owed to other members of the moral community merely as such; (2) a requirement that applied to her no less than to any other member of that community; (3) that, as such, her behavior was morally unacceptable, i.e., of a sort that we, the members of the moral community, cannot and will not accept; (4) that, as a consequence, neither she, nor the other members of the moral community, can carry on just as before; (5) that though she remains a member of the moral community, she is now a member in less good (or even bad) standing; and (6) that it is now morally incumbent on her to acknowledge her violation with the appropriate remorse and alter her conduct and attitudes for the future. In violating a demand concerning the proper treatment of persons merely as such, not only did the wrongdoer damage her relationship with the person she directly wronged; she damaged her relationship with all members of the moral community. At the same time, she remains a member of this community.[6] It is these two facts—the fact that she violated a demand concerning the proper treatment of fellow members of the moral community, and the fact that, in spite of this, she

---

[6] Again, it is crucial that we distinguish between being a member of the moral community, and being a member in good standing. (See n. 3 of this chapter.) It is only to the extent that an agent remains a member of the moral community that her actions can render her morally deserving of reprobation or indignation or, indeed, of any responsibility-related response.

remains a member of the community—that render her morally deserving of the sort of address in question. (While the fact that the wrongdoer continues to be a member of the moral community renders her deserving of moral address—of being addressed and treated as a morally responsible agent—the fact that she violated a demand concerning the proper treatment of persons renders her deserving of moral address with the specific content detailed above.) To deserve moral indignation or reprobation is thus also to deserve an overt response from the moral community that serves to communicate the attitudes in question and the judgments constitutively bound up with them the attitudes. Such a response is what morally responsible wrongdoers deserve merely as such—as full-blown members of the moral community who violated a fundamental moral demand.

Of course, even once it has been established that morally responsible wrongdoers deserve some type of overt response that serves to communicate to them the moral indignation and reprobation they deserve and the judgments bound up with moral indignation and reprobation, there remains the question why this response must take the form of punishment. (This brings us to the second of the three conditions that the communicative understanding has to meet.) Why think that in the face of transgressions of the basic demand in its impersonal, generic, form, non-punitive verbal reproach must be supplemented by the deliberate infliction of suffering in order to communicate to the wrongdoer what must be communicated to her?[7] Why would face-to-face blaming not be perfectly adequate to convey to the wrongdoer the moral indignation or reprobation she deserves?

That non-punitive verbal reproach would be inadequate in cases of serious moral wrongdoing to communicate to the wrongdoer the condemnation she deserves is a claim often put forward by writers attempting to provide an all-things-considered communicative justification of formal institutions of punishment.[8] It is, however, one they have had difficulty defending.

---

[7] There are forms of verbal reproach—e.g., public censure—that are specifically punitive. What makes them specifically punitive is that they involve modes of delivery designed to impose upon the wrongdoers, even if only as means pain additional to the pain of remorse. Even forms of reproach that are not themselves specifically punitive may be deployed punitively—i.e., with the aim of making the reproachee suffer pain or loss additional to the pain of remorse on account of her wrongdoing.

[8] See, e.g., Lucas (1980); Duff (1986); Falls (1987); Primoratz (1989); Kleinig (1991); and Hampton (1992a), (1992b). For an overview of such attempts, see Duff (1996).

While there have been glimmers of what might turn out to be an adequate defense, the majority of those seeking to defend the claim ultimately appeal to further, non-desert-related, ends that we might have in communicating to the wrongdoer the negative reactive attitudes she deserves to explain the need to communicate the attitudes specifically through punishment.[9] Our aim, however, is not to provide a communication-based all-things-considered justification of formal institutions of punishment. It is to explore the possibility of providing a communicative account of moral desert of punishment. Hence, an appeal to non-desert-related ends is not open to us. It is, however, also unnecessary. If we wish to defend the idea that, in cases of serious public moral wrongdoing (transgressions of the basic demand in its impersonal, generic form), non-punitive verbal reproach would be inadequate to convey to the wrongdoer the moral indignation or reprobation she deserves, then we need only look to the content of the judgments with which these attitudes are bound up and that we are trying to communicate. For, I shall argue, the reason that one cannot in such cases adequately convey to the wrongdoer the negative reactive attitudes she deserves except through punishment is that it would be inconsistent with the content of these judgments not to punish her (or to at least make clear that if it were not for countervailing considerations, one would punish her).

In laying out the case for this inconsistency, I shall initially focus on a single judgment: the judgment that, in behaving as she did, the wrongdoer behaved in a way that is morally unacceptable. This judgment lies at the heart of both moral indignation and moral reprobation. What do we mean when we say that certain behavior is morally unacceptable? We mean that the behavior in question is of a type that we, the members of the moral community, *cannot* and *will not* accept; that it and any agent who actively seeks to engage in it *must* and *will* actively be opposed. The judgment that certain behavior is morally unacceptable thus brings with it a commitment not to accept, and, indeed, actively to oppose, the behavior in question, and so a commitment to frustrate the efforts and will of any agent who seeks to engage in such behavior. This commitment is one that applies in both prospect and retrospect. Where the behavior judged

<hr />

[9] E.g., while Lucas (1980) ultimately appeals to the end of deterrence to explain the need to resort to punishment, and Duff (1986) to the ends of reform and reconciliation, Hampton (1992a), (1992b) appeals to the symbolic importance of subjugating the wrongdoer as a means to 'vindicating the value of the victim'.

morally unacceptable is merely in prospect, the commitment to active opposition takes the form of a commitment to preventing the behavior from occurring. Should attempts at prevention fail, the commitment to opposition carries over into the period after the behavior has already occurred. Even after it has occurred, behavior regarded as unacceptable—and, insofar as she continues to stand by the behavior, the agent who engaged it—must face some type of counteraction. As long as the agent continues to stand by the behavior, the offensive will endures. It must be thwarted or frustrated. While the way to thwart unacceptable behavior and the will of its (would-be) agent prior to the behavior's having occurred is to take steps to prevent it from occurring, the way to thwart unacceptable behavior and the will of its agent after the behavior has occurred is to subject the agent to something essentially unwanted, deliberately imposing on her a loss that she would not ordinarily willingly incur.

It is in this connection that punishment becomes necessary: as a way of countering unacceptable behavior, and the efforts and will of those who engage in it and continue to stand by it, after it has occurred.[10] Insofar as the judgment that the agent behaved in a way that is unacceptable brings with it a commitment to countering her behavior and (unless the agent separates herself from the behavior) her will even after the behavior has taken place, it brings with it a commitment to punishment.[11] Given the reason punishment is necessary, talk of punishment being deserved 'in only a derivative way'—or of desert of punishment being 'merely derivative' from desert of the reactive attitudes—seems off the mark. Punishment is deserved *qua* rebuke, where 'rebuke' is intended to retain both its

---

[10] Though his starting point is different from mine, Fingarette (1977) arrives at a similar conclusion concerning the nature and necessity of punishment: viz. that '[p]unishing is the humbling [or frustrating] of the defiant—or at least the disrespectful—will' ((1977), 510). That the non-complying will must be frustrated is something that Fingarette takes to follow from the idea of law as power. It is, as he puts it 'the categorical imperative of law itself': '[i]t is of the essence of the law's power that the will be subject to law, i.e., either conform or in consequence be constrained. Without this there simply is no power of law' ((1977), 510).

[11] It is a consequence of the view that I am articulating that an agent who has genuinely repudiated her wrongdoing is no longer morally deserving of punishment or of the moral indignation and reprobation that punishment communicates. Having said this, there might yet be other reasons (and perhaps even other communicative reasons) sufficient to justify punishing such an agent. Moreover, she would not have ground to complain of unjust treatment if we did punish her. (I am assuming that her wrongdoing was entirely voluntary and that all other compatibilist requirements for moral responsibility are met.)

current sense (viz., condemnation or censure) as well as its original Old French sense of beating back, or checking, or thwarting.

'But', a challenger might ask, 'why should we be committed to thwarting the wrongdoer's efforts and will after the wrongdoing has already occurred?' Remember, insofar as our aim is to provide a communicative account of desert of punishment, we cannot appeal to a non-desert-related end like deterrence to explain the need for punishment. Yet once we've excluded all non-desert-related ends, what reason could we have? A partial answer is that to allow unacceptable behavior to occur without facing counteraction would be to imply that the behavior is morally acceptable and so communicate to the wrongdoer the opposite of what we are trying to communicate.[12] 'But', the challenger might now respond, 'we were never talking about allowing the behavior in question to occur without facing *some* sort of negative response. The need for an overt response communicating to the wrongdoer that her behavior is morally unacceptable was never seriously in dispute. The question was why this response must take the form of punishment. Why couldn't the message that her behavior is unacceptable be adequately communicated to the wrongdoer through non-punitive verbal reproach alone? Indeed, it seems to be the function of verbal reproach to convey just this. Why must we supplement it with the deliberate imposition of suffering or loss?' Because to stop with non-punitive verbal reproach would be to say to the wrongdoer that her behavior was unacceptable and then accept it anyway. Without the imposition of loss, there would be no counteraction. There would be no thwarting or frustrating of the wrongdoer's will. To not even attempt to frustrate the wrongdoer's will is to tolerate her wrongdoing. To adequately express what we mean—and to live up to what we say—when we declare an agent's behavior unacceptable thus requires more than words. It requires us deliberately and pointedly to impose upon the wrongdoer a loss that she ordinarily would not willingly incur.[13] If we

---

[12] The issue of what is likely to deter a wrongdoer from engaging in a certain type of unacceptable behavior is not as separate from communicative issues as this way of putting the point might suggest. Arguably, any decision to limit oneself to hard treatment that one realizes that those who engage in a certain type of wrongdoing are unlikely to find significant despite the availability and moral permissibility of treatment that one believes they would find significant amounts to a decision to tolerate the type of behavior in question.

[13] That what is crucial is imposing on the wrongdoer a loss she would otherwise not willingly incur is what Fingarette (1977) has in mind when he speaks of punishment as 'pure suffering'. He writes:

are to convey to the wrongdoer 'our unqualified insistence that persons not be so treated', we must move beyond non-punitive verbal reproach. What is required, as Margaret Falls argues, is 'a behavioral change . . . away from non-interference or benevolence and towards the infliction of difficult circumstances'.[14]

The fact that the imposition of difficult circumstances involves a change away from the treatment ordinarily accorded and, indeed, owed to fellow members of the moral community is itself significant. Making this change is both a sign and a symbol of the wrongdoer's altered standing within the moral community. It simultaneously reflects and conveys our understanding of the implications of the wrongdoer's behavior for her relationship not just with her victim, but with the rest of the moral community as well. In violating the basic moral demand, the wrongdoer not only failed to accord her victim the respect she was due as a member of the moral community; she failed to respect the humanity in all of us.[15] As long as she continues to stand by her behavior, it cannot but affect her relationship with other members of the moral community, placing her and the relationship in less than good standing. The most natural and appropriate way of communicating this to the wrongdoer is by treating her differently from members of the moral community in good moral standing. This is part of the significance of a behavioral change away from benevolence and non-interference and towards the deliberate infliction of difficult circumstances. It is a clear mark of the negative impact that un-renounced wrongdoing has on an agent's standing within the moral community, and a tangible symbol of the community's reprobation of the agent insofar as she has not separated herself from the wrongdoing.

[I]n the respect that we suffer, we experience what we do not will, or, in a stronger sense, we experience what is *against* our will. It is because certain kinds of experience, such as bodily pain, the deprivation of liberty or property, separation from loved ones, the mutilation of the body, are so generally counter to our will, that they are normally associated with suffering and lend themselves to institutionalization as punishments. Punishment need not be painful, however—capital punishment needn't be . . . It is the humbling of the will that is of the essence. ((1977), 510)

[14] Falls (1987), 43. Cf., Durkheim (1961): 'there is only one way of showing one disapproves of someone, and that is to treat him less well than the people one esteems. This is why punishment almost necessarily implies severe treatment and as a result pain for the person affected . . . [I]t is the external index of the feeling that must assert itself in the face of a violation' (167).

[15] Cf. Kleinig (1991), 411.

I can imagine someone conceding this last point yet nevertheless deny-
ing the need to resort to punishment in order adequately to communicate
to a wrongdoer the negative reactive attitudes she deserves. Granted, in the
face of serious wrongdoing, '[w]e cannot', as John Cottingham emphasizes, 'continue to sit down and eat and drink with [the wrongdoer], to
converse with him as an accepted member of the community'.[16] Nor can
we simply 'admonish or blame the offender and then carry on as before'; to
do so, in Cottingham's words, 'would be the mark of a defect in moral
sensibility'.[17] However, there is a lot of ground between admonishing the
wrongdoer and then carrying on as before, on the one hand, and, on the
other hand, intentionally imposing on the wrongdoer the sort of loss or
suffering constitutive of the hard treatment element of punishment. As
Scanlon notes, 'there is a range of interactions with others that are morally
important but not unconditionally owed to everyone'.[18] Surely it might be
possible to mark a break from the ordinary and, thereby, convey to
the wrongdoer our reprobation and her altered standing within the moral
community without moving beyond this range of interactions, and, so,
without having to impose on her the sort of loss or suffering essential to
punishment.[19] To borrow some examples from Primoratz, we might
mark such a change and, thereby, express, our reprobation 'by adopting
a cool, formal demeanour; by reducing the scope and intensity of our
relations with the person concerned; by failing to render help or support
in situations in which, were it not for the moral offence committed, these

---

[16] Cottingham (1987), 50.
[17] Cottingham (1987), 52.
[18] Scanlon (2008), 143. According to Scanlon, the responses that wrongdoing makes
appropriate fall within this range.
[19] This suggestion is not one Scanlon makes himself and, if I am right, for good reason:
such responses would be inadequate to communicate to the wrongdoer the reprobation she
deserves for violating the basic demand in its impersonal, generic form. At the same time, the
fact that they would be inadequate calls into question Scanlon's suggestion that the responses
that wrongdoing makes appropriate fall within this range and do not involve, as
P. F. Strawson claims they do, 'a modification of the general demand that another, if possible,
be spared suffering'. See P. F. Strawson (1962), 90. Scanlon's one concession in this direction
is in 'cases of mass murder and gross violations of human rights' ((2008), 169). In such cases, he
seems to acknowledge that public expression of blame in the form of punishment is called for.
The argument of this chapter is that in cases far less serious than that of mass murder,
punishment might be required to express adequately to the wrongdoer the moral indignation
or reprobation she deserves.

would be forthcoming without ado; in the most extreme cases, by breaking off all contact and communication.'[20]

Admittedly, we do not typically undertake the changes in behavior with the express purpose of communicating moral indignation or reprobation. With the possible exception of breaking off contact with a person, typically such changes are not ones we deliberately undertake to achieve some further end at all. Where prompted by wrongdoing—and, significantly, such changes are not always so prompted—they are often, rather, a direct effect or reflection of the damage the wrongdoing has done to our relationship with, and feelings for, the wrongdoer. We simply find that we no longer want to spend time with her; that we are not inclined to help her where we are not obligated to do so; that where we previously felt affection, we now feel anger or revulsion or indifference.[21] Still, this is not to say that we couldn't deliberately undertake such changes with the express purpose of communicating to a wrongdoer the moral indignation or reprobation she deserves. If Primoratz is right, we sometimes do just this when words alone 'do not seem up to the task' of expressing our condemnation.[22] The availability of this option might seem to call into question the claim that only punishment can adequately communicate to wrongdoers the moral indignation or reprobation they deserve.

Here we need to be careful. It is true that the changes in behavior under discussion need not be undertaken with the aim of making the wrongdoer suffer a loss, be it as a means to an end. They need not be undertaken with the intention of doing something to the wrongdoer at all. Again, they are a typically direct reflection of the damage the wrongdoer's behavior did to her relationships with others. It is the fact that such changes are typically not undertaken with the intention of doing something to the wrongdoer that makes it incorrect to think of them in the more typical case as forms of punishment. This said, the changes in question do involve deprivations of ordinary treatment and, moreover, deprivations that serve to make the

---

[20] See Primoratz (1989), 198–9. Scanlon's examples of alterations in attitudes and behavior that wrongdoing makes appropriate include 'refus[ing] to make agreements with [the wrongdoer] or to enter into other specific relations that involve trust or reliance' and suspending 'the friendly attitudes that signal a readiness to do so'; modifying, with respect to the wrongdoer, our 'general intention to help others with their projects when this can be done at little cost'; and suspending our ordinary disposition to take pleasure in another's success and hope that things go well for her ((2008), 143–4).

[21] On this point, see Duff (1986), 60–4.

[22] Primoratz (1989), 199.

wrongdoer worse off than she would have been had she not acted wrongfully. (Were it not for their involving such a loss, they would be incapable of communicating to the wrongdoer the moral indignation or reprobation she deserves.[23]) Hence, in the event that such changes are deliberately imposed, *qua* deprivations of this character, upon a wrongdoer in response to her wrongdoing, they come to qualify as punishments. For this reason, the possibility of deliberately adopting such changes in behavior as a way of communicating to the wrongdoer the negative reactive attitudes she deserves would not undermine the claim that only punishment can adequately communicate these attitudes.

At the same time, I think there is reason to question whether such changes would be adequate, other than perhaps in the case of minor transgressions, to convey to wrongdoers the moral indignation or reprobation they deserve for transgressing the basic demand in its impersonal, generic form. The difficulty is that the changes in question are very similar, if not identical, to those an individual might make in her behavior in response to the violation of either a merely personal demand or a non-generic version of the impersonal demand, i.e., a version that applies only to those who stand with one another in some more intimate relationship than that which holds between members of the moral community merely as such. (I have in mind the sort of moral demands that might be taken to apply specifically to friends or colleagues or lovers.) This is not a coincidence. It reflects what, at first glance, might have seemed a virtue of limiting our responses to the type of changes at issue: that they involve changes in attitudes and actions not owed to everyone unconditionally. This is what renders such changes morally permissible even in cases in which violations of the basic moral demand in its generic form are not at issue. Yet, the very fact that it is permissible to undertake these changes where violations of this type are not at issue would seem to undermine the ability of such changes adequately to communicate to wrongdoers the sort of moral indignation or reprobation they deserve where violations of this type are specifically at issue. What must be communicated to the wrongdoer in the face of her having violated the basic demand in its impersonal, generic, form is not merely the judgment that she violated some demand or other, but rather the judgment that she violated *this* demand—i.e.,

---

[23] This claim was argued for in Chapter 4.

a basic moral demand tied to the minimum degree of good will, regard, and respect that she, as a member of the moral community, owes to all other members of the moral community merely as such. Likewise, it must be communicated to the wrongdoer that, given the nature of the violation, she has damaged her standing not just with this or that member of the moral community, but with the moral community as a whole. If our response to violations of the basic moral demand in its generic form is to communicate this to the wrongdoer—i.e., if it is to communicate to the wrongdoer the categorial difference between this type of violation and others—then it must be categorially different from the responses occasioned by, and appropriate to, other types of violation. This requires moving beyond the range of deprivations that are permissible even where violations of the basic demand in its impersonal, generic form are not in question—and so beyond the range of 'interactions . . . not unconditionally owed to everyone'—and into the range of deprivations that would be morally impermissible were it not for the agent's wrongful behavior.[24]

There are several further reasons for thinking that where violations of the basic demand in its impersonal, generic form are at issue, it is necessary to move beyond the range of deprivations that Scanlon has in mind in order adequately to communicate to wrongdoers the moral indignation or reprobation they deserve. If part of what must be communicated to a member of the moral community who has violated the basic demand in its impersonal, generic, form is that, in behaving as she did, she behaved in a way that is morally unacceptable, then the negative consequences we attach to behavior of the type in question must be ones that the wrongdoer herself is likely to find significant. As we've seen, the judgment that a certain type of behavior is morally unacceptable brings with it a commitment not to accept and, indeed, actively to oppose behavior of the type in question, and so a commitment (to attempt) to thwart the efforts and will of any agent who seeks to engage in such behavior. This involves a commitment both to trying to prevent behavior of the type in question from ever occurring and to frustrating the will of any agent who engages in the behavior should the attempt at prevention fail. Just as the way to prevent a certain type of behavior from occurring is to attach negative consequences

---

[24] Based on his examples, I am assuming that when Scanlon speaks of 'a range of interactions . . . not unconditionally owed to everyone', he does not mean a range of interactions unconditionally owed to everyone except wrongdoers.

to it significant enough to deter those who would otherwise engage in it, so the way of frustrating an agent's will after the fact is by subjecting her to hard treatment or deprivation of a sort and magnitude that she would not willingly accept as the price for her behavior. There are, of course, limits on the type and severity of the consequences we might permissibly attach to various offenses. As continuing members of the moral community, even culpable wrongdoers are owed a certain level of respect and concern; torture and other types of dehumanizing treatment are impermissible. There are also other communicative concerns—e.g., that the suffering imposed not be so severe as to overwhelm the message we are trying to communicate, that the severity of the consequences reflect the degree of moral indignation or reprobation deserved—that might impose additional constraints. However, once within the limits set by these constraints, further to limit ourselves to consequences that the majority of those tempted to engage in behavior of the type in question are unlikely to find significant would signal that we were not committed to rejecting the behavior—that we were prepared to tolerate it. It would hardly communicate our 'unqualified insistence' that other persons not be so treated.

There is a final consideration that tells against the communicative adequacy of the deprivations that Scanlon has in mind in cases where transgressions of the basic demand in its impersonal, generic form are at issue. What seems to be required in such cases is not merely informal, essentially individual expressions of moral indignation on the part of discrete members of the moral community, but some more formal response on the part of (or on behalf of) the moral community as a whole that would serve to express the community's collective understanding of the moral significance of the wrongdoer's act and the community's collective indignation or reprobation. This move from the individual to the collective automatically moves us beyond the range of deprivations Scanlon has in mind when he speaks of 'a range of interactions with others that are morally important but not unconditionally owed to everyone' and into the range of deprivations and impositions that would be morally impermissible in the absence of wrongdoing and that would ordinarily be regarded as explicitly punitive insofar as they involve what can only be understood as the deliberate and designed imposition of suffering.

Importantly, taking this view does not commit one to saying that those who engage in moral wrongdoing completely forfeit their rights not to be harmed or killed or deliberately made to suffer. Nothing I have said commits us to this. On the contrary, I have argued that as continuing members of the moral community, culpable wrongdoers continue to be owed a certain level of respect and concern. What I have said does commit us to endorsing P. F. Strawson's claim that the negative moral reactive attitudes, when strong, involve some 'modification . . . of the general demand that another should, if possible, be spared suffering'.[25] Yet all that this claim entails is that there are limits to the rights in question—that the broad right not to be deliberately made to suffer does not include a right not to have deliberately inflicted upon one, in the event of wrongdoing, the suffering that is essential to punishment and that undergirds punishment's ability to communicate to wrongdoers the moral indignation or reprobation they deserve.

Finally—and this brings us to the third condition that I argued must be satisfied for the communicative understanding to be capable of serving as a viable and less morally problematic understanding of desert of punishment than the traditional moral retributivist understanding—, the reason that it is necessary to resort to punishment in order adequately to communicate to wrongdoers, in the event of more serious forms of wrongdoing, the moral indignation or reprobation they deserve is not that the attitudes in question involve an independent desire to see their target suffer or else the belief that this is what wrongdoers non-derivatively deserve. Nor does the explanation of this necessity depend in any other way on the traditional moral retributivist claim that morally culpable wrongdoers deserve to be made to suffer *simpliciter*. The reason that punishment is required is that an essential element of the understanding underlying the attitudes of moral indignation and reprobation—and, hence, an essential element of that which must be communicated to the wrongdoer to adequately convey to her the moral indignation or reprobation she deserves—is the judgment that in behaving as she did, the wrongdoer behaved in a way that is morally unacceptable. This judgment carries with it a commitment not to accept the behavior in question. To allow the wrongdoer's behavior to occur without facing the counteraction of punishment would be to accept the behavior. Hence it would communicate to the wrongdoer the opposite of what must be communicated. It is for this reason that adequately communicating to wrongdoers the moral indignation or reprobation they deserve for violating the basic demand in its impersonal, generic, form requires recourse to punishment.

I conclude that the communicative understanding of the moral desert of punishment is a viable, less morally problematic, alternative to the traditional moral retributivist understanding. However, it is not an alternative to which incompatibilists can (successfully) appeal. As I reminded the reader towards the end of Chapter 4, prior to our noting the connection between moral indignation and reprobation, where strong and the wrong occasioning them public, on the one hand, and a desire or willingness to acquiesce in the infliction of suffering on wrongdoers, on the other, it looked as though desert of moral indignation and reprobation were compatible with determinism. Hence, if it turned out that the desire or willingness to acquiesce and punishment's desert derived from the role of punishment in communicating to wrongdoers the moral indignation or reprobation that (apart from this desire or willingness) they deserved, then desert of moral indignation and reprobation (including the desire or willingness) and the moral desert of punishment (understood in communicative terms) would both be compatible with determinism. If the arguments of this chapter are correct, then the moral desert of punishment and the desire or willingness in question can be seen to derive from punishment's role in communicating to wrongdoers the moral indignation or reprobation that (apart from the desire or willingness) they deserve. Desert of the negative moral reactive attitudes and the moral desert of punishment when it is understood in communicative terms are both compatible with determinism. Where this leaves incompatibilists is the question to be addressed in the book's concluding chapter.

Conclusion:
What's an Incompatibilist
to Do?

In this concluding chapter, I want, first, to review the arguments of the past five chapters, and, second, to assess the options that these arguments leave open to incompatibilists.

As I noted in Chapter 1, prior to Frankfurt's 1969 'Alternate Possibilities and Moral Responsibility', incompatibilists had always based their incompatibilism on the claim that the ability to act, or choose, otherwise is incompatible with determinism. Frankfurt's paper called into question the assumption that to be morally responsible for an action (or choice), its agent must have been able to act, or choose, otherwise. While some incompatibilists responded to the paper by questioning the counterexamples upon which the paper's argument is based, others responded by distinguishing two principles that they had previously failed to distinguish: the principle that moral responsibility requires the ability to act (or choose) otherwise and the principle that moral responsibility requires ultimate responsibility. Proponents of the latter principle argued that not only does it provide sufficient grounds for incompatibilism, but that it is the more basic of the two principles. Hence, if there is reason to be an incompatibilist, it is that moral responsibility requires ultimate responsibility and not that it independently requires alternative possibilities of a sort incompatible with determinism.

But must an agent be ultimately responsible for an action to be morally responsible for it? Must the agent be (or be responsible for) her action's ultimate (determining) cause(s)? The claim that moral responsibility requires ultimate responsibility corresponds with many people's intuitions. One of the principal arguments cited in support of the requirement is that our intuitions endorse it. But, I argued, at least some of the intuitive plausibility of the requirement seems to trade on the ease of sliding between talk of an agent's being 'truly morally responsible' or 'truly deserving of blame' for an action and talk of an agent being 'ultimately responsible' or 'ultimately to blame' for an action. When we examined the arguments of four of the leading proponents of an ultimate responsibility requirement for moral responsibility, we found that their arguments either (a) assume that moral responsibility requires ultimate responsibility (or assume claims just as controversial as the claim that moral responsibility requires ultimate responsibility), thereby begging the question against compatibilists; (b) conflate 'true' moral responsibility with some form of ultimate responsibility; or (c) simply change the topic. If incompatibilists wish to provide a non-question-begging argument in support of the claim that moral responsibility requires ultimate responsibility, then, I argued, they need to adopt a new approach: one that begins by clearly distinguishing moral responsibility from the ultimate responsibility that incompatibilists claim is necessary for moral responsibility and that then proceeds to show why ultimate responsibility is necessary for moral responsibility so understood. To do so, incompatibilists need to turn their attention to what Hart refers to as the 'liability' sense of moral responsibility. To say an agent is morally responsible for an action in the liability sense is to say that she satisfies the causal and capacity conditions an agent must satisfy to be morally deserving of certain responses. To determine whether an ultimate responsibility requirement is among these conditions, one must first supply accounts of the nature of desert and of the moral responses at issue in discussions of moral responsibility. It is not enough to say that moral responsibility relates to the moral desert of such things as reward and punishment, and praise and blame. We need to know what it is to be *deserving* of such responses and the precise nature of that which is *deserved*.

Chapter 2 discussed one way of understanding what is at issue when we claim that an agent is deserving of moral blame. On the understanding discussed, to morally blame an agent for an action is to judge that her action reflects a defect in her as a moral agent: a moral defect or defect of character. Understood in these terms, blame is deserved just in case the judgment constitutive of it is true and so just in case the agent's action does reflect a defect of character. To show that possession of ultimate responsibility is a necessary condition of an agent's being truly deserving of moral blame, one would need to show that, absent ultimate responsibility, an agent's action could never reflect a moral defect or defect of character— that the defects that we ordinarily consider defects of character would not be *moral* defects, properly speaking. This led to consideration of what renders a defect a distinctively moral defect. The answer, I argued, is that unlike other defects, moral defects are ones that an agent is unconditionally obligated to eliminate from her character. The claim that, absent ultimate responsibility, there could be no moral defects can be restated as the claim that, absent ultimate responsibility, there could be no unconditional obligations to have a certain character. But is the claim true? What seems to underlie the claim is the idea that for there to be unconditional obligations to have a certain character (or, in Kantian terms, certain principles), all agents would have to be capable of having the required character (principles), no matter what their character (principles) up to that point. Good character would have to be accessible to all. For it to be so accessible, either agents' present choices with respect to their character (principles) would have to not be determined by the conjunction of their circumstances and their already existing character (principles), or their initial (or perhaps even their entire, temporally unfolding) empirical character (set of principles) would have to have ultimately been chosen by them and them alone.

Against this last claim, I argued that, far from requiring agents to be ultimately responsible for their characters, the capacity to have the required character—good character—is something that belongs to all normal adult human beings simply in virtue of their being normal adult human beings. Even if a particular agent's upbringing was far from good— even if she enters adulthood having already adopted defective principles— still, as a normal adult human being, she enters adulthood equipped with a practically effective understanding of the difference between right and wrong, and the ability (and if there are obligations, the obligation) to critically examine her existing principles and revise them if they are defective. While her capacities as they stand might not be sufficient for virtue, they are sufficient to enable her under normal circumstances to recognize whether a principle is one that she is obligated to reject and to reject it, if it is.

I noted that incompatibilists would object that although being a normal adult human being might guarantee possession of the general capacities needed to recognize and reject defective principles, it does not guarantee possession of the specific ability to exercise these capacities in the circumstances in which the agent actually finds herself. If determinism holds, then this specific ability is absent in any case in which the agent does not exercise her general capacities. And, the objection continues, it is specific ability that agents must possess to stand under obligations. In reply, I argued that the objection depends on understanding 'can' in a theoretical sense whereas the 'can' of 'ought implies can' must be understood in the practical sense. 'Oughts' address agents from inside the practical or deliberative standpoint. The 'cans' that they imply are those that feature in this same standpoint. From the deliberative standpoint, in connection with whether to adopt or reject a given principle, the agent can decide however she sees fit. In fact, from the deliberative standpoint, with respect to the decision currently before the agent, the 'can' of physical (im)possibility cannot so much as appear. Hence the judgment that an agent's action reflects a moral defect is not undermined by determinism, nor by the lack of ultimate responsibility that determinism would entail. Where moral blame is understood in terms of this type of judgment, an agent need not be ultimately responsible for her action to be deserving of moral blame.

Chapter 3 explored a different understanding of moral blame, one inspired by P. F. Strawson's 'Freedom and Resentment'. On this alternative understanding, to morally blame an agent for an action is not to form a negative moral judgment about her on the basis of action. It is to experience negative moral reactive attitudes towards her in response to her perceived violation of the basic demand that all persons be afforded a certain degree of good will, concern, and respect merely as such. The moral reactive attitudes, I argued, have their own internal standards of appropriateness, which are conditioned by the nature of their respective objects. These internal standards fully determine the conditions under which it would be intrinsically just or fitting to hold a given reactive attitude towards an agent and hence the conditions under which the attitude would be deserved. To determine whether an absence of ultimate responsibility would undermine desert of the negative moral reactive attitudes (moral indignation and moral reprobation), we therefore had to determine whether an absence of ultimate responsibility would render the moral reactive attitudes universally inappropriate by their own internal standards. To determine this, we first had to identify the standards of appropriateness internal to the moral reactive attitudes. Following P. F. Strawson, we arrived at two standards that an agent would have to meet to be deserving of moral indignation or reprobation. First the agent would have to have violated the basic demand for good will, concern, and respect in its moral (i.e., impersonal) form. Second, the agent would have to be capable of participation in ordinary adult interpersonal relationships as we normally understand them.

The basic demand is one that regulates ordinary adult interpersonal relationships. It is one that we direct towards those with whom we or others are engaged (or project ourselves as being engaged) on an ordinary adult interpersonal level. In directing the demand to an agent, we assume that she is capable of ordinary adult interpersonal engagement. We assume that she understands the ordinary human needs and concerns that animate such relationships and that determine what would be required to meet the demand in a given set of circumstances. Similarly, we assume that the agent is capable of controlling her behavior in accordance with her understanding. These assumptions are preconditions of the intelligibility of imposing the demand. Where one of these assumptions (or the assumption that the agent violated the demand) is false, the negative moral reactive attitudes are inappropriate by their own internal standards. Insofar as it would not follow from an absence of ultimate responsibility that at least one of these assumptions is always false, an absence of ultimate responsibility would not render the negative moral reactive attitudes universally inappropriate by their own internal standards. It would not render moral indignation or moral reprobation universally undeserved.

While this account was correct as far as it went, it did not go far enough. It failed to address the connection between moral indignation and reprobation, where strong and where the wrong occasioning them is public rather than private, and certain retributive sentiments. The retributive sentiments in question include a 'partial withdrawal of goodwill', 'modification . . . of the general demand that another should, if possible, be spared suffering', a desire or willingness 'to acquiesce in that infliction of suffering on the offender which is an essential part of punishment', as well as the belief that punishment is deserved.[1]) As I noted, some deny that there is connection between moral indignation and reprobation and the retributive sentiments mentioned; others acknowledge that it exists and maintain that this renders it uncivilized to hold the moral reactive attitudes towards anyone, at least in the absence of ultimate responsibility and perhaps more generally. Contrary to those in both camps, I argued that although the connection exists, it does not render it uncivilized to hold moral

---

[1] P. F. Strawson (1962), 90.

indignation or reprobation towards normal adult human beings, either in the absence of ultimate responsibility or more generally. The impression that the connection would render the negative moral reactive attitudes uncivilized stems from a failure to distinguish between a partial (and often temporary) withdrawal of good will and ill will; between modification of the general demand that another, if possible, be spared suffering and wholesale abrogation of the right not to be harmed or killed; between a conditional 'readiness to acquiesce in the infliction of suffering, on an offender, within the "institution" of punishment', if necessary to communicate to the wrongdoer the moral indignation or reprobation she deserves and a readiness to acquiesce in the infliction of suffering on wrongdoers 'in a fashion we saw to be quite indiscriminate or in accordance with procedures which we knew to be wholly useless'; and finally, between a desire to see serious wrongdoers suffer punishment and a desire to see them suffer *simpliciter*. Moral indignation and reprobation, where strong, may well entail the first member of each of the pairs listed; there is no reason to assume that they entail the second. Insofar as they do not entail the second, holding them towards normal adult human beings is not uncivilized even in the absence of ultimate responsibility.

Still, as I pointed out at the end of Chapter 3, even if the connection between the negative moral reactive attitudes and the retributive sentiments discussed does not render the negative moral reactive attitudes uncivilized, it might be enough to generate an ultimate responsibility requirement for their desert. For, incompatibilists might argue, insofar as it is of the nature of moral indignation and reprobation to involve (where they are strong and the wrong occasioning them public) a desire to see their object suffer punishment or the belief that punishment would be deserved, they can only be appropriate by their own internal standards if it is possible for punishment to be morally deserved. The connection between the negative moral reactive attitudes and the retributive sentiments in question inextricably links desert of moral indignation and reprobation to the possibility of the moral desert of punishment. And, according to incompatibilists, no agent can morally deserve to be punished for her actions if she is not ultimately responsible for them.

In Chapter 4, I turned directly to the moral desert of punishment. To claim that an agent morally deserves to be punished for an action, I argued, is not merely to claim that she lacks (a certain type of) ground for complaint of being treated unjustly if she is punished; it is to claim that she has punishment *pro tanto* positively coming to her as what, prior to any institution or formal set of rules, would constitute a just requital for her action. I provisionally defined punishment as the deliberate imposition of 'hard' (i.e., unwelcome or unpleasant) treatment or deprivation upon an alleged wrongdoer for her alleged wrongdoing. Discussion of Morris's argument that, in the face of wrongdoing, punishment might be required to reinstate a fair distribution of the benefits and burdens of non-interference led to my revising our provisional definition of punishment so as to include two further conditions. First, the deprivation or hard treatment imposed upon the wrongdoer for her wrongdoing must be of such a type and magnitude as would normally render a wrongdoer worse off (result in her suffering a net loss of some good) in the short term, relative to the position that she would have been in had she not engaged in wrongdoing. Second, imposition of the treatment or deprivation in question must express moral reprobation of the wrongdoer for engaging in moral wrongdoing. As I explained, while the first of the two provisions is necessary for the hard treatment imposed upon the wrongdoer to penalize the wrongdoer—as it must if it is to express our rejection of her behavior—the second is necessary for the treatment imposed to constitute punishment proper and not just 'mere penalization'.

   With the revised definition of punishment in place, I distinguished two ways of trying to understand the moral desert of punishment. On the first, which I labeled the communicative understanding, moral desert of punishment is seen to derive from desert of the negative moral reactive attitudes, with punishment serving as a vehicle for communicating to a wrongdoer the moral indignation or reprobation that she deserves. On the second understanding, the moral desert of punishment is understood in non-communicative terms. On the non-communicative understanding, it is pre-institutionally and *pro tanto* just, in and of itself, for those who culpably engage in moral wrongdoing to deliberately be made to suffer some type of loss in return for their wrongdoing. Being deliberately made to suffer a loss is deserved by moral wrongdoers in and of itself—i.e., simply *qua* the deliberately imposed suffering of a loss—as what, prior to any institution or formal set of rules, constitutes a just requital for moral wrongdoing. The difficulty with the second understanding, I suggested, is that there seems to be little to distinguish it from a traditional moral retributivist understanding of the moral desert of punishment according to which moral wrongdoers deserve to be made to suffer *simpliciter*.

Although there are some incompatibilists who understand desert of punishment in traditional moral retributivist terms, others, I hypothesized would be reluctant to do so. The traditional moral retributivist understanding strikes many contemporary philosophers as morally objectionable. (Indeed, this way of understanding the moral desert of punishment would collapse the distinction, drawn in Chapter 3, between desiring to see a person suffer punishment and desiring to see a person to suffer *simpliciter*, a distinction that I used to show that the connection between the negative moral reactive attitudes and the retributive sentiments discussed does not render the former 'uncivilized'.) I noted that even on the traditional moral retributivist view, the suffering deserved by wrongdoers need not be thought of as physical or psychological suffering in a narrow sense and that proponents of the traditional moral retributivist view need not be committed to the claim that the *suffering* of wrongdoers is itself intrinsically good or less bad than the suffering of others. One can acknowledge that the suffering of wrongdoers is just as bad and just as much a cause for pity and sorrow as the suffering and losses of others and nevertheless maintain that considerations of justice provide *pro tanto* reason to impose on wrongdoers (and not others) some type of loss or suffering in return for their wrongdoing. However, as I also noted, on the traditional moral retributivist view, being deliberately and pointedly made to suffer a loss is regarded as deserved by wrongdoers in and of itself and not for the sake of its symbolic or communicative function. In the eyes of many, this is enough to render the traditional moral retributivist understanding of desert of punishment morally objectionable. It seems little more than 'tit for tat': you made someone suffer; we'll make you suffer in return. Although the urge to seek such symmetry is perfectly understandable on an emotional (and, as Mackie urges, an evolutionary) level, it is difficult to understand how morality could recommend the return of suffering for suffering, considered merely as such. By comparison it is less difficult to understand how morality could recommend or even require that agents and actions that violate the moral demands not be allowed to stand unopposed. Such agents and actions must face some type of counteraction that communicates 'our unqualified insistence that persons not be so treated', along with the moral indignation and reprobation that violators deserve.[2] If it could be shown that the required communication can only

---

[2] Falls (1987), 43.

take the form of punishment—that it must involve the imposition of some type of loss upon the wrongdoer if it is adequately to communicate to her the moral indignation and reprobation that she deserves—then we would have a way of understanding how pre-institutional considerations of justice could provide *pro tanto* support for the imposition of such a loss. However, this would involve understanding the moral desert of punishment in communicative rather than non-communicative terms. Moreover, understood in communicative terms, the moral desert of punishment would appear not to require ultimate responsibility.

At the end of Chapter 4, I argued that for the communicative understanding of the moral desert of punishment to be capable of serving as a viable, less morally problematic, alternative to the traditional moral retributivist understanding, three conditions would have to be met: first, desert of the negative moral reactive attitudes would have to entail desert of some type of overt response that serves to communicate to the wrongdoer the negative reactive attitudes she deserves; second, as mentioned above, it would have to be the case that, where wrongdoing is serious and public, the negative moral reactive attitudes that an agent has coming to her cannot adequately be communicated except through punishment; and, third, the reason that the negative reactive attitudes deserved cannot be adequate communicated except through punishment cannot be that the attitudes themselves involve a desire to see their object suffer *simpliciter* or the belief that this is what morally culpable wrongdoers independently (i.e., non-communicatively) deserve. I pointed out that if any of these conditions could not be met, then incompatibilists would at least be in no worse of a position than compatibilists. Compatibilists would be left without a viable alternative to the traditional moral retributivist understanding of the moral desert of punishment. And without a viable understanding of the moral desert of punishment, compatibilists would be unable to provide for full desert of the moral reactive attitudes. In fact, if any of the three conditions could not be met, incompatibilists might seem to be in a better position than compatibilists. Incompatibilists might seem to still have the traditional moral retributivist understanding to fall back on as a way of understanding the moral desert of punishment whereas compatibilists would not: if one thing is clear, it is that compatibilist freedom is insufficient for desert of punishment understood along traditional moral retributivist lines.[3] The absence of an alternative way of understanding the moral desert of punishment might persuade incompatibilists to set aside whatever qualms they might have had about committing themselves to the traditional moral retributivist understanding.[4] As I argued at the start of Chapter 4, it is an essential part of the ordinary understanding of moral responsibility that those who culpably engage in serious moral wrongdoing morally deserve not just to be blamed, but to be punished. Faced with a choice between giving up the belief that culpable moral wrong doers (should they exist) would deserve to be punished and giving up the belief that, no matter how much freedom they possess, persons cannot deserve, in and of itself, simply to be made to suffer, some might find that their attachment to the former was stronger than their attachment to the latter.

Still for incompatibilists to confront such a choice, the communicative understanding of the moral desert of punishment would have not to be a viable alternative to the traditional moral retributivist understanding. And, yet, as I argued in Chapter 5, the communicative understanding is a viable alternative to the traditional moral retributivist understanding. The same behavior that gives rise to desert of moral reprobation or indignation— viz., violation of the basic moral demand by a member of the moral community—also gives rise to desert of an overt response intended to communicate to the wrongdoer the moral reprobation or indignation she deserves and the moral judgments underlying moral reprobation and indignation. It is the judgments that underlie moral reprobation and indignation that distinguish them from disapproval and anger more generally. The intrinsically fitting response to a continuing member of the

---

[3] I suppose compatibilists might deny this. Or they might deny that it is any less clear that ultimate responsibility is insufficient for traditional moral retributivist desert than it is that compatibilist freedom is insufficient for such desert and so deny that incompatibilists are in a better position than compatibilists.

[4] It is conceivable that in the absence of an alternative understanding of the moral desert of punishment, a compatibilist might similarly be persuaded to set aside her qualms about the traditional moral retributivist understanding. (Moore may have believed himself to be in this situation.) In the case of the majority of compatibilists, however, it is highly unlikely that they would be so persuaded. As I noted towards the start of Chapter 4, as things stand, the strongest claim concerning desert of punishment that the majority of compatibilists are willing to make is the negative claim that wrongdoers cannot complain of being treated unfairly if they are punished. As long as compatibilists are happy to limit themselves to this claim, they are under no pressure to accept traditional moral retributivism. In fact, their limiting themselves to the negative claim seems to reflect their rejection of traditional moral retributivism.

moral community who violated the basic demand is one that seeks to communicate to the member: (1) that in behaving as she did, she violated a minimum requirement on the respect and regard owed to other members of the moral community merely as such; (2) a requirement that applied to her no less than to any other member of the moral community; (3) that, as such, her behavior was morally unacceptable, i.e., of a sort that we, the members of the moral community, cannot and will not accept; (4) that, as a consequence, neither she, nor the other members of the moral community, can carry on just as before; (5) that although she remains a member of the community, she is now a member in less good (or even bad) standing; and (6) that it is now morally incumbent on her to acknowledge her violation with the appropriate remorse and to alter her conduct and attitudes for the future. Given the content that must be communicated, it can only adequately be communicated through punishment. Indeed, absent an overriding reason to refrain, it would be inconsistent with this content not to punish.

As I argued in Chapter 5, the judgment that certain behavior is morally unacceptable brings with it a commitment not to accept and, indeed, actively to oppose the behavior in question, and so a commitment to frustrate the efforts and will of any agent who seeks to engage in it. This commitment is one that applies both in prospect and in retrospect. Even after unacceptable behavior has occurred, the behavior and (provided she stands by it) the agent who engaged in it must face some type of counteraction. While the way to frustrate unacceptable behavior and the will of its (would-be) agent prior to the behavior's having occurred is to take steps to prevent its occurrence, the way to frustrate unacceptable behavior and the will of its agent after the behavior has occurred is to subject the agent to something essentially unwanted, deliberately imposing upon her a loss she would not otherwise be willing to undergo. It is in this connection that punishment becomes necessary: as a way of countering unacceptable behavior, and the efforts and will of those who engage in it and continue to stand by it, after the behavior has occurred. It is because the judgment that behavior is morally unacceptable brings with it this commitment to countering the behavior and efforts and will of those who engage in such behavior—and not because moral reprobation or indignation bring with it a desire to see the wrongdoer suffer *simpliciter* or the belief that suffering simpliciter is what is deserved—that the moral reprobation or indignation that wrongdoers have coming to them in cases of serious public wrongdoing can only adequately be communicated to them through punishment.[5]

The three conditions that I had argued would have to be met for the communicative understanding of the moral desert of punishment to constitute a viable, less morally problematic, alternative to the traditional moral retributive understanding were thus shown to be met. The communicative understanding is in fact capable of serving as a viable alternative to the traditional moral retributivist understanding—and, moreover, one on which an agent need not be ultimately responsible for an action in order to be morally deserving of punishment for the action.[6] As I further remarked, given the reason that punishment is required to communicate to the wrongdoer the moral indignation she deserves, it is wrong to think of punishment on the communicative account as deserved 'in only a derivative way'. Punishment is deserved *qua* rebuke.

Where does this leave incompatibilists? They might try to show that the communicative understanding of the moral desert of punishment fails to capture the ordinary understanding or fails in some other way to capture 'true' desert of punishment. To vindicate incompatibilism, however, they would also have to show that, correctly understood, moral desert of punishment presupposes ultimate responsibility. This would require incompatibilists to provide their own positive account of the moral desert of punishment. If we bear this in mind, then, at first glance, incompatibilists would seem to have four options: (1) align themselves with the traditional moral retributivist understanding of moral responsibility and desert of punishment despite finding it morally problematic (if, that is, they do find it morally problematic), arguing that it alone captures the ordinary

---

[5] In the case of private moral wrongdoing or violations of the basic demand in its impersonal, non-generic, form, other avenues of communication are available and more appropriate than punishment.

[6] On the account that I provided, the moral desert of punishment and the desire or willingness to punish that belong to moral indignation and reprobation where strong and the wrong occasioning them public both derive from punishment's role in communicating to the wrongdoer the moral indignation or reprobation that (apart from the desire or willingness to punish) she deserves. Insofar as desert of moral reprobation and indignation (apart from the desire or willingness) does not require the agent to be ultimately responsible for her actions, neither the moral desert of punishment nor the desire or willingness to punish that belongs to these attitudes requires an agent to be ultimately responsible for her actions. Moreover, insofar as the desire or willingness to punish does not require an agent to be ultimately responsible for her actions, desert of moral indignation and reprobation even including the desire or willingness to punish does not require an agent to be ultimately responsible for her actions.

understanding; (2) maintain that the traditional moral retributivist under-standing of the moral desert of punishment is not morally problematic (and presupposes ultimate responsibility); (3) show that it is wrong to assimilate the non-communicative (or, perhaps, the 'non-derivative') understanding of the moral desert of punishment to the traditional moral retributivist understanding and that, when not so assimilated, desert of punishment requires ultimate responsibility; or (4) abandon incompatibilism. Whether all of these apparent options constitute genuine options is something that we will have to assess.

Some incompatibilists might resist my framing of their options. To vindicate incompatibilism, they might argue, they needn't provide their own positive account of desert of punishment. Or, at least, they need not provide an account of the same order as the communicative account. It is enough for them to identify 'true' moral desert of punishment as desert of such a type as would be necessary to render punishment just 'all the way through' and then show that without ultimate responsibility, punishment can never be just all the way through.[7] I am not sure that incompatibilists can in this way bypass the need to provide a positive understanding of the moral desert of punishment of the same order as the communicative understanding. Rather than challenge incompatibilists on this point, I want directly to challenge the claim that, absent ultimate responsibility, punishment can never be just all the way through—that punishment would always be in one way unjust.

Why might one think that absent ultimate responsibility, punishment can never be just all the way through—that all punishment must be in one way unjust? According to Smilansky, the answer is that, in the absence of ultimate responsibility, a person's fate is ultimately a matter of luck. In his words, '[t]he fact remains that if there is no libertarian free will, a person being punished *may suffer justly* in compatibilist terms for what is ultimately her luck, for what follows from being what she is—ultimately without her control, a state which she had no real opportunity to alter, hence not her responsibility and fault.'[8] This, he claims, gives us 'good reason to be disturbed by the absence of libertarian free will, for without it people are often subject to the grave injustice of being punished for what is ultimately

[7] For the suggestion that absent ultimate responsibility, punishment cannot be just 'all the way through', see Smilansky (2000), (2003a) and (2003b).
[8] Smilansky (2000), 48.

not under their control, i.e. for what they just happen to be ... The
morally arbitrary, which is not within our control, is in the end what
determines our fate, and this is unjust'.[9]

What are to we make of such claims and the underlying worry
concerning the role of luck? In addressing the issue, it will be important
for us to keep track of just what is (and is not) a matter of luck and just what
the person being punished or held accountable is (or is not) being punished
or held accountable for. In line with our discussion in Chapter 2, we should
also distinguish between a person's moral character, on the one hand, and
those parts of her constitution with which she is simply born (her temperament). If we do, and if by 'what a person is' we mean her moral character,
then the suggestion that a person does not choose what she is is false
(although it is true that her earliest choices regarding her own character
will not have been ones for which she was fully morally responsible or
ultimately responsible). Likewise, we must challenge Smilansky's suggestion
that the truth of determinism would entail that there was 'no real opportunity for us to be people who do differently' than we do. There may be
agents so 'peculiarly unfortunate in [their] formative circumstances', to use
P. F. Strawson's phrase, or so lacking in natural capacity that they had no real
opportunity to turn out differently than they did.[10] However, as Smilansky
himself cautions, cases involving such unfortunates do not provide firm
support for incompatibilism since it is unclear that the agents in question
would qualify as morally responsible by compatibilist standards. Yet, where
agents have not been so unfortunate, they will have had (and, I would add,
continue to have) opportunities to alter their characters in various ways, as
Smilansky also notes. (This is guaranteed merely in virtue of such agents'
being normal adult human beings.) What an agent in this more fortunate
group will not have had an opportunity to change is aspects of her natural
constitution, such as her temperament. But, of course, whether she needs to

---

[9] Smilansky (2000), 97.
[10] P. F. Strawson (1962), 79. The case of Robert Harris, discussed by Watson in his (1987),
may well have been such a case. After describing to a reporter the stunning abuse her brother
suffered at the hands of their father even before he left the womb and the emotional
deprivation that he subsequently suffered at the hands of their mother, Harris's sister Barbara
indicated to the reporter that while all nine of the Harris siblings were, the reporter wrote,
'psychologically crippled as a result of their father ... most have been able to lead useful lives.
But Robert was too young, and the abuse lasted too long, she [Barbara Harris] said, for him
ever to have had a chance to recover' (quoted in Watson (1987), 136).

have had such opportunity for punishing her not to be (*pro tanto*) unjust is part of what is in question.

Returning to the main issue, it is certainly unjust to punish an agent or to hold her accountable for something that (relative to her) is simply a matter of luck in the sense that it is entirely beyond her control.[11] If we define something's being simply a matter of luck (relative to an agent) in terms of its being entirely beyond that agent's control, then an agent's original natural constitution—that part of an agent's constitution with which she was simply born, which again does not include moral character—must be regarded as (relative to her) simply a matter of luck. Hence, to hold an agent accountable or punish her for her natural constitution would, as Smilansky urges, clearly be unjust. But in fact we do not punish agents or hold them accountable for their natural constitutions—at least, not if the claim is interpreted literally. Nor do we literally punish agents for their present moral character. As I argued in Chapter 2, we do hold agents accountable in other senses for their moral character. Yet to the extent that an agent's moral character (principles) at a given time is subject to the direct control of her will, it cannot be regarded as (relative to her) simply a matter of luck. The most serious of Smilansky's charges—viz., that 'in a world without libertarian free will, people are often subject to the grave injustice of being punished for . . . what they just happen to be'—if interpreted literally, is false on multiple counts. People are punished neither for what they happen to be, nor for what they are. What agents are punished for, in the first instance, are intentional actions and, even then, only those that are deemed voluntary (not the product of coercion or compulsion).[12] By their very nature, intentional actions are and must be under the direct control of their agent's will. To the extent that such actions are under the direct control of their agent's will, they also cannot be regarded as (relative to the agent) simply a matter of luck. Thus, even in a world without libertarian free will, we do not punish people for things that are simply a matter of luck.

Having said this, even if the things for which we punish people are not themselves simply a matter of luck, they are (if determinism holds) ultimately determined by causes that (relative to their agents) are simply a matter

---

[11] Part of this, as before, has to do with the reprobative element of punishment: a person cannot be deserving of reprobation for something entirely beyond her control.

[12] In the second instance, we sometimes punish agents for negligence and or other omissions. To avoid unnecessary complications, I shall leave this to the side.

of luck. In punishing people for their actions, we punish people for things the ultimate (determining) causes of which were not subject to their control. The relevant question is whether it is *pro tanto* unjust to punish agents for actions subject to their immediate direct control even though the ultimate (determining) causes were not similarly subject to their control. Tempting though it is for one with incompatibilist intuitions to answer this question in the affirmative, in the end I cannot find a justification for doing so.

At this point in the dialectic, it is natural to point to the 'moral' arbitrariness of our being born with certain constitutions rather than others, and to such counterfactuals as 'If A had been born with B's constitution, then she would not have done what she in fact did' or 'If C had faced all the same (internal and external) circumstances as D, then she too would have behaved as D behaved'. I want to leave to one side the question whether counterfactuals of this form violate the rules of personal identity. Although I suspect that they do, for the sake of argument, I shall assume that they do not.[13] Thus I'll assume that it might be true that if Smilansky's 'Fortunate Criminal'—a Bernard Madoff-type person who cheated many people of their life-savings—had been born with the more easy-going and self-secure temperament of his even more fortunate sister, he would not have felt under pressure to lie to his investors about the health of their investments in order to retain their business. It might also be true that if the Fortunate Criminal's sister had been born with his temperament instead of her own, and had thereafter faced exactly the same circumstances as he faced, she too would have lied to her clients rather than conducting her affairs in the upstanding manner in which she did. We should certainly grant that it was not the fault of our Fortunate Criminal that he was born with his temperament rather than that of his even more fortunate sister. He no more deserved to be born with his temperament than she deserved to be born with hers. The distribution of temperament is, in this sense, morally arbitrary: nor it is not based on desert on moral grounds more generally. Still, this does not render it morally arbitrary of us to punish the Fortunate Criminal and not his sister. Nor does it make it *pro*

---

[13] If such counterfactuals violate the rules of personal identity—as I suspect they do—then this opens up the possibility that there might have been something in B from the start that would have resulted in her not behaving in the same horrible manner as A even if she had faced identical circumstances as A from conception onwards. Still, as Watson emphasizes, this would hardly be something for which B could take credit. See Watson (1987), 141.

tanto unjust for us to do so. However equally innocent our Fortunate Criminal and his sister might be 'on the ultimate level' or with respect to their natural constitution, on the non-ultimate level they are not equally innocent. The Fortunate Criminal engaged in acts that render him genuinely deserving of reprobation and punishment 'on the non-ultimate level', while his sister did not. This difference in non-ultimate level desert is enough to render differential treatment not even *pro tanto* unjust. One morally relevant difference is all that is required to justify differential treatment. The absence of additional differences entails an absence of additional grounds for differential treatment. It does not entail *pro tanto* injustice. 'Non-ultimate level desert'—desert that does not extend all-the-way-back to the ultimate causes of an agent's actions—is the only desert that is needed for punishment not to be *pro tanto* unjust.

Still, even if our Fortunate Criminal cannot complain that we are acting unjustly or unfairly in punishing him (and not his sister), doesn't he have grounds to complain that something—perhaps life or the universe?—is unjust or unfair? Doesn't he at least have grounds for 'metaphysical complaint'? Tempting as such thoughts might seem, if we discount the possibility of a higher power against whom such a complaint might be lodged, the thoughts must be dismissed as confused.[14] Not just anything can be considered just or unjust, or fair or unfair. Moral agents can be considered just or unjust, fair or unfair, as can the actions, practices, and institutions of moral agents. A situation can be unjust insofar as it is the result of the unjust actions, practices, or institutions of moral agents. Apart from this, a situation cannot be considered unjust. Nor can life itself be unjust or unfair apart from these things. It takes an agent (at some point in the proceedings) to make for injustice. Having ruled out the possibility of completely unassignable injustice, we must dismiss the suggestion that in the absence of ultimate responsibility all punishment is *pro tanto* unjust. Once the suggestion is dismissed, incompatibilists are left with the four options that I listed earlier: (1) commit themselves to the traditional moral retributivist understanding of moral responsibility and the

---

[14] Some might object that in ignoring the possibility of a higher power against whom such complaints might be lodged, I am sidestepping the real issue and artificially closing off a potentially fruitful line of argument for incompatibilists. Still, I suspect that the majority of incompatibilists would not want to base their incompatibilism on the existence of God.

moral desert of punishment despite finding it morally problematic (if they do find it morally problematic), arguing that it alone adequately captures the ordinary understanding and that it presupposes ultimate responsibility; (2) show that the traditional moral retributivist understanding of the moral desert of punishment is not morally problematic (and presupposes ultimate responsibility); (3) show that it is wrong to assimilate the non-communicative (or, perhaps, the 'non-derivative') understanding of the moral desert of punishment to the traditional moral retributivist understanding and that, when not so assimilated, the moral desert of punishment requires ultimate responsibility; or (4) abandon incompatibilism.

I conclude with a brief discussion of the first three options. Of the three options, the first option strikes me as the least attractive (if, indeed, it is viable at all). For this reason, I shall treat it as an option of last resort, only to be considered after considering options (2) and (3). To the best of my knowledge, none of the incompatibilists who espouse the traditional moral retributivist terms attempt to show that the understanding is not morally problematic. But Michael Moore, a compatibilist, can perhaps be seen as attempting to provide such a defense.[15] Moore attempts to turn the moral epistemology underlying what even he considers the most serious

---

[15] See Moore (1987) and (1993). My hesitation in ascribing such an attempt to Moore reflects my uncertainty as to the precise form of retributivism he is trying to defend. Much of Moore's language makes it seem as if he is trying to defend the traditional moral retributivist view that morally culpable wrongdoers deserve to be made to suffer *simpliciter*. For example, often he describes the belief associated with virtuous feelings of guilt (a belief to which he assigns great credence) as the belief that the morally culpable 'must suffer'. However, at other points he speaks in terms of the guilty deserving 'the suffering that is punishment' or, simply, 'punishment'. The claim that morally culpable wrongdoers deserve to suffer punishment is neutral between the traditional moral retributivist understanding of desert of punishment and the communicative understanding (though at one point Moore dismisses 'denunciation theories of punishment as disguised forms of utilitarianism'; see his (1987), 181). Perhaps more worrying is Moore's statement in his (1987) that, as he is using the term 'moral culpability', it 'does not presuppose that the act done is morally bad but only that it is legally prohibited' (1987), 181). If this is what Moore means by 'morally culpable', then the view he is defending is not a form of moral retributivism at all. Still, Moore seems to move away from this statement in his (1993). Moreover, much of what he says in both the earlier and the later piece only makes sense if we assume that he is speaking, in this first instance, of moral desert for moral wrongdoing, where this is meant to provide a ground for state punishment. The only (other) contemporary defense of traditional moral retributivism of which I am aware is Davis (1972). According to Davis, the claim that the guilty deserve to suffer is 'very likely' to be true 'on the grounds (a) that there is no convincing argument against it, and (b) that inclination to believe it seems very widespread among the people whose moral intuitions are the main data we have for settling questions of value' (139). If I am right, then the claim that

objection to moral retributivism—viz., that 'if Nietzsche is right', then the emotions on which our retributive judgments are based are 'truly a witch's brew: resentment, fear, anger, cowardice, hostility, aggression, cruelty, sadism, envy, jealousy, guilt, self-loathing, hypocrisy, and self-deception . . .'—into a credential in support of moral retributivism. If the objection is not simply to involve the genetic fallacy, then, Moore argues, there must be reason to believe that our emotions are epistemically connected to morality in such a way that 'the virtue (or vice) of an emotion may often, but not always, be taken as an indication of the truth (or falsity) of the judgment to which it leads'.[16] Moreover, if the objection is to call into question not just particular instantiations of the retributive judgments, but all retributive judgments, then there must be reason to believe that 'retributive judgments are *inevitably* motivated by the black emotions of *ressentiment*'.[17] According to Moore, although we have reason to believe the former, we do not have reason to believe the latter. Even if our retributive judgments are often motivated by the witch's brew described, they need not be so motivated. As he sees it they might instead be motivated by the virtuous feelings of guilt that (we imagine) we would experience if we engaged in serious moral wrongdoing.

In this connection, Moore asks us to imagine that we've just performed some horrible act. (His own example involves intentionally smashing open a person's skull with a claw hammer, as real-life murderer Richard Herrin did to a sleeping Bonnie Garland, who had recently broken up with him.)[18] He then asks us to imagine how we would feel after performing such an act. Moore reports that he hopes that his own response would be that he would 'feel guilty unto death'—that he 'couldn't imagine any suffering that could be imposed upon [him] that would be unfair because it exceeded what he deserved'—that '[s]uch deep feelings of guilt seem to [him] to be the only tolerable response of a moral being', certainly, 'more virtuous than the non-guilty state to which Richard Herrin brought himself, with some help from Christian counseling'.[19] (After having served the first three years of an eight- to twenty-five-year sentence, Herrin

---

our reflective moral intuitions actually endorse is not that wrongdoers deserve to suffer *simpliciter*, but that they deserve to suffer punishment.

[16] Moore (1987), 206.   [17] Moore (1987), 209.
[18] Moore (1987), 212–13.   [19] Moore (1987), 213.

thought he had suffered enough.) According to Moore, '[w]e should trust what our imagined guilt feelings tell us; for acts like those of Richard Herrin, that if we did them we would be so guilty that some extraordinarily severe punishment would be deserved'.[20] More generally, feelings of guilt give rise to the judgment that 'one deserves to suffer because one has culpably done wrong': 'to feel guilty is to judge that we must suffer'. To the extent that these 'feelings of guilt are virtuous to possess, we have reason to believe that this last judgment is correct, generated as it is by emotions whose epistemic import is not in question'.[21] That is, we have reason to believe that, in the event of culpable wrongdoing, 'we deserve the suffering that is punishment', and 'not only in the weak sense of desert—that it would not be unfair to be punished—but also and more important in the strong sense that we *ought* to be punished'.[22] For Moore, it is a first principle of morality that 'the suffering that punishment entails is an intrinsic good when inflicted on those who deserve it'.[23]

Whether our imagined or, indeed, our actual feelings of guilt are as epistemically reliable as Moore takes them to be is questionable. Many people feel guilty about things that they should not. Nor will it help Moore to limit his claims to virtuous feelings of guilt if, as he believes, there are cases in which it would be virtuous for a person to feel guilty even though she had done nothing morally wrong.[24] Certainly a person who has not done anything wrong does not deserve to be punished. When we turn from whether we should feel guilty to how guilty we should feel, our feelings seem even less reliable. Still, for our purposes we can leave such objections to the side. Insofar as moral guilt is just the self-directed form of the negative moral reactive attitudes, we are already committed to saying that there are occasions on which feelings of moral guilt would be appropriate by their own internal standards, viz., occasions on which we have violated the basic demand in its impersonal, self-directed form. We should also admit that just as moral indignation and reprobation, when strong and the wrong occasioning them public, are often accompanied by the judgment that the wrongdoer deserves to be punished and

---

[20] Moore (1993), 26.   [21] Moore (1987), 215.
[22] Moore (1987), 214.   [23] Moore (1993), 24–5.
[24] See Moore (1987), 204–5. We might wish to disagree with Moore's claim that there are cases where it is virtuous to feel guilty even though one has not done something morally wrong.

by a 'preparedness to acquiesce in that infliction of suffering on the offender which is an essential part of punishment', so guilt, where strong and the wrong occasioning it public, is often accompanied by such things.[25] We should further grant that, in cases of serious public wrong-doing, both the judgment and the preparedness to acquiesce are perfectly appropriate—and, moreover, that in a case like Herrin's, to think that one has suffered sufficient punishment after three years in prison or to entertain 'any light-hearted idea of going on as before' is indecent (or else a sign of a lack of moral capacity).[26] The difficulty—at least if the view of desert of punishment that Moore is trying to defend is the traditional moral retributivist view—is that everything that we have granted is just as compatible with the communicative understanding of the moral desert of punishment as it is with the traditional retributivist understanding.[27] Yes, there is something morally wrong with Herrin's thinking he had received the punishment he deserved after a mere three years in prison.[28] Perhaps we do (or should) want Herrin to think that no (finite) punish-ment would be greater than he deserved (though some would certainly dispute this). The explanation of such a desire might be that we want Herrin to recognize the moral enormity of what he has done and that, given that enormity, he is deserving of some of our strongest moral indignation and reprobation, with a three-year sentence being wholly inadequate to convey the indignation and reprobation he deserves.

Indeed, if we look more broadly at the emotions we find virtuous and or non-virtuous, they appear to tell against the traditional moral retribu-tivist understanding of moral responsibility and the desert of punishment. As A. C. Ewing emphasizes, we would not think virtuous a person who dwelled 'frequently with pleasure on the sufferings of criminals, no

---

[25] P. F. Strawson (1962), 90. Even where the wrong occasioning it is not public, guilt typically brings with it the judgment that one deserves to suffer. Fully spelled out, however, the judgment seems not to be that one deserves to suffer or feel bad generically, but to be that one deserves to feel bad in precisely the way in which one feels bad when one feels guilty. It is, in other words, the judgment that one deserves to feel guilt. For a wonderful discussion of guilt, suffering, and punishment, see Morris (1971).

[26] Moore (1987), 216.

[27] It is not entirely clear that the view of desert of punishment that Moore is trying to defend is the traditional moral retributivist view. See n. 15.

[28] I am here assuming that Herrin understood that what he was doing was wrong and was in control of his actions at the time of the murder.

matter how well deserved they might be'.[29] To the contrary, we would think ill of such a person, taking her pleasure to mark a lack of virtue. Yet if 'the suffering entailed by punishment' were 'an intrinsic good when inflicted on those who deserve it', then there would be no reason for us to be of this opinion. As Ewing stresses, if the suffering of wrongdoers were an end in itself, 'it would surely be the part of a good man . . . to rejoice in its intrinsic value; but this is not the case. It is the mark of goodness to rejoice over the defeat of evil but not over the sufferings of the evildoer'.[30] Reflections such as these lead Ewing to conclude that while the punishment of the guilty might be an end in itself, we must not ascribe the 'intrinsic value punishment has to the pain alone, but to the whole fact of punishment', and this because of what the whole of punishment symbolizes and instantiates: the condemnation of evil, as well as its defeat.[31] According to Ewing, to ascribe the intrinsic value of punishment to the pain alone 'would be to commit an illegitimate abstraction, for it is not pain alone that constitutes a punishment, but moral condemnation expressing itself through pain', where the latter is an 'inseparable concomitant' of the defeat of the evil will.[32]

Does the consideration that Ewing points to—that pain alone does not constitute punishment—show that it is impossible to understand the moral desert of punishment in traditional moral retributivist terms? I do not believe it does. Such an understanding is still possible. However, like the communicative understanding that Feinberg envisioned, it would be an understanding on which desert of punishment derived from something else. Rather than deriving from desert of moral reprobation or indignation, it would derive from desert of suffering, with the imposition of suffering being a component of punishment, not the whole, and punishment itself being merely a means of delivering to wrongdoers the suffering they independently deserve. What the fact that pain alone does not constitute punishment shows is that our initial assimilation of a non-derivative understanding of the moral desert of punishment and the traditional moral retributivist understanding is problematic. And this might be good news for incompatibilists. For it would seem to open up a potentially more promising option for incompatibilists—viz., option (3).

To avail themselves of option (3), incompatibilists would still have to show that on the correct non-derivative understanding, moral desert of

[29] Ewing (1970), 35.   [30] Ewing (1970), 111.
[31] Ewing (1970), 111.   [32] Ewing (1970), 111, 108.

punishment presupposes ultimate responsibility. Here is where I foresee difficulties. To my mind, once it becomes apparent why it is wrong to assimilate the non-derivative understanding of the moral desert of punishment with the traditional moral retributivist understanding, the most natural and promising way of understanding what it would be for a wrongdoer to non-derivatively deserve to be punished is by appeal to the idea that the wrongful wills of culpable wrongdoers deserve to be defeated or thwarted. This is the possibility most naturally suggested by Ewing's comments.[33] The considerations brought forward in Chapter 5 also support such an understanding. Yet, in line with the arguments provided in Chapter 5, when understood in these terms, the moral desert of punishment does not require ultimate responsibility.

This brings us back to option (1): that of incompatibilists aligning themselves with the traditional moral retributivist understanding, despite finding it morally problematic (if they do find it morally problematic) on that grounds that it alone captures the ordinary understanding. As I indicated in Chapter 4, I suspect that, pre-reflectively, a majority of Westerners would assent to the idea that culpable moral wrongdoers deserve to be made to suffer *simpliciter*. As I also indicated in Chapter 4, whether the majority of Westerners would reflectively assent to this idea seems to me a different matter. The considerations raised by Ewing further strengthen my doubts. These considerations suggest that the non-derivative understanding described in the paragraph prior to this one has a stronger claim to reflecting the ordinary understanding the moral desert of punishment than the traditional moral retributivist understanding. There are other considerations that tell in favor of the non-derivative understanding's claim to better represent the ordinary understanding than the traditional moral retributivist understanding. For instance, if the traditional moral retributivist understanding accurately reflected the ordinary understanding of the moral desert of punishment, then our sense whether a wrongdoer had received what she morally deserved would not be affected by the source imposing the suffering or, e.g., by whether any effort is made to communicate to her that it is because she behaved badly that the suffering is being imposed. Yet such things seemingly to affect our sense of whether a wrongdoer had received what she deserved. This provides further reason

---

[33] Fingarette (1977) defends a similar understanding of legal desert and state punishment.

to question whether the traditional moral retributivist understanding accurately reflects the ordinary one.

Finally, there is a more serious worry: one that would obtain even if, contrary to what I've argued, the traditional moral retributivist understanding alone captured the ordinary understanding. If the traditional moral retributivist conception is as morally problematic as I and many others take it to be—if it is truly unintelligible how anyone, under any set of circumstances, could deserve in and of itself simply to be made to suffer—then incompatibilists cannot meaningfully claim that ultimate responsibility is a necessary condition of traditional moral retributivist desert. Where a claim is unintelligible, it makes no sense to speak of necessary conditions of its truth. The victor in the debate concerning the compatibility of moral responsibility and determinism would in this event not be incompatibilists, but P. F. Strawson's 'genuine moral sceptic' who insists that 'the notions of moral guilt, of blame, of moral responsibility are inherently confused . . .'.[34]

This, however, is not the situation in which we find ourselves. Although the ordinary understanding of moral responsibility and moral desert involves the idea that those who engage in serious public moral wrongdoing morally deserve to be punished—and this not merely in the weak sense that they lack grounds to complain of unjust treatment if they are punished, but in the strong sense that they have punishment positively coming to them—such desert need not be understood in traditional moral retributivist terms. In fact, it is better understood not in traditional moral retributivist terms. Punishment is deserved by those who engage in serious public moral wrongdoing *qua* rebuke. And *qua* rebuke, its desert, like that of the attitudes it expresses and communicates, does not require ultimate responsibility. The notions of moral guilt, blame, responsibility, and obligation are compatible with determinism.

---

[34] P. F. Strawson (1962), 72.

Bibliography

Anscombe, G. E. M. 1971. 'Causality and Determination'. Reprinted in her *Metaphysics and the Philosophy of Mind*. 1981. Cambridge: Cambridge University Press.

Árdal, Pall S. 1984. 'Does Anyone Ever Deserve to Suffer?' *Queen's Quarterly* 91(2): 241–57.

Ayer, A. J. 1954. 'Freedom and Necessity'. Reprinted in Gary Watson (ed.), *Free Will*, 1st edition. 1982. Oxford: Oxford University Press.

—— 1980. 'Free Will and Rationality'. In Z. van Straaten (ed.), *Philosophical Subjects*. Oxford: Clarendon Press.

Bedau, Hugo Adam. 2002. 'Feinberg's Liberal Theory of Punishment'. *Buffalo Criminal Law Review* 5: 103–44.

Bennett, Christopher. 2002. 'The Varieties of Retributive Experience'. *The Philosophical Quarterly* 52 (207): 145–63.

Bennett, Jonathan. 1980. 'Accountability'. In Z. van Straaten (ed.), *Philosophical Subjects*. Oxford: Clarendon Press.

Bernstein, Mark. 2005. 'Can We Ever Be Really, Truly, Ultimately Free?' *Midwest Studies in Philosophy* 29: 1–12.

Bok, Hillary. 1998. *Freedom and Responsibility*. Princeton: Princeton University Press.

Bradley, F. H. 1927. *Ethical Studies*, 2nd edition. Oxford: Oxford University Press.

Bramhall, John. 1999 (originally published 1655). *A Defense of True Liberty*. Selections reprinted in Vere Chappell (ed.), *Hobbes and Bramhall on Liberty and Necessity*. Cambridge: Cambridge University Press.

Burgh, Richard W. 1982. 'Do the Guilty Deserve Punishment?' *Journal of Philosophy* 79: 193–213.

Buss, Sarah and Lee Overton (eds.). 2002. *Contours of Agency: Essays on Themes from Harry Frankfurt*. Cambridge, MA: MIT Press.

Campbell, C. A. 1938. 'In Defence of Free Will'. Reprinted in his *In Defence of Free Will*. 1967. New York: Humanities Press.

Charvet, John. 1966. 'Criticism and Punishment'. *Mind* 75: 573–9.

Chisholm, Roderick. 1964. 'Human Freedom and the Self'. Reprinted in Gary Watson (ed.), *Free Will*, 2nd edition. 2003. Oxford: Oxford University Press.

Ciocchetti, Christopher. 2003. 'Wrongdoing and Relationships'. *Social Theory and Practice* 29 (1): 65–86.

Clarke, Randolph. 2005. 'On an Argument for the Impossibility of Moral Responsibility'. *Midwest Studies in Philosophy* 29: 13–24.

Cottingham, John. 1979. 'Varieties of Retribution'. *Philosophical Quarterly* 29: 238–46.

—— 1987. 'Just Punishment'. *Proceedings of the Aristotelian Society, Supplementary Volumes* 61: 41–55.

Darwall, Stephen. 2006. *The Second-Person Standpoint: Morality, Respect, and Accountability*. Cambridge, MA: Harvard University Press.

Davidson, Donald. 1971. 'Agency'. Reprinted in his *Essays on Actions and Events*. 1980. Oxford: Clarendon Press.

—— 1973. 'Freedom to Act'. Reprinted in his *Essays on Actions and Events*. 1980. Oxford: Clarendon Press.

—— 1980. *Essays on Actions and Events*. Oxford: Clarendon Press.

Davis, Lawrence. 1972. 'They Deserve to Suffer'. *Analysis* 32 (4): 136–40.

Dennett, Daniel. 1984. *Elbow Room*. Cambridge, MA: MIT Press.

Dolinko, David. 1991. 'Some Thoughts about Retributivism'. *Ethics* 101: 537–59.

Double, Richard. 1996. *Metaphilosophy and Free Will*. New York: Oxford University Press.

Duff, R. A. 1971. 'Psychopathy and Moral Understanding'. *American Philosophical Quarterly* 14: 189–200.

—— 1986. *Trials and Punishments*. Cambridge: Cambridge University Press.

—— 1996. 'Penal Communications: Recent Work in the Philosophy of Punishment'. *Crime and Justice* 20: 1–97.

—— 2001. 'Punishment, Communication, and Community'. Reprinted in his *Punishment, Communication, and Community*. Oxford: Oxford University Press.

—— 2007. *Answering for Crime*. Oxford: Hart Publishing.

—— 2008. 'Responsibility and Liability in the Criminal Law'. In Matthew Kramer (ed.), *The Legacy of H. L. A. Hart*. Oxford. Oxford University Press.

Durkheim, Emile. 1961. *Moral Education: A Study in the Theory and Application of the Sociology of Education*. New York: Free Press of Glencoe.

Ewing, A. C. 1927. 'Punishment as a Moral Agency: An Attempt to Reconcile the Retributive and the Utilitarian View'. *Mind* 36 (143): 292–305.

—— 1970. *The Morality of Punishment*. Montclair, NJ: Patterson Smith.

Falls, M. Margaret. 1987. 'Retribution, Reciprocity, and Respect for Persons'. *Law and Philosophy* 6: 25–51.

Feinberg, Joel. 1962. 'Problematic Responsibility in Law and Morals'. Reprinted in his *Doing and Deserving*. 1980. Princeton: Princeton University Press.

—— 1963. 'Justice and Personal Desert'. Reprinted in his *Doing and Deserving*. 1980. Princeton: Princeton University Press.

—— 1965. 'The Expressive Function of Punishment'. Reprinted in his *Doing and Deserving*. 1980. Princeton: Princeton University Press.

Feinberg, Joel. 1969. 'Sua Culpa'. Reprinted in his *Doing and Deserving*. 1980. Princeton: Princeton University Press.

—— 1970. 'What is so Special about Mental Illness?'. Reprinted in his *Doing and Deserving*. 1980. Princeton: Princeton University Press.

—— 1974. 'Noncomparative Justice'. *Philosophical Review* 83: 297–38.

—— 1980. *Doing and Deserving*. Princeton: Princeton University Press.

Fingarette, Herbert. 1977. 'Punishments and Suffering'. American Philosophical Association, Presidential Address.

Fischer, John Martin. 1994. *The Metaphysics of Free Will*. Oxford: Blackwell.

—— 1999. 'Recent Work on Moral Responsibility'. *Ethics* 110: 91–139.

—— 2002. 'Frankfurt-Style Compatibilism'. In Sarah Buss and Lee Overton (eds.), *Contours of Agency: Essays on Themes from Harry Frankfurt*. Cambridge, MA: MIT Press.

—— and Mark Ravizza. 1998. *Responsibility and Control: A Theory of Moral Responsibility*. Cambridge: Cambridge University Press.

Foot, Philippa. 1959. 'Moral Beliefs'. Reprinted in her *Virtues and Vices*. 1978. Berkeley and Los Angeles: University of California Press.

Frankfurt, Harry. 1971. 'Alternate Possibilities and Moral Responsibility'. Reprinted in his *The Importance of What We Care About*. 1988. New York: Cambridge University Press.

—— 1983. 'What We are Morally Responsible for'. Reprinted in his *The Importance of What We Care About*. 1988. New York: Cambridge University Press.

—— 1988. *The Importance of What We Care About*. New York: Cambridge University Press.

—— 2002. 'Reply to John Martin Fischer'. In Sarah Buss and Lee Overton (eds.), *Contours of Agency: Essays on Themes from Harry Frankfurt*. Cambridge, MA: MIT Press.

—— 2003. 'Some Thoughts Concerning PAP'. In David Widerker and Michael McKenna (eds.), *Moral Responsibility and Alternative Possibilities*. Burlington, VT: Ashgate.

Ginet, Carl. 1996. 'In Defense of the Principle of Alternative Possibilities: Why I Don't Find Frankfurt's Argument Convincing'. *Philosophical Perspectives* 10: 403–17.

Glover, Jonathan. 1970. *Responsibility*. London: Routledge & Kegan Paul.

—— 1983. 'Self-Creation'. Read 8 December 1983. *Proceedings of the British Academy* 69: 445–71.

Haji, Ishtiyaque. 1998. *Moral Appraisability*. Oxford: Oxford University Press.

—— 2009. *Incompatibilism's Allure: Principal Arguments for Incompatibilism*. Toronto, ON: Broadview Press.

Hampton, Jean. 1991. 'A New Theory of Retribution'. In Christopher W. Morris and Raymond Gillespie Frey (eds.), *Liability and Responsibility: Essays in Laws and Morals*. Cambridge: Cambridge University Press.

—— 1992a. 'An Expressive Theory of Retribution'. In Wesley Cragg (ed.), *Retributivism and Its Critics*. Stuttgart: Franz Steiner Verlag.

—— 1992b. 'Correcting Harms Versus Righting Wrongs: The Goal of Retribution'. *UCLA Law Review* 39: 1659–702.

Hanna, Nathan. 2008. 'Say What? A Critique of Expressive Retributivism'. *Law and Philosophy* 27: 123–50.

Hart, H. L. A. 1958. 'Legal Responsibility and Excuses'. Reprinted in his *Punishment and Responsibility*. 1968. Oxford: Clarendon Press.

—— 1959. 'Prolegomenon to the Principles of Punishment'. Reprinted in his *Punishment and Responsibility*. 1968. Oxford: Clarendon Press.

—— 1967. 'Postscript: Responsibility and Retribution'. Reprinted in his *Punishment and Responsibility*. 1968. Oxford: Clarendon Press.

Hegel, G. W. F. 2001. *Philosophy of Right*. Kitchener, ON: Batoche Books.

Herman, Barbara. 1985. 'The Practice of Moral Judgment'. Reprinted in her *The Practice of Moral Judgment*. 1993. Cambridge, MA: Harvard University Press.

—— 1990. 'Obligation and Performance'. Reprinted in her *The Practice of Moral Judgment*. 1993. Cambridge, MA: Harvard University Press.

—— 1993. 'Leaving Deontology Behind'. Reprinted in her *The Practice of Moral Judgment*. 1993. Cambridge, MA: Harvard University Press.

—— 1996. 'Making Room for Character'. Reprinted in her *Moral Literacy*. 2007. Cambridge, MA: Harvard University Press.

—— 1998. 'Responsibility and Moral Competence'. Reprinted in her *Moral Literacy*. 2007. Cambridge, MA: Harvard University Press.

—— 2001. 'The Scope of Moral Requirement'. Reprinted in her *Moral Literacy*. 2007. Cambridge, MA: Harvard University Press.

—— 2007a. 'The Will and its Objects'. In her *Moral Literacy*. 2007. Cambridge, MA: Harvard University Press.

—— 2007b. 'Obligatory Ends'. In her *Moral Literacy*. 2007. Cambridge, MA: Harvard University Press.

Hieronymi, Pamela. 2004. 'The Force and Fairness of Blame'. *Philosophical Perspectives* 18: 115–48.

—— 2007. 'Rational Capacity as a Condition on Blame'. *Philosophical Books* 48 (2): 109–23.

Hobart, R. E. 1934. 'Freewill as Involving Determinism and Impossible without it'. In Bernard Berofsky (ed.), *Free Will and Determinism*. 1966. New York: Harper & Row.

Honderich, Ted. 1984/1989. *Punishment: The Supposed Justifications*. Cambridge: Polity Press.

Honderich, Ted. 1988. *A Theory of Determinism.* Oxford: Clarendon Press.

Hornsby, Jennifer. 2004a. 'Agency and Actions'. In Helen Steward and Jon Hyman (eds.), *Agency and Action.* Cambridge: Cambridge University Press.

—— 2004b. 'Alienated Agents'. In M. De Caro and D. Macarthur (eds.), *Naturalism in Question.* Cambridge, MA: Harvard University Press.

Hume, David. 1977. (originally published 1777). *An Enquiry Concerning Human Understanding.* Eric Steinberg (ed.). Indianapolis: Hackett.

—— 2000. (originally published 1739–40). *A Treatise of Human Nature.* David Fate Norton and Mary J. Norton (eds.). Oxford: Oxford University Press.

Husack, Douglas. 1992. 'Why Punish the Deserving?' *Nous* 26: 447–64.

Kane, Robert. 1985. *Free Will and Values.* Albany: SUNY Press.

—— 1994. 'Free Will: The Elusive Ideal'. *Philosophical Studies* 75: 25–60.

—— 1996. *The Significance of Free Will.* Oxford: Oxford University Press.

—— 1999. 'Responsibility, Luck, and Chance: Reflections on Free Will and Indeterminism'. *Journal of Philosophy* 96: 217–40.

—— 2000. 'The Dual Regress of Free Will and the Role of Alternative Possibilities'. *Philosophical Perspectives* 14. Oxford: Blackwell Publishers, 57–80.

—— 2004. 'Agency, Responsibility, and Indeterminism: Reflections on Libertarian Theories of Free Will'. In Joseph Keim Campbell, Michael O'Rourke, and David Shier (eds.), *Freedom and Determinism.* Cambridge, MA: MIT Press, 70–88.

—— 2005. *A Contemporary Introduction to Free Will.* Oxford: Oxford University Press.

Kant, Immanuel. 1960 (originally published 1803). *Religion within the Bounds of Reason Alone.* Trans. T. Greene and H. Hudson. New York: Harper & Rowe.

—— 1996. (originally published 1797). *The Metaphysics of Morals* in *The Cambridge Edition of the Works of Immanuel Kant.* Trans. Mary J. Gregor. Cambridge: Cambridge University Press.

—— 1997 (originally published 1788). *Critique of Practical Reason.* Trans. Mary J. Gregor. Cambridge: Cambridge University Press.

Keller, Pierre. 2010. 'Two Conceptions of Compatibilism in the Critical Elucidation'. In Andrews Reath and Jens Timmermann (eds.), *Kant's Critique of Practical Reason: A Critical Guide.* 2010. Cambridge: Cambridge University Press.

Kelly, Erin. 2002. 'Doing without Desert'. *Pacific Philosophical Quarterly* 83: 180–205.

Klein, Martha. 1990. *Determinism, Blameworthiness and Deprivation.* Oxford: Oxford University Press.

Kleinig, John. 1973. *Punishment and Desert.* The Hague: Martinus Nijhoff.

—— 1991. 'Punishment and Moral Seriousness'. *Israel Law Review* 25: 401–21.

Kneale, William. 1967. 'The Responsibility of Criminals'. Reprinted in H. B. Acton (ed.), *The Philosophy of Punishment.* 1969. London: MacMillan.

Korsgaard, Christine. 1989. 'Morality as Freedom'. Reprinted in her *Creating the Kingdom of Ends*. 1996. Cambridge: Cambridge University Press.

—— 1992. 'Creating the Kingdom of Ends: Reciprocity and Responsibility in Personal Relations'. Reprinted in her *Creating the Kingdom of Ends*. 1996. Cambridge: Cambridge University Press.

Latham, Noa. 2004. 'Determinism, Randomness and Value'. *Philosophical Topics* 32 (1–2): 153–67.

Lenman, James. 2002. 'On the Alleged Shallowness of Compatibilism, A Critical Study of Saul Smilansky: *Free Will and Illusion*'. *The Jerusalem Philosophical Quarterly* 51: 63–79.

Levy, Neil. 2005. 'The Good, the Bad, and the Blameworthy'. *Journal of Ethics and Social Philosophy* 1(2): 1–16.

Lucas, J. R. 1980. *On Justice*. Oxford: Clarendon Press.

Mabbot, J. D. 1939. 'Punishment'. *Mind* 48 (190): 152–67.

McKenna, Michael. 1998. 'The Limits of Evil and the Role of Moral Address: A Defense of Strawsonian Compatibilism'. *Journal of Ethics* 2: 123–42.

—— 2005. 'A Critique of Pereboom's 'Four-Case Argument''. *Analysis* 65: 75–8.

—— 2008. 'A Hard-Line Reply to Pereboom's Four-Case Manipulation Argument'. *Philosophy and Phenomenological Research* 77 (1): 142–59.

—— and Paul Russell (eds.). 2008. *Free Will and Reactive Attitudes*. Burlington, VT: Ashgate.

Mackie, J. L. 1982. 'Morality and the Retributive Emotions'. Reprinted in his *Persons and Values: Selected Papers Volume II*. 1985. Oxford. Clarendon Press.

Manser, A. R. 1962. 'It Serves You Right'. *Philosophy* 37: 293–306.

Margalit, A. 1996. *The Decent Society*. Cambridge, MA: Harvard University Press.

Mele, Alfred. 2003. 'Agent's Abilities'. *Nous* 37 (3): 447–70.

Metz, Thaddeus. 2000. 'Censure Theory and Intuitions about Punishment'. *Law and Philosophy* 19: 491–512.

Meyer, Susan Sauvé. 1993. *Aristotle on Moral Responsibility*. Oxford: Oxford University Press.

Moberly, Walter. 1968. *The Ethics of Punishment*. London: Faber & Faber.

Moore, Michael S. 1982. 'Closet Retributivism'. Reprinted in his *Placing Blame: A General Theory of the Criminal Law*. Oxford: Oxford University Press.

—— 1985. 'Causation and the Excuses'. *California Law Review* 73: 1091–149.

—— 1987. 'The Moral Worth of Retribution'. In Ferdinand Schoeman (ed.), *Responsibility, Character, and the Emotions*. Cambridge: Cambridge University Press.

—— 1993. 'Justifying Retributivism'. *Israel Law Review* 27 (1–2): 15–49.

—— 1997. *Placing Blame: A General Theory of the Criminal Law*. Oxford: Oxford University Press.

Morris, Herbert. 1968. 'Persons and Punishment'. Reprinted in his *On Guilt and Innocence*. 1976. Berkeley: University of California Press.

—— 1971. 'Guilt and Punishment'. *The Personalist* 52: 305–21.

—— 1976. *On Guilt and Innocence*. Berkeley: University of California Press.

—— 1981. 'A Paternalistic Theory of Punishment'. *American Philosophical Quarterly* 18 (4): 263–71.

—— 1999. 'Some Further Reflections on Guilt and Punishment'. *Law and Philosophy* 18 (4): 363–78.

Mundle, C. W. K. 1954. 'Punishment and Desert'. Reprinted in H. B. Acton (ed.), *The Philosophy of Punishment*. 1969. London: MacMillan.

Murphy, Jeffrie G. 1971. 'Three Mistakes about Retributivism'. Reprinted in his *Retribution, Justice, and Therapy*. 1979. Dordrecht: Reidel.

—— 1972. 'Kant's Theory of Punishment'. Reprinted in his *Retribution, Justice, and Therapy*. 1979. Dordrecht: Reidel.

—— 1973. 'Marxism and Retribution'. Reprinted in his *Retribution, Justice, and Therapy*. 1979. Dordrecht: Reidel.

—— 1987. 'Does Kant Have a Theory of Punishment?'. *Columbia Law Review* 87 (3): 509–32.

—— 1999. 'Moral Epistemology, the Retributive Emotions, and the "Clumsy Moral Philosophy" of Jesus Christ'. In Susan Bandes (ed.), *The Passions of Law*. NY: NYU Press.

—— 2007. 'Legal Moralism and Retribution Revisited'. *Criminal Law and Philosophy* 1: 5–20.

—— and Jean Hampton. 1988. *Forgiveness and Mercy*. New York: Cambridge University Press.

Nagel, Thomas. 1979. 'Moral Luck'. Reprinted in Gary Watson (ed.), *Free Will*, 1st edition. 1982. Oxford. Oxford University Press.

—— 1986. *The View from Nowhere*. Oxford: Oxford University Press.

Narayan, Uma. 1993. 'Appropriate Responses and Preventive Benefits: Justifying Censure and Hard Treatment in Legal Punishment'. *Oxford Journal of Legal Studies* 13 (2): 166–82.

Nino, C. S. 1983. 'A Consensual Theory of Punishment'. Reprinted in A. John Simmons, Marshall Cohen, Joshua Cohen, and Charles R. Beitz (eds.), *Punishment*. 1995. Princeton: Princeton University Press.

Nowell-Smith, P. H. 1948. 'Freewill and Moral Responsibility'. *Mind* 57 (225): 45–61.

Otsuka, Michael. 1998. 'Incompatibilism and the Avoidability of Blame'. *Ethics* 108: 685–701.

Parfit, Derek. 2011. *On What Matters: Volume I*. Oxford: Oxford University Press.

Pereboom, Derk. 1995. 'Determinism Al Dente'. *Nous* 29: 21–45.

—— 2001. *Living without Free Will*. Cambridge: Cambridge University Press.

―― 2003. 'Source Incompatibilism and Alternative Possibilities'. In David Widerker and Michael McKenna, (eds.), Moral Responsibility and Alternative Possibilities. 2003. Burlington, Vermont: Ashgate.

―― 2005. 'Defending Hard Compatibilism'. Midwest Studies 29: 228–47.

―― 2008. 'A Hard-line Reply to the Multiple-Case Manipulation Argument'. Philosophy and Phenomenological Research 77 (1): 160–70.

Primoratz, Igor. 1989. 'Punishment as Language'. Philosophy 64: 187–205.

Ravizza, Mark. 1994. 'Semi-Compatibilism and the Transfer of Non-Responsibility'. Philosophical Studies 75: 61–93.

Reid, Thomas. 2011. (originally published 1788). Essays on the Active Powers of Man. Cambridge: Cambridge University Press.

Rosen, Gideon. 2004. 'Skepticism about Moral Responsibility'. Philosophical Perspectives 18: 295–314.

Russell, Paul. 1992. 'Strawson's Way of Naturalizing Responsibility'. Ethics 102: 287–302.

―― 1995. Freedom and Moral Sentiment. Oxford: Oxford University Press.

Scanlon, T. M. 1988. 'The Significance of Choice'. In Sterling M. McMurrin (ed.), The Tanner Lectures in Human Values. 1988. Salt Lake City. University of Utah Press.

―― 1998. What We Owe to Each Other. Cambridge, MA: Harvard University Press.

―― 2002. 'Reasons, Responsibility, and Reliance: Replies to Wallace, Dworkin, and Deigh'. Ethics 112: 507–28.

―― 2008. Moral Dimensions: Permissibility, Meaning, Blame. Cambridge, MA: Belknap Press of Harvard University Press.

Schlick, Moritz. 1939. Problems of Ethics. New York: Dover Publications, Inc.

Sher, George. 1987. Desert. Princeton: Princeton University Press.

―― 2006. In Praise of Blame. Oxford: Oxford University Press.

Skillen, A. J. 1980. 'How to Say Things with Walls'. Philosophy 55: 509–23.

Skorupski, John. 1999. Ethical Explorations. Oxford: Oxford University Press.

―― 2005. 'Blame, Respect, and Recognition: A Reply to Theo van Willigenburg'. Utilitas 17 (3): 333–47.

Smart, J. J. C. 1961. 'Free Will, Praise, and Blame'. Reprinted in Gary Watson (ed.), Free Will, 2nd edition. 2003. Oxford: Oxford University Press.

Smilansky, Saul. 1990. 'Discussion: Is Libertarian Free Will Worth Wanting?' Philosophical Investigations 13 (3): 273–6.

―― 1991. 'Free Will and Being a Victim'. Journal of Moral and Social Studies 6 (1): 19–32.

―― 2000. Free Will and Illusion. Oxford: Clarendon Press.

―― 2003a. 'Compatibilism: The Argument from Shallowness'. Philosophical Studies 115: 257–82.

―― 2003b. 'On Free Will and Ultimate Injustice'. The Jerusalem Philosophical Quarterly 52: 41–55.

Smith, Angela. 2005. 'Responsibility for Attitudes: Activity and Passivity in Mental Life'. *Ethics* 115 (2): 236–71.

—— 2007. 'On Being Responsible and Holding Responsible'. *Journal of Ethics* 11: 465–84.

—— 2008. 'Control, Responsibility, and Moral Assessment'. *Philosophical Studies* 138: 367–92.

Stern, Lawrence. 1974. 'Freedom, Blame and Moral Community'. *Journal of Philosophy*, 71: 72–84.

Strawson, Galen. 1986. *Freedom and Belief*. Oxford: Oxford University Press.

—— 1994. 'The Impossibility of Moral Responsibility'. *Philosophical Studies* 75: 5–24.

—— 1998. 'Free Will'. *Routledge Encyclopedia of Philosophy*.

—— 2000. 'The Unhelpfulness of Indeterminism'. *Philosophy and Phenomenological Research* 60: 149–56.

—— 2001. 'The Bounds of Freedom'. In Robert Kane (ed.), *The Oxford Handbook of Free Will*. Oxford: Oxford University Press.

Strawson, P. F. 1962. 'Freedom and Resentment'. Reprinted in Gary Watson (ed.), *Free Will*, 2nd edition. 2003. Oxford: Oxford University Press.

—— 1980. 'P. F. Strawson Replies'. In Z. van Straaten (ed.), *Philosophical Subjects*. Oxford: Clarendon Press.

—— 1985. *Skepticism and Naturalism*. New York: Columbia University Press.

Tasioulas, John. 2006. 'Punishment and Repentance' *Philosophy* 81: 279–322.

Taylor, Richard. 1966. *Action and Purpose*. Englewood Cliffs, NJ: Prentice-Hall.

van Inwagen, Peter. 1978. 'Ability and Responsibility'. *The Philosophical Review* 87: 201–24.

—— 1980. 'The Incompatibility of Responsibility and Determinism'. Reprinted in John Martin Fischer (ed.), *Moral Responsibility*. 1986. Ithaca, NY: Cornell University Press.

—— 1983. *An Essay on Free Will*. Oxford: Clarendon Press.

Vargas, Manuel. 2004. 'Responsibility and the Aims of Theory: Strawson and Revisionism'. Reprinted in Michael McKenna and Paul Russell (eds.), *Free Will and Reactive Attitudes: Perspectives on P. F. Strawson's "Freedom and Resentment"*. Burlington, VT: Ashgate.

Walker, Nigel. 1991. *Why Punish?* Oxford: Oxford University Press.

Wallace, R. Jay. 1994. *Responsibility and the Moral Sentiments*. Cambridge, MA.: Harvard University Press.

—— 2000. 'Moral Responsibility and the Practical Point of View'. Reprinted in his *Normativity and the Will*. 2006. Oxford: Oxford University Press.

Wasserstrom, Richard. 1980. *Philosophy and Social Issues*. Notre Dame, IL: University of Notre Dame Press.

Watson, Gary (ed.). 1982. *Free Will*, 1st edition. Oxford: Oxford University Press.

—— 1987. 'Responsibility and the Limits of Evil: Variations on a Strawsonian Theme'. Reprinted in John Martin Fischer and Mark Ravizza (eds.), *Perspectives on Moral Responsibility*. 1993. Ithaca, NY: Cornell University Press.

—— 1996. 'Two Faces of Responsibility'. *Philosophical Topics* 24: 227–48.

—— (ed.). 2003. *Free Will*, 2nd edition. Oxford: Oxford University Press.

Widerker, David. 1995a. 'Libertarian Freedom and the Avoidability of Decisions'. *Faith and Philosophy* 12: 113–18.

—— 1995b. 'Libertarianism and Frankfurt's Attack on the Principle of Alternative Possibilities'. *Philosophical Review* 104: 247–61.

—— 2000. 'Frankfurt's Attack on the Principle of Alternative Possibilities: A Further Look'. *Philosophical Perspectives* 14: 181–201.

—— and Michael McKenna (eds.). 2003. *Moral Responsibility and Alternative Possibilities*. Burlington, VT: Ashgate.

Williams, Bernard. 1965. 'Morality and the Emotions'. Reprinted in his *Problems of the Self*. 1973. Cambridge: Cambridge University Press.

—— 1997. 'Moral Responsibility and Political Freedom'. *Cambridge Law Journal* 56 (1): 96–102.

Winch, Peter. 1972. 'Ethical Reward and Punishment'. In his *Ethics and Action*. London: Routledge & Kegan Paul.

Wolf, Susan. 1981. 'The Importance of Free Will'. In John Martin Fischer and Mark Ravizza (eds.), *Perspectives on Moral Responsibility*. 1993. Ithaca, NY: Cornell University Press.

—— 1990. *Freedom within Reason*. Oxford: Oxford University Press.

—— 1997. 'Sanity and the Metaphysics of Responsibility'. In Ferdinand Schoeman (ed.), *Responsibility, Character, and the Emotions*. Cambridge: Cambridge University Press.

Wood, Allen. 1984. 'Kant's Compatibilism'. In Allen Wood (ed.), *Self and Nature in Kant's Philosophy*. 1984. Ithaca, NY: Cornell University Press.

Wyma, Keith. 1997. 'Moral Responsibility and Leeway for Action'. *American Philosophical Quarterly* 34: 57–70.

Zimmerman, Michael. 1988. *An Essay on Moral Responsibility*. Totowa, NJ: Rowman & Littlefield.

—— 2002. 'Taking Luck Seriously'. *The Journal of Philosophy* 99 (11): 553–76.

Index